The Cross,
The Flag,
and The Bomb

Recent Titles in
Contributions to the Study of Religion
Series Editor: Henry W. Bowden

Private Churches and Public Money: Church-Government Fiscal
Relations
Paul J. Weber and Dennis A. Gilbert

A Cultural History of Religion in America
James G. Moseley

Religious Mythology and the Art of War: Comparative Religious Sym-
bolisms of Military Violence
James A. Aho

Saints, Slaves, and Blacks: The Changing Place of Black People Within
Mormonism
Newell G. Bringhurst

Southern Anglicanism: The Church of England in Colonial South
Carolina
S. Charles Bolton

The Cult Experience
Andrew J. Pavlos

Southern Enterprise: The Work of National Evangelical Societies in
the Antebellum South
John W. Kuykendall

Facing the Enlightenment and Pietism: Archibald Alexander and the
Founding of Princeton Theological Seminary
Lefferts A. Loetscher

Presbyterian Women in America: Two Centuries of a Quest for Status
Lois A. Boyd and R. Douglas Brackenridge

Marchin' the Pilgrims Home: Leadership and Decision-Making in an
Afro-Caribbean Faith
Stephen D. Glazier

Exorcising the Trouble Makers: Magic, Science, and Culture
Francis L. K. Hsu

The Cross,
The Flag,
and The Bomb

American Catholics
Debate War and
Peace, 1960–1983

WILLIAM A. AU

CONTRIBUTIONS TO THE STUDY OF RELIGION, NUMBER 12

Greenwood Press
Westport, Connecticut ● London, England

Library of Congress Cataloging in Publication Data

Au, William A.
  The cross, the flag, and the bomb.

  (Contributions to the study of religion, ISSN 0196-
7053 ; no. 12)
  Bibliography: p.
  Includes index.
  1. Nuclear warfare—religious aspects—Catholic Church
—History of doctrines. 2. War—Religious aspects—
Catholic Church—History of doctrines—20th century.
3. Peace—religious aspects—Catholic Church—History
of doctrines—20th century. 4. Catholic Church—
United States—History—20th century. 5. United States
—Church history—20th century. 6. Catholic Church—
Doctrines—History—20th century. I. Title.
II. Series.
  BX1795.A85A9 1985   261.8′73   83-25290
  ISBN 0-313-24754-4 (lib. bdg.)

Library of Congress Catalog Card Number: 83-25290
ISBN: 0-313-24754-4
ISSN: 0196-7053

First published in 1985

Greenwood Press
A division of Congressional Information Service, Inc.
88 Post Road West
Westport, Connecticut 06881

Printed in the United States of America

10 9 8 7 6 5 4 3

To my parents—
William, my father
Annabell, my mother
Peter, my stepfather
this first effort is gratefully dedicated

Contents

Series Foreword

Roman Catholics have constituted the largest single denomination in America since the middle of the nineteenth century, but they have operated essentially as a minority group in the twentieth century in a culture dominated by Protestants. As a minority, often suspected of foreign loyalties and accused of un-American sympathies, Catholics have usually tried to counteract prejudice by cooperating fully with the country's social and economic programs. For generations they tried to overcome stigmas of alien origins and an unpopular faith by offering unquestioning acceptance of patterns not of their own making. Since World War II things have changed. American Catholicism has at last come of age, and this new confidence can be seen no more clearly than in debates about values in national life.

One of the more crucial areas of recent national concern has been that of warfare, especially the use of nuclear weapons. Catholics have engaged in discussions about justifiable military action, international ideological conflicts, nationalist aggression, and the ends and uses of armed intervention to retain a global balance of power. More importantly, they no longer reinforce majority opinion but now voice ideas along the whole spectrum of attitudes toward the uses of war, the goals of peace, and America's place in that continuing challenge.

This study by William Au provides a descriptive, carefully balanced analysis of Catholic contributions to this important debate. Moreover, it is one of the first books to provide historical background for emerging Catholic participation in the question that has profound consequences for all citizens. Au shows that his co-religionists slowly emerged from their minority-conscious shell by engaging in some peace activism between the world wars. Papal pronouncements by Pius XII and the Second Vatican Council sparked more reactions from several factions that had emerged by the 1950's. As technology produced nuclear weapons of greater destructive capacity and the conflict in Vietnam exacerbated questions about justifiable intervention, Catholics added their weight to opinions expressed by both hawks and doves. Particularly noticeable in all these events have been the actions of the Catholic Worker Movement and the Catholic Association for International Peace. The recent publication of the Bishops' Letter on War and Peace is the latest in a long line of such activities.

The most important value of William Au's work on these events is his ability to treat them as linked phenomena. His historical overview allows us to see them as steps in continuous development, not as separate party lines lacking a common denominator. This study discloses a unity of concern, a growth of perspectives that reaches back several decades and mounts to contemporary urgency because nuclear power has raised the stakes. Au confines his interest primarily to the American context; he notices some input from the larger Catholic community, but concentrates basically on the American denomination as it struggles both to guide consciences of adherents and to participate in a crucial question that involves the whole population.

History gives us long-range perspective, and Au makes it possible to understand more clearly the recent, ongoing aspects of questions as they unfold. He matches an ability to explain the cumulative process with an evenhanded fairness in analyzing and assessing major positions along the way. This careful overview is not a tract or diatribe for one side or the other. Its historical depth affords background for understanding how positions have emerged; its analytic balance clarifies their pertinence to contemporary application; its expertise in both theological and cultural affairs exemplifies the ways in which Catholic Americans have become full participants in this crucial debate.

Henry W. Bowden

Acknowledgments

I would like to express my gratitude to Monsignor John Tracy Ellis, Dr. Thomas R. West, and Reverend J. Bryan Hehir for their help and insights in the research and composition of this work. I would also like to give thanks to my relatives and friends whose love, patience, and faith have supported me in this work and in so many other things. Finally, I would like to thank all of those who, in their deep yearning for peace and justice, have provided the subject matter of this book.

Introduction

"Next to the production of food, which sustains life, the family, which nurtures life, and religion, which hallows life and gives it meaning, no sphere of activity has so occupied man's thoughts and usurped his energies as war, which degrades life as it destroys it."[1] Today, when the advance of technology has equipped the world's major powers with weapons of mass destruction, the issue of war has become the issue of human survival on this planet. The Second World War ended with the acceptance of the obliteration bombing of cities as a legitimate means of waging war, and the advent of nuclear weapons had made present to many the ominous words of Albert Einstein, "The splitting of the atom has changed everything save our modes of thinking, and therefore we drift toward unparalleled catastrophe."[2]

The ethical problems of war and the Christian participation in it have always been the source of some of the most divisive issues and complex dilemmas for the Catholic Church. In a world now conscious that war could destroy it, the Church cannot ignore the imperative to re-examine its own understanding of the issue of war. This re-examination must focus not only on the intrinsic demands of the Gospel but also on the social and ideological perspectives within which the Church has historically analyzed and understood the issue of war and related questions.

For American Catholics, such an examination of the issue of war is perhaps as new as it is vital. While American Catholics have had a strong tradition of involvement in issues of domestic reform, they have never been represented in large numbers or by a strong institutional presence in American anti-war movements. The tradition of Catholic nationalism which accounted for this is well documented in Dorothy Dohen's *Nationalism and American Catholicism*.[3] This nationalism was particularly strong among Catholic liberals who, while interested in domestic reform, were anxious to prove the compatibility of Catholicism and American society. In his study of the social thought of Catholicism in colonial and revolutionary America, C. Joseph Nuesse has documented the preoccupation with conformity to the general patterns of American society that from the beginning dominated Catholic social perspectives.[4] Conscious of being a minority in an anti-Catholic milieu, and eager to be an accepted part of it, Catholic reformers historically did not challenge the place of the nation in the international community, nor did they challenge its basic social system. They wanted reform within the boundaries of the American tradition, and generally looked to the government for help rather than to criticize it. It was thus inevitable that the responsibility of the United States on issues of war and peace would be one of the last issues which Catholic reformers would confront.[5]

In the 1960's American society experienced a tremendous upheaval in which were questioned most of the cultural and religious principles and ideals which had previously undergirded it. Henry Steele Commager has claimed that "... it was the sixties that broke dramatically and even convulsively with the world that had been fashioned in the previous three-quarters of a century."[6] "In the realm of religion and ethics," said Sydney Alhstrom in describing the American era which began with the inauguration of John Kennedy, "one could justify the adjective revolutionary. Never before in this country's history have so many Americans expressed revolutionary intentions and actively participated in efforts to alter the shape of American civilization in almost every imaginable way."[7]

In this same period the Catholic Church experienced some of the greatest challenges to its relevance for daily life on the issues of war and social justice. In the past two decades issues raised by the continuing nuclear arms race and the domestic divisions over the Vietnam War caused many Catholics to respond to what they saw as the challenge of Vatican II to look at war "with an entirely new attitude."[8] The past twenty years have witnessed an unprecedented growth of a pacifist position within the American Catholic community. By the beginning of the eighties, Catholic bishops, who had previously been viewed as a monolithic, nationalistic body, were numbered among the most prominent advocates of the anti-nuclear and disarmament movements. In these same years prominent voices within the Church rejected American society as inherently racist and warlike, and considered the Church to have become a corrupted part of that society. They called upon their fellow Catholics to embrace revolutionary agendas for transforming America and establishing world peace.

The events and controversy of these years not only brought the issue of war to the forefront of consciousness and debate within the Catholic community, but also revealed a great deal of confusion and disagreement over the basic terms with which the issue of war was to be defined and understood.

One of the causes of the current conceptual confusion and disarray on the subject of war and peace is what Gunnar Johnson has categorized as the often made and unjustified assumption that we all mean or understand the same thing when speaking of peace.[9] We ignore the fact that the values frequently associated with peace often conflict, for we do not sufficiently grasp the different theoretical frameworks within which different groups and individuals are operating. Consequently it often seems we are using the same words, but speaking different languages.

American Catholics who have argued over issues of war and peace in the past two decades have been far apart on questions that make up the social issue of war: the intrinsic demands of the Christian faith on the use of violence and the appropriate attitude toward the state; the moral character of American society and its international role; nuclear weapons and modern war; the world conflict defining international relations; the degree and method of social change necessary to achieve peace; and even the definition of peace itself. In such a situation the need for conceptual clarity is of paramount importance. Crucial to achieving such clarity is an historical investigation into the intellectual perspectives through which American Catholics have understood and approached the issues of war and peace. Only a keen grasp of the worldviews shaping the different schools of thought on the peace issue will enable us to give unity to the debates of the last two decades, and to evaluate the adequacy of Catholic attempts to address the threat of war in the nuclear age.

The purpose of this study will be to examine the basic trends, developments, and possible contradictions of American Catholic thought on the issue of war in the years 1960–1983. It will begin with an examination of the intellectual heritage within which American Catholics approached the issues of war and peace at the beginning of the sixties, and will follow the development of the chief schools of thought on the subject up to and including the issuance of the American bishops' pastoral letter, *The Challenge of Peace*, in 1983. The objective will be not to provide a narrative of all that Catholics did or said on the issue, but to isolate and critically examine the major intellectual perspectives within which Catholics conceptualized the nature of war as a social issue within American society. No attempt will be made to account for everyone who spoke or wrote on the issue. Rather, those authors will be chosen whom the research revealed to be representative of the major currents of American Catholic thought on war and peace.

At issue will be the evaluation which each school of thought made of American society and its place in international conflict, and the view which each school had of the place of the Church in modern society and its role in addressing issues of war and peace. The stance which each school took on these two points determined how it dealt with specific issues constituting the peace debates, such as American nuclear policy. It was their differing judgments on the moral quality of American society, and the consequences which these had for the social role of the Church, which constituted the major dividing line in the Catholic debates on war and peace over the past two decades. In their views of American society these conflicting groups of Catholics revealed that they saw the issue of war to be part of a larger cultural issue concerning the type of society which is compatible with the Christian view of the human person and human community, and the degree to which their own society did or did not conform to this. Because the debates of these years often tended to focus on issues of weapons and defense policies, this larger cultural concern was not always evident. Yet the stances which Catholics took on these issues were always directly governed by their prior ideological commitments to the maintenance or transformation of their society. To set forth these conflicting social visions and their consequences for the American Catholic response to the pre-eminent crisis of our times is the task to which this study turns.

NOTES

1. Albert Marrin, ed., *War and the Christian Conscience* (Chicago: Henry Regnery Co., 1971), p. 1.
2. An account of Einstein's views on peace is found in O. Nathan and H. Norden, eds., *Einstein on Peace* (New York: Avenel Books, 1981), p. 376.
3. Dorothy Dohen, *Nationalism and American Catholicism*, with an introduction by Joseph P. Fitzpatrick, S.J. (New York: Sheed and Ward, 1967).
4. Celestine Joseph Nuesse, *The Social Thought of American Catholics 1634–1829* (Washington, D.C.: The Catholic University of America Press, 1945). Nuesse concluded:

In the development of the plantation system the Catholic families, like others, became enmeshed in the institution of land tenure, indentured servitude, slavery, and social ease, which it implied. Only in the matter of religious liberty . . . was there a conscious progressive departure from conformity, since it was intended to remove the most difficult barriers to normal relations between Catholic colonists and others. The growth of the Maryland Tradition . . . indicated not only their desire for justice, but also their desire to be identified with American life as a whole. Far from proclaiming uniqueness they were anxious to convince their neighbors that they were not different from them, except in creed. (p. 283).

5. Patricia F. McNeal, *The American Catholic Peace Movement* (New York: Arno Press, 1968), p. 12.
6. Henry Steele Commager, "America in the Age of No Confidence," *The Saturday Review/World*, August 1974, 16.

7. Sydney E. Ahlstrom, "The Traumatic Years: American Religion and Culture in the 60's and 70's," *Theology Today* 36 (January 1980): 511.

8. *Gaudium et Spes*, #80, in Joseph Gremillion, ed., *The Gospel of Peace and Justice: Catholic Social Teaching since Pope John* (New York: Orbis Books, 1976), p. 317.

9. L. Gunnar Johnson, *Conflicting Concepts of Peace in Contemporary Peace Studies* (Beverly Hills: Sage Publications, 1976), p. 43.

The Cross,
The Flag,
and The Bomb

1

Background

Before examining the development of American Catholic thought on war in the past two decades, it is important to appreciate the *major* theoretical perspectives which constituted the intellectual heritage of Catholic thought on war at the beginning of the sixties. These perspectives are those of the Catholic Association for International Peace and the Catholic Worker Movement. The membership of both groups were a minority within the Catholic community, but together they represented articulate American Catholic opinion on the issue of war. These two bodies represent conflicting world views for interpreting the issue of war and the role of the Church in society, and can be seen as representing the two major polarities in American Catholic social thought. This chapter will seek to chart the major outlines of their differing approaches to the issue of war and peace and the conceptual elements which they bequeathed to the debates which erupted in the sixties.

THE CATHOLIC ASSOCIATION FOR INTERNATIONAL PEACE

Founded in 1927 at the instigation of the Reverend John A. Ryan at the Catholic University of America, the Catholic Association for International Peace (CAIP) was the first Catholic peace organization in American history. The CAIP was established in the wake of the debates over the League of Nations, which prompted Ryan and others associated with the Social

Action Department of the National Catholic Welfare Conference (NCWC) to attempt to move the American Church to address issues of war and peace. They sought to link traditional liberal Catholic emphasis on domestic reform with work for peace through international agencies like the League, and in so doing went against the strong current of isolationism which ran through the Catholic community.[1]

The objective of the organization was primarily educational, to bring to the consciousness of the Catholic community the Church's traditional teaching on war and international relations. Its methodology was somewhat elitist. It focused on the cultivation of highly trained laymen to work with priests in furnishing educational material for the reconstruction of the social order, and on urging these Catholics to seek positions of influence in business and civil life to bring the Church's teaching to bear on social policies.[2]

At the beginning of the period with which this study is concerned the CAIP represented the mainline liberal Catholic social thought on the problem of war. The operating premise of the organization was that, contrary to the avidly held but fatal assumption of the inevitability of war, peace is feasible, and that within the Catholic Church there is to be found a workable *moral* program for international peace and justice.[3] It was the concrete explanation and application of this Catholic view of society which the CAIP sought to effect through the work of its various committees. The CAIP accepted the just war theory of Aquinas as its operative theological position from which to oppose both pacifism and isolationism, both of which were seen as being contrary to papal teaching and to the world responsibilities and interests of the United States. In its opposition to pacifism and isolationism, the CAIP manifested two salient characteristics which it is important to explore here—its liberal internationalism and its Americanism.

Internationalism

From their inception the CAIP efforts could be described as an attempt to justify to the American people, and especially to American Catholics, the principle of collective security, and the principles of justice and charity on which it would rest. These principles were seen as set forth by Pope Benedict XV in his encyclical *Pacem Dei Munus* of May, 1920, in which he called for the world's nations to join in a mutual league for protection and the maintenance of general peace.[4]

The establishment of a world organization which would have the power to maintain order and protect the rights of nations was seen as necessary to eliminate the international conflict inherent in a world community based on the absolute sovereignty of the nation state. Such an organization was further demanded by the spiritual unity of the human race, which unbridled nationalism and materialistic competition negated. Thus the internationalist outlook of the CAIP was clearly set forth in its strong endorsement of the feasibility and the necessity of a world federal government. Peace was seen as the tranquility of order. Yet the world order which it envisioned was not the mechanical imposition of a new juridical structure on the international community. It was rather the fruit of charity and of the right ordering of human relationships with God and neighbor.

Following the lead of Benedict XV, and especially Pius XII, the CAIP stressed that the needed world juridical order must be based on the recognition of true social, moral, and economic principles and harmonized with the natural order which governs the relations between peoples and states, and which is articulated in the traditional Catholic teaching on the natural law. A world state based solely on the elimination of outside aggression, but not based on the development of a just social order in accord with the nature of human needs and rights, would produce even greater evils than the present international situation. As the Reverend John A. Driscoll summarized this danger for the 1953 CAIP symposium on "The Role of the Christian in the World for Peace":

In very short order and by a logical necessity, a Godless, secularistic world state would set itself up as man's final end. It would thus become the source of man's rights and the sole arbiter of when these rights would begin and when they would cease. There would be no inimitable foundation for true moral, social and economic principles. The effects of entering such a world government would be immeasurably worse than the results of an atomic war. There are many things more precious than life.[5]

Thus, while its internationalist ideal caused the CAIP to endorse the necessity of a world government to establish lasting peace, it also was cognizant that the necessary road to a world without war could also lead to the final tyranny of a managerial world state. To avoid such a development, CAIP members stressed the need to link the political principle of a reformed international order to the traditional Catholic natural law teaching on the principles of social organization necessary to a just society. The peace that comes from the tranquility of world order must also be the fruit of justice.

The CAIP constantly urged the Catholic community to accept its unique role in the development of a new world order. A constant theme of many CAIP publications was that international law and the concept of the familial unity of the world's nations were a Catholic invention. More than any other group, Catholics were seen as having a tradition of moral teaching which offered the world a concept of unity based on charity and the recognition of the universal worth and dignity of the human person. It was the duty of the Church in international affairs to insist upon the recognition of God as the end of the human race, and upon the existence of natural and divine laws as the basis of human rights and duties, and the foundation of all positive law. Through its witness to the proper moral and spiritual foundation of human society, the international family of the Church could point the way to a family of the world's nations.[6]

To implement its internationalist vision the CAIP worked against American neutrality and isolationism in international affairs, and endorsed American participation in the League of Nations and the Court of International Justice. Its endorsement of these international institutions, however, was far from unqualified. The CAIP saw the League as favoring the international *status quo* and, therefore, the wealthier nations and the colonial powers. The League, moreover, had no real power to curb aggression on the part of its members. Likewise, the

CAIP found the International Court to be more symbolic than effective. Yet the CAIP in these years insisted on the need to work within existing international institutions and seek to further their development into more adequate structures.[7] Prior to World War II, the CAIP called for an alteration of the American policy of neutrality, and for amendment of the Neutrality Act to allow for the distinction between aggressor and victim among nations at war. Thus, when Japan attacked China in 1937, the CAIP called for an economic boycott of Japan. After the war, CAIP members claimed that neutrality, which they had opposed, had encouraged Hitler and Japan and had actually brought on the last war.[8]

Following World War II, the CAIP became a staunch supporter of the United Nations, as it had previously defended the earlier short-lived League. The post-war world, the CAIP believed, was aware of the need to create a new world order at the same time that it was increasingly threatened by the unequal distribution of the world's resources and by the newly invented atom bomb.[9]

Yet the CAIP criticized the U.N. for not having gotten beyond the structural defects of the League. The CAIP's attitude toward the newly created U.N. found expression in the statement of the American bishops on November 18, 1945. The bishops complained that the U.N. charter did not provide for a sound institutional organization of international society. It was in effect an alliance of the great powers to maintain order, and the great powers themselves enjoyed a status above the law. United States participation was nonetheless endorsed, as the U.N. was better than chaos. The bishops hoped that in the revision of the U.N. charter slated for 1955, its defects would be eliminated and a world order could be established upon a legally binding recognition of the rights and duties of international society, and not upon the voluntary concessions of the nations.[10]

The consistent criticism which the CAIP brought against the U.N. continued to reflect its fear that the world organization's structural defects would prevent it from ever becoming a true world authority capable of suppressing war and fostering the material and spiritual development of the world community.

Yet the association could not abdicate its hope that the con-
stituent countries could learn to accept the principles of a true
federation of nations. The CAIP continued to hold to its ideal
of a world without war, conceived within the framework of
traditional Catholic teaching on the possibility of a true federal
world government, founded on an acceptance of human rights,
and articulated in papal social teaching from Leo XIII to Pius
XII.

Americanism

Yet it was its Americanism which determined how the CAIP
attempted to apply Catholic social principles to the international order. The CAIP understood the conflict defining contemporary international relations (and therefore providing the
context for interpreting all international issues) to be the struggle between the Western democracies and communism. Within
this conflict the United States was clearly equated with the cause
of the West and of Christianity. The CAIP gave its utmost
commitment to the containment of communism as the first
prerequisite to the establishment of a world order of justice
and peace.

Viewing the present nature of international conflict in this
way decidedly affected the CAIP's approach to collective security. While it called for revision of the U.N. charter for the
effective control of war, for the short run it defended Western
alliances such as the North Atlantic Treaty Organization
(NATO). This was to ensure protection against Soviet expansionism, as the CAIP had no doubt that Russia was bent on
world domination.[11] The CAIP reconciled its endorsement of
American defense policy with its call for world government by
arguing that alliances like NATO ultimately served to make
a revision of the U.N. charter possible by curbing Russian expansionism and forcing the communists to see the necessity of
world co-operation through the U.N. The communist powers
were consistently seen as the aggressive party and Western
alliances were consistently given the mantle of moral rectitude
as being only defensive in nature.

Most of the CAIP's advocacy of limited federation of nations into mutual security alliances thus had the purpose of getting non-communist nations to accept the need for co-operation and federation, and to resist the spread of communist influence. To these ends, it advocated the creation of a United States of Europe and an Organization of American States, and it adamantly opposed the admission of Red China to the U.N.[12]

The CAIP was aware that the policy of containment was limited and insufficient by itself to prevent the spread of communism and ensure world peace. The fundamental problems of Asia, Africa, and Latin America, it held, were poverty and the under-development of resources. Consequently, a constant theme in the CAIP's efforts to foster international co-operation and simultaneously undercut the advance of communism was the call for universal economic reform and social development. The association endorsed the Marshall Plan and stressed that an essential element in opposing communism was reform in the Western capitalistic system.[13]

In this respect, the Americanism of the CAIP, while endorsing the cause and major policies of the United States, was not without criticism. Russia was described as communist, imperialistic, anti-religious, dictatorial in its rule of its satellite nations, and sure of what it wanted. The United States was described as post-capitalistic, not sure of what it wanted, anti-imperialistic, individualistic, vaguely secularistic and vaguely religious, against war, eager to cooperate with other countries, and not dictatorial at home or abroad.[14] While benignly viewed, American society was criticized for its individualism and materialism. If the Soviet Union ignored the dignity of the individual, Americans ignored the obligation of the individual to serve the common good. Short of war, the CAIP believed the East-West struggle would be decided by whether or not the West would use its wealth and ability for the general welfare without sacrificing individual dignity in the process.[15]

The common good which the CAIP stressed was not a mere abstraction, but the concrete product of a social order built on the recognition of the dignity of the human person and providing to individuals, not an abundance of material goods, but rather the real opportunity to satisfy their material and non-material needs.[16] Securing the common good, the CAIP recognized, required significant change in the principles and practice of the Western and world economy. Yet no specific program was advocated by the CAIP for securing this objective. Neither did the association outrightly condemn capitalism as a system, while it criticized American materialism. The CAIP merely reasserted the principles of economic reconstruction set forth in Pius XI's *Quadragesimo Anno* as a moral guideline for an effort to develop the resources of all nations. The CAIP's dual call for world economic reform and the creation of a world federal government were in effect a demand for a spiritual revolution, consisting of the individual and institutional recognition that all people are subject to the requirements of human rights and the common good.[17]

The CAIP's criticism of the individualism and materialism of American and Western culture reflects traditional Catholic criticism of the philosophical liberalism which stood as midwife for the modern era.[18] Beneath the struggle between East and West, which immediately determined international relations, was a more fundamental struggle between Christian and secularist culture. Communism was itself seen to be the ultimate expression of the changes that occurred in Western culture in the transition from the medieval to the modern era. This outlook was summarized by John C. H. Wu at a CAIP symposium in 1953:

The process of disintegration has been going on in Europe for several centuries, and in America for about a century. Matter has taken the place of God, the State or the dominating class has taken the place of the Messiah, and the spirit of naturalistic secularism has taken the place of the Holy Spirit. The atheistic communism is but the culminating point of the whole downward tendency, in which the whole world seems to be engulfed.[19]

Here the analysis of the CAIP suggests that of R. H. Tawney in *Religion and the Rise of Capitalism.*[20] The social ideal of Catholic medieval Europe, Tawney argued, upheld the spiritual unity and dignity of the human race, the necessary linkage of economics with the moral law, and the importance of religion to the maintenance of a just and human social order. The rise of modern bourgeois culture was made possible by the shattering of the normative power of this social ideal. An individualistic conception of religion and the human person severed economic and other social activity from the moral supervision of the Christian Church. The individualism of the new culture destroyed the sense of social obligation and the common good upheld by medieval society, and substituted for the concept of the Mystical Body as the ideal of society the Calvinist division of people into the elect and the unelect. The result of this individualism in extracting the human person from his natural context of rights and duties within community was actually to destroy the sense of the individual's intrinsic worth. The capitulation of Christians to this new culture was seen as the source of all the nationalisms and materialistic economic systems and resultant wars and revolutions of the modern era.[21]

Yet in applying to American society this critical assessment of modern culture the CAIP was ambiguous. The association was committed to the Catholic principles of social organization which were expounded in the modern tradition of papal social teaching and which sought to call Western society back to the ideals of medieval Europe. Consequently it was troubled by American historical roots in the Calvinistic-bourgeois business culture which it sought to oppose. Yet the CAIP was also committed to being a part of American society, and saw it as the best hope in the struggle against communism. The association's criticism of America, while sometimes expressing great fears for its future course of development, never led to the point of even intimating a need for a radical break with American society. To the extent that America was criticized as representing the secularist culture the CAIP opposed, the association never saw this as being the society's determining essence. The best elements of the Western democracies, of which America was the exemplar, were linked by the CAIP to the older Christian tradition of the worth of the individual and emphasis on social obligations. It viewed the democracies as giving the greater freedom to move towards an era of human solidarity and to construct institutions which promote human dignity and social obligations. Despite what criticism could be made of them, the CAIP pointed out that in the democracies there are no Siberias or crematories.[22] Thus the association was able to mesh a traditional and radical Catholic critique of twentieth-century society with a firm support of the American social system and basic agreement with almost all of its major defense and foreign policies.

One of the clearest expressions of this outlook of the CAIP was its evaluation of relations between the United States and Latin America. The association's committee on Latin America recognized two historical contrasts between North and South America which reflect the major differences in culture and society between the two great divisions of the New World. Those contrasts are in the way in which they have dealt with the native Indians and Negro slaves, and in their response to the new regime of liberal-bourgeois society described above.[23] In North America the colonists brought with them

new, unformed, individual and various religions with little traditional teaching and based upon personal interpretations of a book that itself contained two diverse dispensations, the harsh history, code and prophecies of a segregated people, and the good tidings of universal redemption. Save for rare exceptions, they were able to wrest from the Bible new and personal interpretations which would permit them to do as pleased them to the native Indians and imported Negroes.[24]

Armed with these interpretations, they waged wars of annihilation against the Indians and reduced Negro slaves to the status of chattels, without human rights or dignity. In Latin America the influence of a Catholic culture militated against treating the Indians and Negroes as animals. Despite much cruelty they were accorded human status, and efforts were made to protect their family life. Both were converted in accord with an ideal which sought the creation not of a white but of a Catholic society.[25] In this the CAIP judged Latin America as having a greater tradition of respect for the individual, regardless of color, a fact which the continuing social exclusion of the Negroes in the United States was indicated as proving.

The same factors which allowed the North Americans to treat the Indians and Negroes as they did and still do, reads the committee report, allowed the United States to more easily evolve in the scientific-business culture of the nineteenth century. In Latin America Catholic culture was a greater obstacle to those who would divorce economics from religion. Because of this more intense cultural struggle, Latin America "came into the modern era" in the past century through bloody revolutions. Yet even today Latin American culture is more inclined not to make the rights of property absolute, and control of industry and finance is mostly in the hands of foreigners.[26]

The CAIP's analysis thus compares unfavorably the moral quality of the culture of the United States with that of Latin America. The CAIP also condemned the policy of intervention which has marked the history of the relations between the United States and Latin America.[27] The United States was accused of having related to Latin America with the rapacious acquisitiveness of the worst elements of bourgeois culture, rather than with a will to mutual harmony and development. The CAIP credited the Monroe Doctrine with freeing Latin America from European colonial control, but charged the United States with replacing European colonial control with its own economic aggression. The violent struggles currently infecting Latin America were a reaction to the rape of its traditional culture and the expression of twentieth-century aspirations for a better social order. They were in fact part of a worldwide struggle to overcome the evils of a generation which, in the ordinary life of work, rejected law, morals, and God.[28]

Yet despite the clear criticism of the United States in its Latin American relations, the CAIP was not led to see this nation as a "bad guy" in the international community. United States policy, claims the committee report, was reflective of the objective of containing communism throughout the world. As such, the objective of the Monroe Doctrine, to keep any threatening foreign influence out of Latin America, was seen as acceptable. What the CAIP condemned was the willingness of the U.S. to rely on economic domination to achieve this objective.

The association called for a policy of reconciliation for the two Americas. It saw the United States as having to offer Latin America a tradition of stable government and religious freedom, and greater technical knowledge. In turn, the United States could learn from Latin America's traditions of respect for the dignity of the person, appreciation of leisure, and a greater sense of justice. The creation of an Organization of American States could provide genuine security and cooperation and eliminate any premise for U.S. intervention.[29] The unity of the Americas would be especially important in the event of another world war, when, in the view of the CAIP, the Americas would be a likely last refuge for Christianity and Western civilization.[30]

Thus, the CAIP's evaluation of the relations between the United States and Latin America balanced criticism and support. The association criticized American foreign policy as imperialistic, yet believed in the ultimate justice of the nation's struggle against communism. To the extent that the United States was criticized as representing secularist-bourgeois culture, it was also extolled for maintaining the best hope for returning to a true social order based on a genuine solidarity of the world's people. The CAIP's sense of communism as the chief threat to peace in the world and its commitment to the United States as the best agent of Christianity's cause insured that no critical analysis of American society would lead the CAIP away from support for the major elements of American foreign policy as being good for the world.

Modern War and the Atomic Age

In regard to the question of modern war and nuclear weapons, the most significant and typical statement of the CAIP (prior to the 1960's) came shortly after World War II and the beginning of the atomic age.

At the beginning of his essay "The Ethics of Atomic War," Wilfred Parsons, S.J., recalled the prophetic words of Pius XII, who in a speech before the Pontifical Academy of Science in 1943 had warned against ever using the newly discovered power of the atom as a weapon.[31] Slightly more than two years later, on August 6, 1945, what the Pope declared unthinkable became reality in Hiroshima. In Parsons' estimation, the deployment of the atom bomb made a practical possibility of the modern conception of total war. Parsons was unequivocal in his belief that any major future war would be an atomic one and therefore

total. Another contributor to the same CAIP pamphlet, Edward
A. Conway, S.J., used War Department reports to show that
nuclear weapons were not designed as tactical weapons but
were meant to serve as terror weapons aimed at cities, and
that there was no defense against them.[32]
A purely emotional rejection of total war was unreliable,
Parsons insisted, for emotional revulsion is ephemeral. It was
necessary to develop a clear ethical standard to evaluate and
judge modern war. Parsons assaulted any attempt to justify
the modern theory of total war (a war in which the entire
population of any enemy country is seen as a military target)
as incompatible with any traditional moral standard of justice.
The distinction of non-combatants from military forces and
their inviolability from direct, deliberate attack must be maintained. Because he saw any future war as being atomic and
therefore total, Parsons doubted that any future war could be
moral. He further maintained that the existence of the United
Nations, however imperfect it may be, would itself invalidate
any just claim to start a war.[33]

Yet despite his condemnation of total war and of atomic war
as total, Parsons did allow for the possible use of nuclear weapons against an aggressor nation's cities under certain conditions. Following a nuclear attack against a nation a retaliatory
nuclear strike against the aggressor could be justified, if it was
the only possible and necessary means to prevent further
aggression or an enslavement of the remaining population.
Such a nuclear counter-strike would be justified only if the
cities so attacked contained the enemy's military productive
capacity, and the objective of the attack was the necessary
neutralizing of the enemy's military capacity for further
aggression. Such a situation, argued Parsons, would provide a
proportionate reason for the unintended but permitted destruction of the non-combatants in the victim cities.[34]

Parsons claimed that such a defensive use of nuclear weapons
against cities was not total war in the condemned sense. That
the use of nuclear weapons against cities could result in the
same annihilation of most of a nation's population as the total
war he condemned was not a question which Parsons addressed.
It should also be noted that the position which Parsons took

here ran directly counter to that taken by Father John Ford,
S.J., who during World War II had stood almost alone among
American Catholics in publicly condemning the obliteration
bombing of cities, which had become accepted Allied policy.[35]
Ford maintained that the traditional principle of non-combatant immunity, and the requirement that any use of lethal force
in war be proportionate to the good sought, could never allow
the obliteration of civil populations.

Parsons' position reflects the tension that permeated much of
the CAIP's efforts to uphold traditional Catholic principles of
morality and the social order, and at the same time provide
support for the necessities of American defense and foreign
policies. He sought to condemn the total or annihilating character of modern war and yet still provide for a legitimate defensive use of nuclear weapons in an era when the chief
adversaries of the United States would also be armed with such
weapons. Writing at the beginning of the atomic era, Parsons
did not, of course, reflect the more detailed and nuanced debates
over the morality of nuclear deterrence which would exercise
Catholic moralists in the sixties and seventies. Yet he reflected
the consistent attempt of the CAIP, and many who would follow
it in later decades, to reconcile the abhorrence of traditional
Catholic morality for weapons of mass destruction and the desire to provide moral legitimacy to some possession and use of
them by the United States in its own defense.

Parsons did condemn what he saw to be the beginning of the
greatest arms race in the history of the world, and viewed a
nuclear arms race as itself being the greatest potential cause
of World War III. He criticized the continuing production of
nuclear weapons by the United States as a cause of Russian
suspicion of America and the motive behind Russian behavior
at the U.N. Parsons called for the United States to cease production of nuclear arms or bear the responsibility for the outbreak of another war. The Reverend John K. Ryan,[36] another
prominent member of the CAIP Ethics Committee which Parsons chaired, dissented from this conclusion, and the CAIP
generally seems not to have endorsed it. A later CAIP position
paper declared that the Soviet Union's obduracy toward any
realistic international supervision and control of atomic energy

made it unwise for the United States to stop the production of atomic weaponry.[37]

The CAIP did support the international control of nuclear arms and energy development as the only final solution to the threat posed by the arms race. It endorsed the early proposals of the United States, Canada, and the United Kingdom for the establishment of a United Nations Atomic Energy Commission to control the proliferation of atomic energy technology, and believed the United States to be leading the way in good faith on this issue. The association also envisioned the logical conclusion of the concern over nuclear energy as extending to a need to control all weapons of mass destruction (chemical and biological), and ultimately leading to the necessity of general disarmament through the creation of a world authority.[38]

Thus, in its consideration of the specific problems of modern war and the nuclear age, the CAIP was consistent with both its internationalist aspirations for the necessity of a world government and its Americanist sentiments in viewing the United States as genuinely working for peace in the face of threats from a basically untrustworthy communist foe. Its sense of the threat of nuclear war was subordinate to its sense of the threat of communist aggression, and its desire to control the proliferation of modern technological arsenals was controlled by its deeply felt need to accommodate the stated needs of American defense policy.

In the end, the CAIP's Americanist sentiments determined its internationalist aspirations. Its vision of a world order to end war and ensure international development was controlled by its hope that the current East-West conflict would end with the defeat of communism, if not its physical annihilation. Consequently, its optimism about the ability of the national states to create an international world order without war was decidedly tempered by its belligerency toward what it saw as the chief ideological opponent of that world order's possibility.

In the fifties the CAIP tended to concern itself more with the underlying causes of war in economic and social deprivation, and in rearticulating its call for the creation of viable international structures, than with a consideration of nuclear weapons and related issues.[39] In 1955 the Reverend George G.

Higgins, the CAIP's executive secretary, was appointed head of the Social Action Department of the National Catholic Welfare Conference. Under his leadership the CAIP became virtually undistinguishable from the NCWC. In 1969, following the reorganization of the NCWC into the National Conference of Catholic Bishops and the United States Catholic Conference in 1966, the CAIP ceased to exist as a separate organization.

THE CATHOLIC WORKER MOVEMENT

Founded in 1933 by Dorothy Day to implement the social philosophy of Peter Maurin, the Catholic Worker was the first American Catholic pacifist group, and has been the most long-lived radical movement in American Catholicism. While decidedly a minority within Catholicism, the Catholic Worker has exercised, over the years, a tremendous influence on the thinking of many Catholics concerned with social reconstruction.

The social perspective of the Catholic Worker is quite at odds with that represented by the CAIP. In the early sixties the movement provided the most radical Catholic intellectual heritage available to those Catholics seeking to formulate a more revolutionary stance toward American society, and its influence was significant among many whose names are associated with the Catholic Left of the late sixties and early seventies.

The summary which follows will not seek to present a systematic study of the writings of Dorothy Day, Peter Maurin, and the contributors to the *Catholic Worker* paper. Rather, it will seek to present the major outlines of the social perspective of the Catholic Worker tradition, as it entered the period with which this study is concerned and formed one of the major polarities of Catholic thought on the issues of war and peace.

Despite various points at which she differed from Maurin in practice and emphasis, Dorothy Day insisted that it was his ideas which underlay the Catholic Worker. The Catholic Worker movement was in no way an orthodoxy demanding an absolute ideological adherence of all who worked within it, and among its affiliates could be found a variety of viewpoints on various issues. Yet the major philosophical orientations of the movement and the critique it brought to American society have their sources in the thoughts of Peter Maurin.[40]

The son of a French peasant, Maurin had become a Christian Brother and was involved for some time with the Sillon Movement of Marc Sangnier. He eventually broke with this movement, prior to its 1910 condemnation by the papacy, because he became disillusioned with its emphasis on political action as a means to social justice. Under the anticlerical repression of the government of Emile Combes, Maurin left the order, and began a wandering emigration which landed him in New York in the mid-twenties. It was here that he began composing his "Easy-Essays," which are the only written statements of his social philosophy and interpretation of history. In New York Maurin met Dorothy Day in 1933, and proposed the establishment of a newspaper to blunt the influence of the communists among Catholic workers and to publicize the Church's teachings on social justice.[41]

It is paradoxical of the ideology of Peter Maurin and the Catholic Worker that, while it is associated with the radical elements of American Catholicism, it is actually a product neither of the American Left nor liberal Catholicism, but rather of the European Right. The Catholic Worker ideology rests upon the repudiation of most of the ideas developed during the Enlightenment which became the fundamental tenets of the philosophical liberalism underlying the structure of American economics, politics, and society. In that lay the radicalism of the Catholic Worker.[42]

Maurin's social philosophy was grounded in a conviction of the validity and centrality of Roman Catholicism's role in the reconstruction of the social order. Yet, for the most part, he saw the Church as having reneged on its prophetic role and having sold out much of its own tradition to become part of the establishment. Too often its involvement in social issues has been marked by a readiness to rationalize the *status quo*.[43]

The Catholic social ideal to which Maurin looked blended a literal interpretation of the Christian Gospels with medieval ecclesiastical institutions and modern papal social teaching. Maurin believed that the Gospel provided a blueprint for the social order, and that under the guidance of the Church, me-

dieval society had succeeded in creating a social order based
on personal responsibility and cooperation in seeking the common material and spiritual good. The medieval order was shat-
tered by the Protestant Reformation, whose evil effects Maurin
found symbolized in John Calvin. Following R. H. Tawney's
study,[44] Maurin interpreted the social legacy of Calvinism to
be the legitimation of capitalism and individualism, and the
subordination of all values to economic considerations. For
Maurin the social effects of this cultural transformation were
totally disastrous and culminated in a society characterized by
a spirit of selfishness that was never given such free reign in
the Christian world of the Middle Ages.[45]

   The bourgeois culture which supplanted that of the medieval
world was judged by Maurin and the Catholic Worker to be
fundamentally opposed to human fulfillment, because it in-
culcated a spirit of competitive exploitation, and demanded
that there always be a class of exploited at the mercy of the
powerful. Thus, the Catholic Worker, unlike most American
Catholic liberals, viewed capitalism as a wholly bad force, inimical to Christian love, for it organized life around the profit
motive.

   The centrality of financial power and motive was understood
as having been made possible by ignoring the Church's traditional condemnation of usury. Drawing on Thomistic teaching, Dorothy Day summarized the movement's view: "That
money is fruitful, is the central doctrine of the capitalist heresy."[46] For Maurin, it was usury and not private property which
was the central problem of capitalism, and he judged the financial structures based upon it to be systematically responsible for the inflationary cycles which plague capitalist countries.
To return to the medieval ideal and a more human social order,
it would be necessary to undo the commercial revolution on
which the present economic system is based.[47]

   To combat the dehumanization of modern Western civilization Maurin took as a model medieval Irish monasteries, which
had laid the foundation for the Christian social order of the
Middle Ages. In Maurin's view the early Irish monasteries
formulated an intellectual synthesis and technique for action
which combined agrarian labor with intellectual development,

adherence to the liturgy for spiritual growth, and the providing of hospitality to all who sought it. What the Irish monks had done to re-establish the foundations of Christian culture in Europe after the fall of the Roman Empire, Maurin believed the Christian community could do today in the face of the failure of modern empires.[48]

To achieve this goal, the Catholic Worker sought to provide not a strategy for dealing with particular social problems, but rather a "total idea" or way of life aimed at the regeneration of society. The core of the Catholic Worker's social ideal was the concept of Christian personalism. For Maurin, the heart of the Christian life was personal responsibility, which the chaotic conditions of modern bourgeois society have destroyed. The mission of the Christian was to restore personal unity and responsibility to the world through integrating the spiritual and material aspects of life through his participation in the political, economic, and social concerns of the world.[49] What this meant was an attempt to live a literalist interpretation of the New Testament. To be personalist was to live actively the self-giving qualities which Jesus called for in the Gospels, which alone can bring about human community, and which are summarized in the Sermon on the Mount.

The Catholic Worker rejected the traditional dualism of Christian spirituality which separated precepts and counsels. Instead, it maintained that love was a commandment, and that to be poor, chaste, and non-violent was part of the literal command of Jesus to love one another.[50]

The movement rejected the liberal theory of history as progress and the state as the source of community. For the Catholic Worker, time has in a sense come to a standstill with the literal inbreaking of the Kingdom of God in Jesus Christ. The Christian community must therefore see itself as living at the end of time and seek to live outside of that time which is the progress that the modern technological world is bent on making.[51] In the face of the liberal myths of the nation, technology, and progress, the Catholic Worker posited the Christian myths of the garden and the fall, the light of the beatitudes, the sacred community, and sinful alienation. It was the eschatological vision of a community whose goals would only be fully realized

at the end of time, and which demanded that history submit
to it. Like the early Christians, the Catholic Worker held out
the hope that by their fidelity to Christ, history itself would be
sped to its consummation.[52] In this eschatological hope, the
movement proclaimed the possibility of establishing a com-
munion with God and neighbor which seemed impossible to
common sense.

Yet despite its eschatological orientation, the vision which
Maurin imparted to the Catholic Worker stressed the possibility of living Christian community here and now, and effecting change in the present order. The concrete forms which
this effort at Christian community took were the establishment
of farm communes and houses of hospitality for the service of
the poor. These communities, Maurin hoped, would forge a
movement which brought together scholars and workers to
clarify thought in the light of the Gospel and to unite theory
and praxis in living voluntary poverty and practicing the cor-
poral works of mercy. It was the works of mercy that Maurin
saw as the real tools of revolution, and Dorothy Day spoke of
what she saw as the difference between the peace movement
and the Catholic Worker as being precisely its wider vision
and a way of life based on the works of mercy.[53]

The use of farm communes as the ultimate vehicle for implementing his anti-industrialist ideal also reflects Maurin's opposition to the assimilationist tendencies of American
Catholicism, and especially liberal Catholicism. For Maurin,
it was the job of the Church not to adapt to the world, but to
call the world to conform to Christian principles of social living.
He therefore eschewed any reformist program seeking to work
within the present social framework through progressive leg-
islation or welfare programs. Maurin's aim was the creation of
alternative centers of living, in which the Christian community
would confront modern society with the radically different mode
of communal living that had existed in medieval society.[54] In
this way Maurin sought to "build the new in the shell of the
old."

It was on this point that Dorothy Day and others within the
Catholic Worker perhaps most openly diverged from Maurin's
philosophy. While agreeing with his priority of fashioning al-

ternative social structures, Day believed that it was necessary
to support efforts for immediate justice for the oppressed, even
though it meant working for justice within an unjust system,
which must itself be rejected. For this reason Dorothy Day and
the Catholic Worker movement consistently gave support to
labor strikes and the civil rights movement, and participated
in the American peace movement.[55]

Maurin's rejection of capitalistic-bourgeois culture also extended to current social ideologies which presented themselves
as revolutionary alternatives to capitalism, especially socialism and communism. Maurin's criticism of modern society in
certain ways resembled that found in the early writings of
Marx, such as his view of the modern person as having been
alienated from his own productive labor. Yet Maurin saw Marxism and its products, socialism and communism, as trapped in
the same intellectual and spiritual cul-de-sac as capitalism. All
were essentially materialistic philosophies. Socialism and communism may be able to bring about limited reform and the
abolition of abject poverty, but they still appealed to the same
economic motives as capitalism. Both capitalism and its ideological rivals were seen as focusing on people's acquisitive desires and being premised on class conflict rather than cooperation.
For Maurin, the only solution to modern social problems was
to construct a new type of society based not on economic motives, but on the desire of people to develop together their common human nature. None of the competing ideologies of
contemporary society were capable of providing the spiritual
basis for such a renewed society, viewing the human person as
a child of God, rather than as an economic being, and rooting
moral values in natural and divine law.[56] Thus, Maurin's call
to build a new type of community is a rejection not only of the
status quo of capitalist society, but also of the entire intellectual
framework within which the modern world has conceived of
both that society and any possible alternatives to it.

In its development of its understanding of the human person
and community, two characteristics emerged as typifying the
philosophy of the Catholic Worker: anarchism and pacifism.
During the forties and fifties both words became terms by which
the movement described itself. Its anarchism flowed from the

Catholic Worker's belief in freedom as the gift of God, given in Christ, which must be prophetically affirmed in the face of all determinist philosophy. For the Catholic Worker, freedom, despite all of its misuses and perversions, is the central theme of history. The movement's rejection of the modern philosophies of capitalism, fascism, and communism is in part based on their reliance on coercion, which is the practical denial of freedom. To live in modern society, therefore, demands resisting the implicit and explicit ways society controls individuals and forces them to conform to standards which demean them as persons and destroy the sense of personal responsibility.[57]

Intimately connected with the anarchism of the Catholic Worker was its pacifism. From the beginning, Dorothy Day insisted that pacifism was the only philosophy in accord with the Christian life demanded by Christ in the Sermon on the Mount. To love as Christ did is to see clearly the whole of life and to see what is lacking in social structures as well as in individuals. Yet this way of love also demands that justice be achieved by pure means. For Day, this could only be by a non-violent love, which extended even to the enemy. Only such a pacific love could respect the freedom of the human person and provide a foundation for any true and lasting change in society.[58]

Because of the anarchistic nature of the personalism of the Catholic Worker, the movement showed little interest in the larger social forces or units of social organization outside of the state, which it viewed as a negative force. Beyond the individual, the Catholic Worker posited the Mystical Body of Christ, before which the state stood as a coercive and divisive force which destroyed personal responsibility and the spiritual unity of the human race. This rejection of the state and any sort of controlling organizational form to social life has been criticized as not going far enough in probing the dialectic of person and society. Too quick a move to the eschatological dimension fails to deal with how the Mystical Body becomes real in social relations or even how the power structure of society is itself a context for the exercise of personal responsibility.[59]

The anti-state anarchism of the Catholic Worker would seem necessarily to lead radical Christian protest into a stance of apocalyptic sectarian response to modern society. This tendency is seen in the work of Paul Hanley Furfey, who with his acquaintance with the Catholic Worker in the thirties, became perhaps the best known systematic expositor of its philosophical outlook. In works such as *Fire on the Earth* and *The Mystery of Iniquity*, Monsignor Furfey stressed the responsibility of the Christian not to participate in sinful social structures, and advocated, as a revolutionary strategy, the Pauline admonition: "Come out from among them and be ye separated." (II Cor. 6:17).[60]

For the Catholic Worker, the process of cultural change involves an essentially religious commitment to a counter-cultural community, which seeks by its witness to invite individuals to convert to its way of life. While the sectarian posture of the movement has incurred the criticism that an apocalyptic withdrawal has little actual effect on existing social structures, such criticism would not be a deterrent to the movement's stalwart adherents. The Catholic Worker ethic is basically a commitment to the "foolishness" of the cross and not a search for success. Success is always secondary to moving in the direction of the truth. In the end, what is of consequence for the movement is the constant reassertion of the value of the person in the face of a depersonalizing mass society.[61]

Nevertheless, there is a tension between Maurin's harking to the ideal of medieval society and the anarchistic personalism of the Catholic Worker. The social synthesis of medieval Christian Europe clearly recognized a positive role of the state in the maintenance of a just social order, as well as the need for strong intermediate structures between the state and the individual (family, church, guild, commune, etc.). The social philosophy of the Catholic Worker has not clearly addressed the question of how to combine its personalist approach, which preserves the values of person and community, with the necessity of the state and the creation of intermediate social structures.

A similar tension exists in the Catholic Worker's philosophy of non-violence. The movement had little concern for working out a theory of force and its use, and simply presupposed all coercion to be destructive. It regarded the state's use of force in law enforcement and punishment as self-evidently unjust, but did not deal with the state's role in restraining evil or how this was to be done.[62]

The movement's paper attacked the traditional Catholic just war theory as inadequate to the era of modern war, even though it would use the theory to the extent that the editors believed that its categories could be interpreted as invalidating modern war. The movement developed no theoretical bridge between its evangelical, eschatologically oriented pacifism and rational institutional attempts to limit or eliminate war.[63] This, together with its anarchistic personalism, probably accounts for the Catholic Worker's neglect of the questions involved with the establishment of an international government, which so preoccupied the CAIP.

Yet tensions within the Catholic Worker position can be seen in Dorothy Day's support of the Cuban revolution. In her justification, Day said she did not reject her adherence to the ideal of non-violence, but that she could still recognize that violence for the poor was better than violence against them.[64] That she could so complicate, without rejecting, her commitment to non-violence promised that pacifist Catholics would continue to chafe against the constraints of that stern creed as they sought to explore the limits and means of a non-violent revolution.

A final feature of the Catholic Worker tradition to be noted here was its adherence to a self-consciously Catholic identification. Under the strong influence of Dorothy Day, the movement opposed the secularization of religion and stressed the importance of religious externals. This did not mean that the movement was not willing to take issue on occasion with the official Church. In 1956, Dorothy Day dissented from Pius XII's rejection of conscientious objection. She also admitted that much of the persecution of the Church by the Cuban revolution (and by revolutionary movements elsewhere) was itself in part due to the betrayal by churchmen of their mission and their insensitivity to the poverty around them. Similarly, the relationship of the Catholic Worker and its home Archdiocese of New York was often quite strained because of chancery disapproval of many of the political involvements of the movement's members.[65] Yet Dorothy Day, even when most disappointed with the Church's moral leadership, would maintain that there was no place else to go for the spiritual truth and sustenance of the Gospel.

During the sixties, however, Day observed that the increasing influx of youth who came to the Catholic Worker to protest war and social injustice could no longer identify with the Church. For many of them, the meaning of Christ and the Church (to the extent that they still had meaning) was reduced to their usefulness as catalysts for change. Day was concerned that the youth who were attracted to the movement, and who were so concerned with establishing community, knew nothing of the spiritual foundation of human community. She was particularly distressed that many brought drugs and habits of immorality. Day felt that the moral and spiritual disintegration which she observed in these youth was itself the product of the inner collapse of bourgeois culture, and all the more she lamented the Church's failure to reach modern society.[66]

SUMMARY

The CAIP and the Catholic Worker together present the two major ways in which American Catholics understood the issue of war as the nation and the Church entered the decade of the sixties. In presenting these conflicting conceptual perspectives it is important to see the chief ways in which they both coincide with and contradict one another, as well as the chief internal tensions within each. Both contain fundamental elements of traditional Catholic teaching on war and the social order, as well as differing interpretations of how that teaching applied to contemporary American society and international relations. How Catholics preserved, developed, ignored or contradicted the major elements of these two perspectives is a major feature of recent Catholic attempts to grapple with the issue of war.

Both the CAIP and the Catholic Worker traditions concur that the issue of war looks beyond the question of the morality or immorality of particular weapons or the just use of force. Both present the issue of war as being part of the issue of the creation of a just social order based on the recognition of the humanity of all people and the mutual development of our human nature. For each, the issue of war is ultimately the issue of culture. The unique significance of modern war is not only in the unprecedented horror of modern weapons, but also in the historically unprecedented nature of modern secular culture and its ability to destroy the spiritual bonds and foundations of the human community.

Both the CAIP and the Catholic Worker rooted their understanding of the historical origin of the modern social problem in the traditional Catholic critique of the Protestant Reformation and the philosophical liberalism of the Enlightenment. For both, the Protestant Reformation is represented not so much by Luther as by Calvin, and the cultural transformation which swept over Western civilization at that time was represented in the rise of an individualism which destroyed the communalism of medieval Europe and made possible the rise of modern capitalism.

For both, the solution to the social problem, of which war was the deadliest expression, required a rolling back of these historical changes, and a return to the social ideals and sense of the common good. In its essence, the social foundation for peace and justice, which both the CAIP and Catholic Worker saw as paramount, was the re-establishment of a sense of relatedness among the world's peoples, both within and among states. It was this fundamental human kinship which modern society was seen as negating in its substitution of materialistic competition for human cooperation. The absence of this cultural awareness and fostering of basic human kinship was credited as the single most important factor in the creation of the materialistic and nationalistic competition of nations and social ideologies, which inevitably culminated in war. Only a spiritual revolution, which created a social consciousness of God as the true end of man and the common dignity of all the world's peoples, could fashion a cultural condition in which the control or elimination of war was possible.

Intimately connected to this understanding of the historical roots of the modern social crisis is the relation of the problem of war to racism. The Catholic Worker consistently condemned racism as one of the most outstanding features of modern society's inhumanity and alienation from God. In its own analysis, the CAIP recognized that the development of bourgeois culture had made possible the denial of human status to Negroes and Indians, which allowed their enslavement and annihilation. Implicit in the perspective of both the CAIP and the Catholic Worker is the recognition that the Calvinist culture which produced capitalism also, in destroying the sense of universal human kinship, gave birth to contemporary racism, which, in turn, added a further dimension to warfare. To the extent that full human status could be denied to whole groups of people, there would be no realistic limit to the violence that could be directed against them. Prior to the sixties, however, neither the CAIP nor the Catholic Worker clearly defined the relation of war and race as a cultural expression of American and Western society. This question would become a significant focus of social criticism for many American Catholics addressing the issue of war in the sixties and seventies.

Yet, while there is much similarity in their understanding of the historical origins of the present social crisis and in their vision of the Christian ideal for social reconstruction, there is obviously a radical difference in their application of this social vision to American society and the international situation. This difference is rooted, in large measure, in their different judgments on the United States as either perpetuating the destructive developments within Western civilization or leading the way to a renewed world order. Their judgments on the United States, in turn, determined the understanding which the CAIP and the Catholic Worker each had of the conflicts which structured the character of current international relations. In the relationship of Church and world, these conflicting interpretations of American society and its place in the international community determined the understanding of the "world" in which the CAIP and the Catholic Worker saw the Church as situated.

For the CAIP the conflict determining international relations was the struggle against communism, which it viewed as the pure distillation and ultimate product of the spiritual degeneracy of Western civilization. While willing to apply its critique of secular culture to America, the criticism of the CAIP was muted by its belief that America and the Western democracies still retained enough of the Christian heritage to provide leadership in the reconstruction of a just world order. Its Americanist commitment determined that the CAIP could condemn the abuses of American capitalism, but not reject the capitalist system. It could condemn previous imperialistic adventures of the United States, but not the objectives of American foreign policy. While often expressing an uneasy conscience over domestic injustice and the future course of American society, the CAIP usually turned from a thorough critique of American society to reasserting the need for international institutions and a moral renewal based on Catholic social principles.

In this, it would seem to incur the criticism which Adrian Cunningham and Terry Eagleton have made of the inadequacy of traditional liberal social thought. This inadequacy, they claim, was often clearly exemplified in debates on the problem of war:

These are either conducted with great energy in the abstract realm of natural law and just war theory, or, as a slight advance on this, in terms of international institutions like the U.N. or personal protest and "change of heart." The point is that *all* these attitudes completely evade the social issues involved in war, and the necessity of political action within, as well as between states. The interrelation of war and a permanent war-economy, and ultimately, of exploitation, violence, and divisiveness in war and in the structures of capitalism, is frequently missed.[67]

It is true that the CAIP consistently called for economic reform, and its outcries often implied that this would mean significant change in the present mode of social organization. The implications of this call for reform, however, were never pursued to the point of ever threatening a serious critique of American social institutions. Neither was the CAIP's critique of capitalist practices carried to the point of threatening a condemnation of American foreign policy objectives. Similarly, its rejection of the modern concept of total war and weapons of mass destruction could not override its need to defend American involvement in the nuclear arms race and to provide a justification for the use of such weapons, even against civil targets. In the end, the CAIP commitment to traditional Catholic teaching on the social order and international relations was often at odds with its support of the American and Western

cause against communism. Where these two conflicted remained
an area mostly either ignored or unexplored.
The Catholic Worker presents a rather different problem.
The conflict defining the relations between nations and peoples,
it believed, was not the struggle between East and West, but
the struggle between Christianity and modern culture. The
critique which the CAIP applied to communism the Catholic
Worker applied to Western society as well. America and Russia
were seen as competitors who exemplified different ideological
forms of the same dehumanizing technological culture, which
reduced people and society to considerations of material wealth
and power. To correctly understand the struggle for the world's
future meant to reject the false choice between capitalism and
socialism, and to build a genuine alternative for a human community built on respect for the freedom and dignity of the
human person.
Yet in its anarchistic personalism, the Catholic Worker in-
vites the criticism that Terry Eagleton has made of much of
radical Christian social thought since the nineteenth century:
it has been unable to translate a radical consciousness into the
terms of actual institutional change, and has been hostile to
all ideas of programs and institutions as significant elements
of social thinking. According to Eagleton:

The basic contradiction in Christian socialism was that it attempted
a radical critique of contemporary society in the context of an ultimate
disbelief in social reality as an object worthy of absolute attention.
Christian socialism was so concerned to assert, against the pressure
of merely utilitarian change, that socialism was about human morality and relationship, that it tended to forget that it is only in the
detailed institutional process of society that feelings and relationships
are negotiated.[68]

The failure of the Catholic Worker to develop its ideas into a
theory of society and social change which admitted a place to
the state and other institutions left it in a position of being a
source of personalist protest rather than a focus for the development of a wider movement for social change.
If their differing assessments of American society determined

the CAIP's and the Catholic Worker's understanding of the world in which the Church finds itself, their differing approaches to addressing the world situation also reflect different conceptions of the necessary relationship of the Church to the world. The CAIP clearly saw the Church as being a part of the structure of society and as having a positive role to play in the building of a just and peaceful society. Its view placed no inherent contradiction between the obligations of citizenship and Christian discipleship. In contrast, the Catholic Worker placed the Christian community in a sectarian, counter-cultural position that assumed that the obligations of the citizen and the disciple of Christ are at least in constant tension and very often in outright conflict. To the extent that the CAIP stressed that there was no conflict between being an American and being a Catholic, the Catholic Worker stressed that Catholics should come away and be separated from a social order incompatible with the demands of faith.[69] This difference is most manifest in their attitudes toward pacifism.

Strict adherence to pacifism as an ethical imperative of the Gospel obviously places a breach between the Christian community and society by requiring the Christian to refuse certain fundamental obligations which the state places upon the citizen for the maintenance of its order and security. The sectarian position which absolute pacifism imposes has traditionally been exemplified by the Protestant "peace churches," such as the Mennonites. Interpreting the New Testament as demanding non-violence of the followers of Christ, the Catholic Worker readily accepted the sectarian consequences which this would impose on the Church. The assumption of a sectarian position within American society was greatly facilitated by the Catholic Worker's interpretation of the structures, values, and goals of that society as inimical to human development and world peace.

In contrast, the CAIP's rejection of pacifism and acceptance of the traditional just war ethic presupposed that the Church and the state should collaborate to promote human welfare, and, as such, the Christian must be willing to use force to protect the common good. This fusion of the responsibilities of the citizen and the Christian was, in turn, reenforced by the CAIP's view of American society as offering the best hope of the establishment of a just world order. Its struggle against the threat of communism demanded the moral sanctioning of American objectives as the "secular arm" providing defense against the great heresy of the modern world. Thus in the CAIP and the Catholic Worker are presented two contrasting pictures of the Church-world relationship, featuring differing understandings of both the world situation which the Church faces and the manner in which the Church should seek to relate to its world. Their fundamental interpretations of society and Church provided the framework for approaching the issue of war. In them is manifested the fact that how these Catholics evaluated the specific issues of war and peace was in large part determined by prior judgments on the quality of American society, and the intrinsic demands of the Christian faith regarding the use of force and the Christian's relationship to the state. The contrasts and tensions of these conflicting perspectives provided the intellectual background for the American Catholic consideration of war in the turbulent decades of the sixties and seventies.

NOTES

1. McNeal, Patricia F. *The American Catholic Peace Movement* (New York: Arno Press, 1968), pp. 14–19.
2. Ibid., p. 32.
3. *The Catholic Church and Peace Efforts*, a report of the History Committee, by John Tracy Ellis, Chairman (Washington, D.C.: The Catholic Association for International Peace, 1934), p. 32.
4. Charles G. Fenwick, "A Program for Peace, 1927–1952," in *The Role of the Christian in the World for Peace* (Washington, D.C.: The Catholic Association for International Peace, 1953), pp. 16–19.
5. John A. Driscoll, O.P., S.T.M., "Catholics and World Federal Government," in *The Role of the Christian in the World for Peace*, p. 106. Driscoll cited Pius XII's address to the Fourth Congress of the World Movement for World Federal Government in Rome, April 6, 1951:

...no organization of the world could live if it were not harmonized with the whole complex of natural relations, with that normal organic order which rules the particular relations between men and men and between different people.... We should like to invite those to reflect on this point, precisely from the federalist viewpoint, who dream of setting up a world parliament. Otherwise they would subject themselves to the play of those disintegrating forces from which our political and social order has already suffered so much. They would only add one more legal automaton to the many others which threaten to stifle nations and reduce men to the condition of inert instruments.

6. *International Ethics*, Preliminary Report of the Committee on International Ethics, by John A. Ryan, Chairman (Washington, D.C.: The Catholic Association for International Peace, 1928), pp. 5–6; Driscoll, "Catholics and World Federal Government," p. 107.

7. Fenwick, "Program for Peace," pp. 17–18.; also C.J. Nuesse, "American Catholic Opinion on World Order," *The Role of the Christian in the World for Peace*, p. 130.

8. Fenwick, "Program for Peace," p. 18.; McNeal, *American Catholic Peace Movement*, p. 29. McNeal states that the CAIP fight to amend the Neutrality Law actually contributed to helping prepare the nation for war by its emphasis on collective security rather than neutrality.

9. *Toward an Integrated World Policy*, Joint Report (Washington, D.C.: The Catholic Association for International Peace, 1950), p. 5.

10. Edward A. Conway, S.J., "Revision of the U.N. Charter," in *The Role of the Christian in the World for Peace*, pp. 122–123.

11. Thomas H. Mahoney, "Strengthening the Free World," in *The Role of the Christian in the World for Peace*, p. 94; *Integrated Policy*, p. 26.

12. *Integrated Policy*, pp. 22–23.

13. Mahoney, "Strengthening the Free World," p. 95; *Integrated Policy*, pp. 27–28; Rev. Raymond A. McGowan, "Economic Organization for Well-Being and Peace," in *The Role of the Christian in the World for Peace*, pp. 66–69. McGowan pointed out that Pius XI's encyclical on *Atheistic Communism* only devoted one-third of the text to a discussion of communism. The remaining two-thirds of the encyclical were addressed to the need for economic reform (p. 67).

14. *Integrated Policy*, p. 12.

15. Ibid., pp. 12–13.

16. Ibid., pp. 13–14.

17. Ibid., p. 14; McGowan, "Economic Organization for Well-Being and Peace," p. 68.

18. The CAIP used various terms interchangeably to refer to that modern culture which was the product of the Protestant Reformation and the Enlightenment and which replaced the culture and social order of the Middle Ages. It listed terms commonly used: "The new regime, the era of progress, the age of science, bourgeois society, liberalism, industrialism, capitalism, the century of the individual, etc.,"

in *Latin America and the United States,* Preliminary Study by the Committee on Latin-American Relations (Washington, D.C.: The Catholic Association for International Peace, 1929), p. 3.

19. John C. H. Wu, "The Role of the Christian in the World for Peace," in *The Role of the Christian in the World for Peace,* p. 8.

20. R. H. Tawney, *Religion and the Rise of Capitalism* (New York: Harcourt Brace & Co., 1952).

21. *Integrated Policy,* p. 18; *Latin America and the United States,* pp. 3–27.

22. *Integrated Policy,* p. 18.

23. *Latin America and the United States,* p. 3.

24. Ibid., p. 11.

25. Ibid., pp. 11–72.

26. Ibid., pp. 12–16.

27. Ibid., pp. 27–41. The same type of analysis is found in *An Introduction to Mexico,* report by the Committee on Latin America by Anna Dill Gamble, Chairman (Washington, D.C.: The Catholic Association for International Peace, 1936).

28. *Latin America and the United States,* pp. 23–24.

29. Ibid., p. 26; pp. 50–53.

30. *Integrated Policy,* p. 11.

31. Wilfred Parsons, S.J., "The Ethics of Atomic War," in *Peace and the Atomic Age,* three reports (Washington, D.C.: The Catholic Association for International Peace, 1947) p. 5: "Above all, therefore, it should be of utmost importance that the energy originated by such a process (atomic fission) should not be let loose to explode—but a way found to control such power by suitable chemical means. Otherwise there could result not only in a single place, but also for our entire planet, a dangerous catastrophe."

32. Edward A. Conway, S.J., "The International Control of Atomic Energy," in *Peace in the Atomic Age,* pp. 21–23.

33. Parsons, "The Ethics of Atomic War," pp. 8–11.

34. Ibid., pp. 11–15.

35. John C. Ford, "The Morality of Obliteration Bombing," *Theological Studies* 5 (September 1944): 261–399.

36. Parsons, "The Ethics of Atomic War," p. 16.; Ryan was noted for his study, *Modern War and Basic Ethics* (Milwaukee: The Bruce Publishing Company, 1940). In this study Ryan strongly condemned any direct attack on civil populations, and dismissed the various efforts of other moralists to justify attacks on cities by the principle of double effect (chapter 9).

37. *Integrated Policy,* p. 17.

38. Conway, "International Control of Atomic Energy," pp. 31–32.; Thomas H. Mahoney, "The Atomic Bomb and the United Nations—Can the United Nations Keep the Peace?" in *Peace and the Atomic Age*, pp. 33–43.

39. A significant example of this is seen in the 1953 symposium, *The Role of the Christian in the World for Peace*. The symposium considered the problems of migration, food production, the economic system, communism, the U.N., and technical development, but gave no attention to the question of nuclear arms, or modern war as such.

40. Some biographical material on Maurin (1877–1949) can be found in William D. Miller, *A Harsh and Dreadful Love: Dorothy Day and the Catholic Worker Movement* (New York: Liveright, 1983), and in Dorothy Day's autobiography, *The Long Loneliness* (San Francisco: Harper and Row, Publishers, 1952); also in Arthur Sheehan, *Peter Maurin, the Gay Believer* (Garden City, New York: Hanover House, 1959).

41. Day, *Long Loneliness*, pp. 169–175; Anthony Novitsky, "Peter Maurin's Green Revolution: The Radical Implications of Reactionary Social Catholicism," *The Review of Politics* 37 (January 1975): 86. Novitsky provides the most systematic attempt to treat the thought of Peter Maurin. This article is based on his doctoral dissertation, "The Ideological Development of Peter Maurin's Green Revolution: From Le Sillon to the Catholic Worker" (the State University of New York at Buffalo, 1976).

42. Novitsky, "Green Revolution," pp. 83–84.

43. Peter Maurin, "Easy Essays," in Thomas C. Cornell and James H. Forest, eds., *A Penny a Copy: Readings from the Catholic Worker* (New York: The Macmillan Co., 1968), pp. 15–16. These selections give an example of the "Easy Essays," which were the only form in which Maurin wrote down his social theory.

44. Tawney, *Religion and the Rise of Capitalism*.

45. Novitsky, "Green Revolution," pp. 87–89.

46. John Stuart Sandberg, "The Eschatological Ethic of the Catholic Worker" (Ph.D. dissertation, The Catholic University of America, 1978), pp. 50, 146–148.

47. Novitsky, "Green Revolution," pp. 97–98. Maurin interpreted Calvin's justification of usury as the foundation of the modern commercial revolution.

48. Maurin, "Easy Essays," pp. 11–14; Novitsky, "Green Revolution," p. 90.

49. McNeal, *American Catholic Peace Movement*, p. 36.

50. Sandberg, "Eschatological Ethic," pp. 25–29.

51. Miller, *Harsh and Dreadful Love*, pp. 2–3.
52. McNeal, *American Catholic Peace Movement*, p. 67.
53. Ibid., p. 190; Sandberg, "Eschatological Ethic," p. 12.
54. Novitsky, "Green Revolution", p. 96.
55. Ibid., p. 100; Sandberg, "Eschatological Ethic," pp. 149–151.
56. Novitsky, "Green Revolution," pp. 96–97, 101.
57. Miller, *Harsh and Dreadful Love*, p. xi; Sandberg, "Eschatological Ethic," pp. 38–41.
58. Sandberg, "Eschatological Ethic," p. 97.
59. Ibid., pp. 79–81.
60. Paul Hanley Furfey, *Fire on the Earth* (New York: Macmillan, 1936); *The Mystery of Iniquity* (Milwaukee: Bruce, 1944).
61. Sandberg, "Eschatological Ethic," pp. 60–62.
62. Ibid., pp. 253–256.
63. Ibid., pp. 290–294.
64. Miller, *Harsh and Dreadful Love*, p. 305.
65. Ibid., p. 305; also William D. Miller, "The Church and Dorothy Day," *The Critic* 35 (Fall 1976): 63–70; Sandberg, "Eschatological Ethic," pp. 160, 190.
66. Miller, *Harsh and Dreadful Love*, pp. 335–338.
67. Adrian Cunningham and Terry Eagleton, "Christians against Capitalism," in Adrian Cunningham et al., *Catholics and the Left*, with an introduction by Neal Middleton (Springfield, Ill.: Templegate Publishers, 1966), p. 42.
68. Terry Eagleton, "The Roots of the Christian Crisis," in *Catholics and the Left*, pp. 69–70.
69. A classic treatment of differing models of church-state relations can be found in Ernst Troeltsch, *The Social Teaching of the Christian Churches*, 2 vols. (New York: The Macmillan Company, 1950). Two of the ecclesial organizational forms treated by Troeltsch are the church and sect types. The differing attitudes of these two types of ecclesial structures toward relations with the state are represented by the CAIP and the Catholic Worker respectively.

2

Catholic Americanism: Realist

As the decade of the 1960's dawned, secular and religious peace movements had already begun to experience a revival in the United States and Western Europe. In reflecting on the rise of the Catholic Left in Britain and the United States, Brian Wicker cited the factors most immediately responsible for this development to be the political climate of the post–1956 years and the moral problem of nuclear warfare and deterrence. He concluded, "It could be said that the Catholic Left was born out of the recognition that there was no possibility of effectively separating the moral from the political problems of the cold war."[1]

In the United States the immediate impetus to this development was the atmospheric testing of the hydrogen bomb. Beyond concern for the immediate effects of radioactive fallout from these tests, many ideologically disparate persons sought to focus attention on the problem of thermonuclear weapons themselves. From these efforts, and extending into the subsequent two decades, emerged a renewed examination of national policy, the morality of modern war and nuclear weapons, and the relationship of the causes of war to American national values and goals. From the mid-sixties to its termination in 1975, the escalating American intervention in Vietnam provided the strongest and most divisive stimulus to the debates of this period.[2]

Besides sharing the concerns of their secular counterparts, those American Catholics who engaged in these debates had the added incentive of the thrust of the papal and conciliar teaching of these years. The encyclicals of Pope John XXIII, *Mater et Magistra* (1960) and especially *Pacem in Terris* (1961), focused attention on the growing interdependence of the world's peoples, and the need to construct a renewed international order to foster mutual development and to avoid the irrational recourse to nuclear war. The Second Vatican Council's "Pastoral Constitution on the Church in the Modern World" (*Gaudium et Spes*—1965) recognized the need to look at war in the modern era "with an entirely new attitude."

As American Catholics took up a renewed examination of the issues relating to modern war in this period, several schools of thought emerged which constituted the chief ways in which they interpreted the meaning of war as an issue in American society. These intellectual perspectives continued to reflect the polarities seen in the conflicting views of the CAIP and the Catholic Worker, as well as providing significant developments upon them. This and the following chapters will seek to present these conflicting schools of thought in terms of those Catholic writers who emerged as most representative of them from 1960 to 1983. The major positions which will be examined here can be generally classified as Catholic realism, nuclear pacifism, and radical pacifism and resistance. These general classifications can, in turn, be subdivided according to nuances and developments among those falling within them.

This chapter and the next will focus on presenting the development of the positions which can be classified as realist and nuclear pacifist. The more radical pacifist positions will be treated in the following two chapters. This division is made primarily in accordance with the level and extent of the critique which the advocates of these positions made of American society in their interpretation of the issue of war, and secondly the implication of their positions for the place of the Church in society.

The realist and nuclear pacifist positions treated here differ in certain fundamental judgments which they make in such matters as the application of the just war theory to the conditions of modern war, their view of the qualitative problem posed by nuclear weapons, and the approaches they take to the amelioration of international conflict. Yet they converge in their

rejection of pacifism, their belief in the superiority of the tradition of Western liberal democracy, and the acceptance of the
clash between Western democracy and communism as the defining cultural-political-moral struggle determining international relations today. Thus, despite the often acrimonious
debates between representatives of these perspectives, they can
be examined together as conflicting positions, still sharing certain fundamental presuppositions.

While many pacifist spokesmen were found in the ranks of
those calling for a rejection of the development and use of (or
threat to use) nuclear weapons (nuclear pacifism), their actual
positions extended beyond the question of nuclear weapons to
a rejection of all force in international relations, and in many
cases to a negative assessment of American society. The more
radical perspectives of the Catholic pacifist and resistance
movement will, therefore, be given separate treatment. This
format of presentation will hopefully allow the primary line
dividing Catholic interpretations of the issue of war, and the
significant division within each major school of thought, to be
more clearly delineated.

Since the debates between realists, nuclear pacifists, and
pacifists presuppose the background of the just war teaching
as the dominant approach of the Catholic Church to evaluating
the relationship of war and morality, it is necessary to state
briefly the traditional criteria of the just war theory. Particularly
for the realists and nuclear pacifists treated here, the just war
categories provided the criteria for determining the parameters
of the moral use of armed force in a world where pacifism was
not seen as a realistic option.

The Just War

The tradition of Catholic just war teaching presumes against
the use of armed force, but allows that, under certain circumstances, that presumption may be overridden. The criteria determining the moral resort to armed force generally dealt with
two factors: the right to go to war, *jus ad bellum*; and the moral
limits on the use of force in waging a just war, *jus in bello*. The
conditions of the *jus ad bellum* are as follows:[3]

1. Competent authority—war is to serve the public interest and must be declared by the legitimate public authority.

2. Just cause—there must be a real and grave wrong to be corrected or right to be defended.

   Traditionally three types of just causes were recognized: war of self-defense against an aggressor, offensive war to restore rights previously lost to aggression or to seek restitution for past wrongs, and offensive war to punish evil doers.

   In 1954, however, Pius XII declared that in light of the vast destructiveness of modern war, it can no longer be considered morally legitimate to resort to war except in self-defense. He therefore eliminated all but the first definition of a just cause—the repelling of an aggressor.[4]

3. Proportionality—the requirement to assess that the likely good effects of war will outweigh the obvious evil effects. Related to this is the requirement that the just party have a reasonable chance of success. Yet most authorities hold that the victim of aggression has a right to even a hopeless defense.

4. Exhaustion of peaceful remedies—war must be the last resort.

5. Right intention—the war is to be continued only as long as is necessary to achieve the just end, and nothing is to be done to imperil the goal of the war which is the establishment of a just and lasting peace. The war must not become an occasion for indulging in the uncharitable attitudes and practices usually unleashed in war.

The conditions of the *jus in bello* are:

1. Proportionality between the means used to prosecute the war and the likelihood of achieving just ends.

2. Any means which is immoral in itself may not be used, no matter how militarily effective it is. The most important characterization of immoral means concerns the killing of innocents (or non-combatants, in the language of international law). These are to be immune from direct intentional attack.

   Traditional teaching has allowed the use of a principle of moral reasoning, called the double effect, by which an action which killed innocents could be morally allowed if: its intended object was a legitimate military target which could not be dealt with in any other way, and the deaths of innocents were incidental to the intention of the attacker.[5] This principle in particular, as well as the application of the total just war criteria in the nuclear age, and even to conventional modern warfare, would be a major area of controversy within American Catholic debates on war. How these criteria were understood and applied depended on the perspective within which American Catholics viewed the meaning of war as an issue within their society.

REALISTS

The term realism has been used to designate a moral-political perspective associated with the name of Reinhold Niebuhr in American Protestant thought, and also with political analysts such as Hans Morgenthau and George Kennan. The "realism" which they represented arose after World War II as a reaction to the political idealism (internationalism) of the interwar period. This idealism was often summed up in the term "Wilsonian diplomacy," which focused on the establishment of trust in international relations, and the creation of international structures and laws to limit and eventually to eliminate war. The subjection of the world order to the rule of reason and love was dismissed as a presently unattainable goal, and pacifism was viewed as being not a Christian attitude, but a form of Renaissance optimism.[6]

In contrast to the optimism of the idealists who sought to transform the international order, the realists held that the present world order of competing nation states and ideologies was here to stay for the foreseeable future. Consequently, war and the "balance of power" would remain realities with which the moral person would have to deal. The realists, therefore, argued for a more "realistic" power-politics approach to the problems of war and international relations, which stressed the moral and political obligations of the decision maker to use power responsibly. Thus, rather than the quest for systemic change in the world order, the realist's chief task is charting the moral limits of the use of force in providing security within a stabilized balance of world powers.

As the previous chapter showed, the CAIP's approach to the

issue of war was very much characterized by the idealist internationalism which the realist school of thought rejected. Yet
other salient characteristics of the CAIP, namely its Americanism, its adherence to the just war tradition, and its view of
the ecclesial community's relationship to society, would be continued by those American Catholics who attempted to articulate a realist perspective in the last two decades.

The Catholic realist perspective that is charted here includes
individuals who, while sharing certain basic assumptions and
goals, also markedly differ in some important conclusions. Yet
together they reflect a distinct moral-political perspective which
constituted one of the major worldviews within which American Catholics have interpreted the issue of war in recent years.
This section will attempt to present the most representative
expressions of this Catholic realism and the lines of development within this school of thought.

At the beginning of the sixties the most authoritative expression of the realist position in American Catholic thought was
found in the work of John Courtney Murray, S.J. Murray did
not write extensively on the question of war and peace, but the
few articles he did write were of great significance and influence.[7] The focus of Murray's work was on bringing the tradition
of Catholic thought on the interrelation of Church and state
into creative dialogue with the "American proposition" of pluralist democracy. He is most remembered for his work to reconcile traditional Catholic teaching on Church-state relations
with the American concept of religious liberty. Yet his work
also had definite implications for approaching the issue of war
and related questions.

Father Murray's analysis of the present dimensions of the
issue of war must be seen in the context of his understanding
of the current state of the "American proposition." For Murray,
American society and its form of government were a unique
historical manifestation. A republic, he argued, rests upon a
necessary social consensus, for debate and dialogue between
conflicting views and interests can only take place, constructively, within a general consensus of values that are not in
doubt. The existence of such a consensus as the basis of American pluralist democracy is evidenced in the words of the Dec-

laration of Independence, "We hold these Truths to be self-evident." Murray saw the social consensus underlying American society as combining the classical principles of constitutional government, as preserved in the American liberal tradition, and the principle of republican virtue found in the medieval social synthesis. This consensus, in fact, was interpreted by Murray as resting on the principles of natural law which find their fullest articulation in traditional Catholic teaching.[8]

For Murray, the problem of the present historical moment in American society lay in the fact that the social consensus necessary to its existence is no longer so self-evident. The crisis of society resulted from the social confusion and doubt over the moral basis of the American proposition of pluralist democracy. Society always exists on the edge of barbarism, which Murray defined as the end of all rational standards and the loss of clarity about the larger aims of life. Murray characterized a society which has slipped over into barbarism as one in which men live in fear, economic interests become primary, technology assumes an autonomous exploitative existence without the guidance of higher principles of morality and politics, and the state becomes all powerful, but unable to achieve rational ends. It was into such a crisis that Murray saw American society as having entered. This crisis was new in American history and struck at the very core of the identity of the American people.[9]

The crisis became most keen in the conflict between the type of civilization represented in the American proposition and world communism. Murray viewed communism as an apostasy from civilization, in that it rejected the principles necessary to civil society. That is, it rejected the moral-social consensus that makes pluralist democracy possible.

In the face of this world struggle, the internal crisis of American society becomes most crucial. Murray argued the need for a renewed understanding of the basic principles of the American liberal tradition of constitutionalism and the tradition of natural law teaching on the dignity and rights of the individual, on which the American proposition was founded. He feared that the actual conduct of America in the world reflected the fact that Americans no longer had a clear doctrine or moral consensus directing their policies. It was, therefore, of paramount importance that such a moral-political focus be restored to government and society. Because of their heritage of natural law tradition on the nature of the human person and society, Catholics were seen as having an especially valuable role to play in this task.[10]

Thus far Murray echoes many of the themes of the CAIP's attitude toward American society and contemporary Western culture. The best of the American liberal tradition was seen as having its roots in values originating from the Christian tradition. The present social crisis is not rooted in the traditional values and historic practice of American society, but rather in America's alienation from its own heritage. The task of social reconstruction is thus essentially to clarify and reappropriate a wedding of the genuine tradition of American liberalism with the Christian tradition of natural law, to provide a moral consensus that can support pluralist democracy.

In moving to a specific analysis of the issue of war, Murray argued that one of the most important questions one must ask is the exact nature of the conflict which defines international life today, for the answer to this question in large measure provides the context in which all other issues of foreign and defense policy will be interpreted. In defining the conflict, Murray follows Pius XII in describing it as that rupture dividing the world into opposed blocs, between which "co-existence in truth" is not possible, because there is no common acceptance of a "norm recognized by all as morally obligatory and therefore inviolable."[11]

As can be seen from Murray's view of the internal crisis of American society, this line of moral rupture also ran through the West and not just between East and West. It was this internal crisis of the West that constituted its greatest vulnerability in the confrontation with Eastern communism.

While in line with the CAIP in seeing communism as the chief nemesis of Western civilization, Murray disagreed with many who considered communism to be a Western heresy. His more radical assessment held communism to be a conscious apostasy from Western civilization, whose forerunner was Jacobinism. The aim of the communist movement, through its

chief vehicle, the Soviet Union, was to succeed where Jacobinism had failed in bringing the history of the West to an end,
by destroying civilization constructed on the traditions of
Christianity and Western liberalism. Murray saw this objective
reflected in the cardinal tenet of communism that there are no
bounds to the omnipotence of government.

One of Murray's great fears was that pragmatically minded
Americans would fail to understand this profoundly ideological
essence of communism and, consequently, not understand the
Soviet Union, which as the chief vehicle of communism was,
therefore, the chief adversary of the West. Murray argued that
Americans did not comprehend that in the Soviet Union they
did not confront another nation state but rather an empire, in
which one half of its subjects were ethnically non-Russian,
colonized peoples. This empire, as Murray analyzed it, was
unique as an empire and a state power. As a state power, it
was based on a complete despotism of a centralized government
devoid of any understanding of law to a degree unprecedented
in history. As an empire it was also unique in that it was
grounded on a revolutionary doctrine. In the Soviet Union,
Murray perceived a consciously erected atheistic materialism,
that, for the first time in history, was the practical political
and legal principle forming the substance and procedure of the
state. This revolutionary doctrine provided an account of history and the nature of historical change, and was inherently
aggressive, for it saw itself as destined to be the sole surviving
political force in the world. Murray concluded that it is this
doctrine and the doctrinal nature of the Soviet empire that
made it unappeasable, and therefore a threat to the Western
powers.[12]

Murray's analysis of the nature and structure of the Soviet
Union also reveals the rationale behind his departure from the
internationalism of the CAIP. For Murray, Soviet doctrine and
social structure were an organic whole, and could not be significantly altered without destroying the whole system. For
example, the official atheism of the state could not be altered
because to do so would admit a power higher than the state.
This, in turn, would provide a basis for the individual to make
claims against the state, which communist doctrine cannot al-

low. Murray concluded that the Soviet empire must remain governed by communist doctrine, if it was to remain intact.

Consequently, Murray could see the Soviet leaders yielding to nothing except calculations of power and success. It was necessary, therefore, to put an end to the Wilsonian era of diplomacy, with its exaggerated trust in world assemblies and international conferences. Instead, Murray argued, we must deal directly with the Soviet Union, for if any disarmament agreement is reached, it would be as a result of bilateral talks between the Kremlin and the White House, without the "confusing assistance of additional nations and alliances."[13]

While Murray did not overtly reject the ideal of establishing an international authority for the control of war, his "realist" approach could not sustain the optimism of holding such a goal as practically realizable. Consequently, he favored a more power-oriented approach to confront an ideological opponent that was seen as inherently incapable of responding to anything else. This attitude was clearly reflected in Murray's response to John XXIII's encyclical *Pacem in Terris*. The Pope strongly upheld the internationalist ideal, which had been a consistent dimension of Pius XII's teaching, and urged the world's nations to eliminate any excuse for war by establishing an international authority to adjudicate disputes. Murray's response echoed those of Reinhold Niebuhr and others in arguing that the Pope was failing to take realistic account of the actual schism which divided the contemporary world.[14]

Rather than pursue the impractical ideal of a new international order, Murray argued the need to develop a strategy of continuous American engagement with Soviet attempts at expansion, as well as the formulation of a *moral* policy to guide the conduct of this strategy. This engagement did not necessarily mean a military confrontation. In fact, to avoid the military level of confrontation, Americans needed to appreciate the doctrinal nature of the present world conflict. Murray argued that the threat posed by the Soviet Union was not world domination in the traditional sense of overt military expansion, but rather world revolution, in the spreading of its ideology and fostering revolutionary struggles. To meet the threat of world revolution Americans had to be able to formulate a doctrinal reply to communism.[15]

The problem for Murray was that the West had not yet formulated such a reply, in large measure because of its own internal confusion and lack of perception of its own cultural and moral heritage. He agreed with Arnold Toynbee that the West had identified itself with technology as its cult and sole export. This constituted a self-contradiction in which Western civilization was rejecting its own soul. The attempts of Western countries to engender anti-communist movements were considered by Murray to be a dismal failure because of their emotional character. Their significant weakness was their intellectual failure to clarify what is the difference between Western civilization and communism, and what were the reasons that allowed communism to obtain a foothold in the West.[16]

When the confrontation of East and West did turn to the question of armaments and war, Murray feared that the same lack of intellectual clarity which kept Americans from formulating a doctrinal reply to communism also resulted in malformed or even immoral defense policies. Murray maintained that the Soviets had shown a greater understanding than Americans of the problem of using force in the modern era, by developing a defense policy he characterized as "maximum security and minimum risk." That is, Soviet policy reflected their doctrine in believing in the inevitability of the progress of world revolution. They, therefore, would not jeopardize that progress by a major war over anything less than the Soviet homeland itself. The Soviets consequently followed the policy of not allowing any confrontation to be pushed to the point of all-out war. Even in the case of military confrontation, Soviet policy, according to Murray, allowed the tactical use of nuclear weapons, but would terminate their use short of an all-out nuclear exchange, which would devastate their homeland. Murray concluded that the United States, because of its own massive nuclear deterrence, did not stand in danger of a surprise Soviet attack on the West. This did not mean, for Murray, that the Soviets did not want war, but rather that they only wanted that war which furthered the interest of world revolution, and which did not jeopardize their own survival.[17]

In effect, Murray saw the Soviets as having solved the policy problem that bedeviled American strategists, in having separated the problem of survival from the problem of war. The

Soviets had no intention of making survival a question to be
settled by war. Americans, on the other hand, still grappled
with the question of how to use force and withdraw before
survival was at stake. The problem lay in the fact that in their
approach to war Americans adopted the opposite attitude to
that of the Soviets. Murray lamented that, historically, war for
Americans has always been either a crime or a crusade. That
is, as a people they have tended to reject all wars before the
fact, but having entered into one would recognize no limits in
its prosecution.[18] In effect, Americans tend to resort to war only
when survival is seen to be at stake, and always make war a
matter of survival. In so doing, Murray felt, the West had
surrendered to the East its own doctrine that survival should
never be a matter of arms. He argued that survival should not
be left in the lap of the Department of Defense or the Atomic
Energy Commission. To conceive of strategic defense only in
apocalyptic terms served only to make American power
impotent.[19]

Instead, Murray maintained, a true understanding of Soviet
doctrine should lead the United States to follow a policy of
maximum risk and minimum security. That is, knowing that
the Soviets will not risk a major war for less than the defense
of their homeland, America should directly counter any communist attempt to use force to expand their sphere of hege-
mony. He felt that this was the basis of the American entry
into Korea, but that the United States backed away to a policy
of minimum risk.[20]

To mount such a strategy of maximum engagement required
the one thing which the United States had failed to do—the
development of a doctrine of the limited use of force, including
nuclear weapons. This failure, Murray argued, was based on
the false assumption that any use of nuclear weapons would
lead to an unlimited use of them. The result was to leave the
United States caught in a choice between renouncing all use
of nuclear weapons or launching a world holocaust. Murray's
attitude toward the use of nuclear weapons was perhaps best
summed up in the often quoted passage, "since nuclear war
may be a necessity, it must be made a possibility. Its possibility
must be created.... To say that the possibility of a limited

nuclear war cannot be created by intelligence and energy, under the direction of a moral imperative, is to succumb to some sort of determinism in human affairs."[21] The failure to develop this possibility for a moral use of nuclear weapons was seen as the direct result of the tragic linkage of war and survival in the American mind, which prevented the development of a strategy for the use of force (even nuclear force) within rational limits. Murray felt that the general public's sense of the irrationality of rooting our strategic defense policies in the threat of global suicide led to focusing their deep disapproval on what he saw as the relatively minor question of nuclear testing.[22]

For Murray the heart of the problem of creating the possibility of limited war lay in the fact that our military and political thinking lagged behind our technology. Our military policies were, in fact, governed by the mad rush of expanding technology, rather than harnessing technological development to serve the needs of policy. The lack of a moral doctrine only made the situation worse, for it meant we were developing immense power without a sense of direction. The only conclusion could be the destruction of humanity.[23]

In arguing for the need to construct a clear model of limited war in the nuclear era, Murray defended the validity of the traditional just war teaching of the Church as essential for this task. Drawing almost completely from the teaching of Pius XII, Murray argued that the Pope's limitation of the *jus ad bellum* to purely defensive wars did not rule out the use of atomic, biological, or chemical weapons in such a defense. Pius also taught that a just defensive war included the right of strong nations to come to the defense of weaker ones. Murray stressed that Pius's recognition of the extreme destructiveness of modern warfare did not lead to a denial of the right to just defense in the absence of a world authority.[24]

The present questioning of the just war teaching by Catholics was attributed by Murray to the fact that in the past it was not used for a sound critique of public policies.[25] The traditional teaching, Murray argued, could be a solvent for false dilemmas that offer no alternatives to pacifism and bellicism, both of which banish morality from war. Furthermore, the just war categories could provide the clarity necessary to public debates

on international relations and defense policies. Murray insisted
that a reappropriation of the just war tradition was essential
to the development of the moral-political consensus necessary
to America's ability to mount a strong and moral military deterrent. Yet, given the internal crisis of American society, Murray ended on a note of pessimism that this moral clarification
of American goals and policies would ever occur.[26]

Thus in John Courtney Murray is set forth what is perhaps
the most systematically thought out realist perspective within
American Catholic thought at the beginning of the sixties.
While departing from the internationalism of the CAIP, Murray clearly continued its Americanism in his definition of the
conflict constituting contemporary international relations. Here
he was also consistent with the CAIP in approaching the issue
of war within the context of the cultural struggle of Western
civilization with what was seen as the antithetical culture of
communism. As such, the issue of war remained the issue of
culture, and the creation and defense of a just social order.

Yet, as is typical of the realist approach which Murray set
forth, his discussion of the problem of war focused not on elim-
inating the causes of war, but on developing moral means of
providing security. With the rejection of internationalist solutions for providing an alternative to war as a means of settling conflicts, the problem became one of making the inevitability
of war a moral possibility.

In this perspective the specific problem of nuclear weapons
and modern war, while presenting a unique threat, does not
represent a unique moral problem. Nuclear weapons are not
seen as *mala in se*, nor is their use a qualitatively different
moral problem from the use of other weapons. They are subject
to the same norm as the use of all other weapons. The problem
is seen to be not the weapon, but the moral clarity of those
formulating policy for its use. Murray shared the abhorrence
of the extreme destructiveness of modern warfare which led
Pius XII to limit the *jus ad bellum* to purely defensive war.
Yet rather than focusing on the absence of an international
authority, which was the only reason Pius XII said defensive
war was still permissible, Murray focused on the Pope's rec-

ognition of the right of self-defense and the technical tasks of how this could take moral shape in the nuclear age.

In ending on a note of pessimism as to whether or not American society and its leaders would develop the moral and doctrinal clarity necessary to competent and moral foreign and defense policies, Murray echoed the mixed feelings of the CAIP. In both is found the conviction that the American cultural heritage contains a consensus of values at one with those of the Christian tradition as seen in its medieval synthesis. Both insisted on a conscious clarification and reappropriation of those values as essential to the survival of American society as the vessel in which they placed their hopes for Christian civilization. Yet both Murray and the CAIP expressed fears and doubts about the ultimate significance of the materialism and moral confusion which they criticized as a major feature of American society.

Despite his muted doubts about America's future prospects, Murray has been criticized by more recent commentators for his lack of critical perspective in his views of both the American capitalist system and the Cold War. In embracing the American liberal tradition and public philosophy, Murray was criticized as also embracing its bias for liberty at the expense of justice.[27] Because of his focus on blending the liberal tradition and the Catholic natural law tradition to create a renewed social consensus for American democracy, Murray did not raise or pursue substantive questions about the justice of American economic and social arrangements.

Present here is also a strong ecclesiological dimension in Murray's thinking. In attempting to unite the Church's tradition of natural law teaching with the public philosophy of the American liberal tradition, Murray demonstrated how he saw the Church must enter the realm of public debate in a pluralistic society. For Murray, the Church could not attempt to use specifically religious symbols or theological language to address public issues, for the state in a pluralist society is not based upon an acceptance of the religious truths which the Church holds. Rather, the latter must translate its social teachings, based on religious insights and convictions, into categories of philosophical discourse, which can address the state in its own language and in terms of its own perceived interests. Only in this way can the Church contribute to the creation of a language of civil discourse, in which all segments of a pluralist society can engage, and formulate a common conception of their common good.

Yet as Murray approached this task, he reflected a basic act of trust in the compatibility of the American liberal tradition with the realization of the Christian vision of a just society. This overriding confidence in the doctrinal base of the American cultural heritage as essentially at one with the Christian view of the human person and society served as a determinative characteristic of Murray's work. Consequently, his criticisms of American society would remain focused, not on the injustices of the economic or political system, but on the extent to which Americans had lost faith in their own liberal traditions. The clarification of the moral and philosophical dimensions of the American proposition was all the more imperative in the face of the challenge to Western civilization that Murray saw being posed by communism.

In 1960 Murray's major article on modern war appeared in *Morality and Modern Warfare*, edited by William J. Nagle.[28] This volume, which was one of several "state of the question" books published during the sixties and seventies, provides perhaps the best reflection of the American Catholic consensus on the issue of modern war at the beginning of the sixties. Only one contributor, Gordon Zahn, represented a pacifist perspective. The majority of the contributors developed positions basically in accord with that of Murray, and which adhered to the just war approach to the defense of American nuclear and defense policies.

In his introduction Nagle referred to a similar book published in England the year before, which was much more pacifist in its orientation.[29] He credited the difference to the differing contexts within which American and English Catholics must assume their moral positions. Nagle explained that the unanimity among the few American Catholics and Protestants who had written on the subject reflected the American sense of responsibility before the communist threat. The pacifist positions of people like Gordon Zahn and Dorothy Day were praised by Nagle, not for being able to offer solutions to the problem, but for prodding the consciences of others to come to terms with the problems of modern war.[30]

It should be noted that Nagle's recognition of the noticeable difference in tone between his volume and its British counterpart was significant. Nagle's sense of the unanimity among the few American Catholics and Protestants writing on the subject at that time is testimony to the very American character of the Catholic realist perspective being charted in this chapter. His explanation for the unanimity among Catholic, Protestant, and secular realists also serves to highlight a major characteristic of Catholic realist thinking, that is, an overriding sense of the moral righteousness and responsibility of America in the face of the communist threat to Western civilization. This theme was strongly present in the work of John Courtney Murray and would continue to shape the development of Catholic realism over the following two decades. As this Americanism distinguished the consensus of American Catholic thought on war and peace from that of their British co-religionists in 1960, that same Americanism would pit Catholic realists against the rise of nuclear pacifist and pacifist sentiment within the American Catholic community during the sixties and seventies.

The unanimity among Catholic and Protestant realists which impressed Nagle was also indicative of the fact that the Catholic debate on war and peace, on which this study concentrates, did not occur in a vacuum. Particular mention should be given to the contribution of the Council on Religion and International Affairs (CRIA) for fostering interchange between Catholic and Protestant moralists. Especially in the sixties, this New York based interdenominational group sponsored a series of studies which brought together Catholic, Protestant and Jewish scholars and moralists along with members of the military and policy making communities to debate issues of nuclear war and deterrence, and modern conventional and counterinsurgency warfare. The CRIA served both to stimulate debate among Catholics and to help integrate Catholic thought into the larger American debate through the publication of papers by Catholic realists such as John Courtney Murray and William O'Brien and nuclear pacifists and pacifists such as Justus George Lawler and Gordon Zahn.

Perhaps a most significant feature of the Protestant-Catholic interchange fostered by the CRIA was its aid in facilitating interaction with the thought of Paul Ramsey. Ramsey is generally regarded by most American moralists as the most prominent and systematic expositor and proponent of the just war theory. More than any other contemporary Protestant ethician, Ramsey showed a great interest and appreciation for Roman Catholic ethical thought and natural law theory. During the sixties, his work on the morality of war provided both challenge and support for the differing schools of American Catholic thought addressing that issue.[31] Despite their disagreements with him, many of the diverse individuals treated later in this study, such as realist William O'Brien and nuclear pacifist Justus George Lawler owe much to their interaction with Ramsey. For Catholic realists, who based their position on the continuing validity of the just war theory and the need to integrate that moral tradition with the necessities of an adequate defense in the nuclear age, this interaction with Ramsey and non-Catholic American realists was vital to the development of the thinking treated in this chapter.

In Nagle's 1960 volume the majority of the contributors defined the conflict determining international relations in the same manner as Murray. The overarching conflict between the United States and the Soviet Union was seen as going beyond purely economic competition to constitute a conflict of two antithetical ways of life. As James E. Dougherty concluded, as long as the West remained pluralist and free, and as long as the Soviets remained committed to the philosophy of Lenin, no settlement was possible. In the end, communism must be resisted because no spiritual tradition could survive under it.[32] Because the majority accepted the view of America as the best hope for preserving Judeo-Christian civilization, they could not escape the compelling need to support United States defense policies and attempt to fit a nuclear defense into a framework that Catholics could call moral.

All of these contributors admitted the special problems posed by nuclear weapons, and the main concerns of their critiques of present policy centered on two themes, which Murray also stressed: 1) American defense policies and weapons production are not being directed by clearly formulated policies based on sound moral principles, but by the undirected development of technology; 2) there is a need to move the international struggle from a military level to the diplomatic and spiritual level—strengthening the moral tradition of the West is its best defense against communism.

In the contributions to this volume can also be seen a move toward consideration of the specific problems of nuclear deterrence and the use of nuclear weapons that would become much more the center of debate in the subsequent years of the decade. James E. Dougherty recognized the problem posed by the nuclear defense policy of "massive retaliation" announced by Secretary of State John Foster Dulles in the 1950's. According to this defense doctrine, the United States sought to deter a Soviet attack by threatening that any such attack on the United States or its allies would be met with an all-out nuclear strike against Soviet society (that is, against civilian population centers), with the objective of destroying the Soviet Union as a viable society.

Dougherty observed that this deterrence policy had, in fact, "worked" in so far as it could be credited with having prevented any major Soviet aggression. The trouble which Dougherty recognized with this policy was that while it was morally acceptable as long as it deterred, if deterrence failed it would be immoral to resort to such indiscriminate and total destruction. Furthermore, reliance on massive strategic retaliation to the detriment of both a conventional and a more flexible nuclear response would leave American power impotent in a host of crisis situations. Dougherty argued that it was the recognition of the moral and practical limits of massive retaliation which had led to the debate on the possibility of limited war. He held that only the development of the policy and the technical capability of waging limited conventional and nuclear war would be able to resolve the schism in the Western mind between pacifism and total war.[33] In this position Dougherty echoed the sentiments of the majority of his fellow contributors, who felt that the development of a nuclear deterrence that could effectively deter, and be morally usable should deterrence fail, was

not only morally necesary but also practically feasible. As
Thomas E. Murray concluded, to believe otherwise was to deny
man's rational ability and the ability of the American military
to make a moral use of weapons.[34]

In these statements it is possible to see the major thrust of
the realist perspective as it emerged among American Catholics in the early years of the sixties. Adopting a strongly Americanist and anti-communist position, Catholic realists focused
on the need to develop a defense policy and technical capability
to provide the West with sufficient security in its global struggle against a nemesis culture. In essence this meant a move
to apply the just war criteria to a war which could include
nuclear weapons.[35]

In its final session the Second Vatican Council debated the
issue of modern war and nuclear deterrence as part of the draft
of its "Constitution of the Church in the Modern World" (Gaudium et Spes). The final document issued in 1965 called for
approaching war with an entirely new attitude. Yet the Council
did not really resolve the moral questions raised concerning
modern war and nuclear deterrence. The Council condemned
weapons of mass destruction (designed to destroy whole areas
and their populations), but grudgingly acknowledged that the
existing systems of military deterrence, which were based on
such weapons, had preserved a peace of sorts through a balance
of terror. It also condemned the escalating arms race as a danger to peace and cause for draining resources away from vital
human needs, and urged serious efforts towards arms control
and disarmament.[36]

In the debate that arose during and after the Council's consideration of Gaudium et Spes, American Catholic realists
squared off against those Catholics who argued for a rejection
of nuclear weapons and those who called for a stance of total
pacifism. In the developing arguments of Catholic realists of
the sixties and seventies there was a noticeable shift of tone
from that found in John Courtney Murray, whom many Catholic realists regarded as the leading figure of their school of
thought. Murray, writing little on the issue of war, showed a
greater interest in analyzing American culture, and in focusing
on the ecclesiological concern of how the Church remains a

part of, and speaks to, a pluralist society. The Catholic realists who followed Murray tended to focus on the more specific and narrower question of security and how to make the right of self-defense a moral possibility in the nuclear age. In this they saw themselves as following out the task charted by Murray, namely, that since nuclear war may be a necessity, it must be made a moral possibility. The tone and direction which the Catholic realist position took is found in two articles in 1964 by James E. Dougherty and William V. Kennedy.

Dougherty attacked the contention of those who argued that the traditional criteria of the just war demanded the rejection of nuclear weapons.[37] He argued that those who claim to be nuclear pacifists really tended to shade off into total pacifism, and that therefore the attempt to present a position of nuclear pacifism, based on adhering to the moral limits of the use of force prescribed by the just war teaching, was really a ruse. The only choice was between pacifism and an acceptance of the just war, which could also be limited nuclear war. Pacifism, he argued, was rejected by the Church's tradition, and could not really claim Christian credentials.

Dougherty further rejected, as implicit in most pacifist positions, the attempt to blame both the United States and the Soviet Union as *equally* responsible for the Cold War. He strongly upheld the fundamental realist theme that Western liberal civilization was superior to that created under communism, and that any improvement in the international situation would come only as a result of the communist world becoming more liberal and pluralistic. Consequently, the defense of the West was worth the amassment of sufficient military deterrence power.

Citing Pius XII, Dougherty argued that it was not the introduction of nuclear weapons into world conflict that must be condemned as intrinsically evil, but rather the act of aggression which unjustly initiates war. He held, therefore, that, while "city busting" (using nuclear weapons indiscriminately against population centers) was immoral, it was not immoral to initiate the use of nuclear weapons in a discriminating manner in the course of a defensive war.[38] Dougherty stressed that John XXIII (*Pacem in Terris*) did not rescind the teaching of Pius XII, and even recognized that the intentions of world leaders in building nuclear arsenals was not to wage but to deter war.

For Dougherty, the pacifist rejection of deterrence and the morality of the intentions of Western military and political leaders was a step down from a moral argument to an interpretation of history and strategic policy. It was precisely on this level of historical and political analysis that Dougherty saw most pacifists as generally incompetent. He felt that pacifists generally took the easy way out by arguing policy questions in moralistic terms. Dougherty argued that pacifist calls for trust and disarmament never dealt with Soviet recalcitrance toward inspection, and that prophecies of doom were no substitute for rational systems of arms control. International control of nuclear weapons would only come when men desired the same kind of peace, built upon a common treasure of truth. Until then, Dougherty insisted, to reject our nuclear deterrent would amount to unilateral disarmament and, therefore, surrender to communist domination.

Later in the same year, William V. Kennedy endorsed Dougherty's position, and went even farther in rejecting the nuclear pacifist and pacifist positions.[39] Kennedy felt that Christian pacifists were irresponsible in that their position would effectively take the Christian community out of the political arena in which they could make a moral difference. His statements exhibited the implicit ecclesiological concern that consistently ran through the Catholic realist position, even though most realists after Murray did not explicitly treat ecclesiological questions in great detail.

For Catholic realists, the implication of the nuclear pacifist and pacifist rejection of nuclear weapons (both in actual usage and the deterrent threat to use) was the effective elimination of American Catholics from the realm of defense and foreign policy making, since nuclear weapons were seen to be a permanent part of the world balance of power. Catholic realists consequently argued in a way that made clear that the acceptance or non-acceptance of nuclear weapons involved more than the Catholic attitude toward a particular type of weapon. It involved a decision about the effective participation or non-participation of Catholics in the political life and policy making apparatus of the nation.

Kennedy went even further in his charge of irresponsibility in saying that the nuclear pacifist and pacifist positions not only reneged on the responsibility to defend the West, but also reneged on Western responsibility toward freeing those already under communist rule. He went so far as to claim that it was necessary to destroy the public myth that America could not justifiably strike first against the Soviet Union or China. He argued that it was possible to have the intelligence information to foretell a coming communist attack, and that in such a case it would be morally justified to launch a pre-emptive strike. In this Kennedy was specifically negating then Secretary of Defense Robert McNamara's 1964 testimony to the Senate Armed Services Committee, in which he disavowed any justification for an all-out American attack prior to a nuclear strike against ourselves.[40]

In his attack on McNamara, Kennedy also clearly exhibited the major point of Catholic realist contention with American defense policy. McNamara had stated that the essential basis of American deterrent policy was the visible capability of United States forces to decisively destroy Soviet society (retaliate against cities), even after a massive nuclear attack upon this country (the doctrine of mutually assured destruction—MAD). The rationale was that this assurance of mutual destruction made any major nuclear confrontation unlikely, and thus allowed more flexible responses to communist incursion.[41] Kennedy argued that the MAD form of deterrence could not be reconciled with traditional Christian morality, which only legitimates direct attacks against military targets. While its defenders claimed that the MAD policy of deterrence allowed the United States to save money on having to maintain larger conventional forces, Kennedy stated that it built into American strategy murderous, city-busting policies. He stressed that we were morally limited to those military and political targets by which the adversary maintained its power, and we should announce a defense policy of limiting ourselves to such targets. Furthermore, he advocated larger expenditures on developing the flexible conventional forces that would be able to follow up a limited nuclear strike on Soviet targets with an invasion into Soviet territory.

In this he strongly represented the Catholic realist's contention that the American military deterrent must only threaten what can morally be done. This required the development of a flexible capacity to respond to a Soviet attack by engaging in "limited" nuclear war with the means to destroy Soviet military capability without the indiscriminate obliteration of Soviet society. In this sense Catholic realists saw themselves as both upholding the defense of the Western cause against pacifists and insisting on the rational limitation of armed force against the advocates of total war.

In delineating the moral limits to the use of armed force, the majority of Catholic realists observed the traditional categories of the just war tradition, and particularly observed a strict interpretation of its twin principles of proportionality (the good defended must outweigh the evil effects of the war) and discrimination (between military targets and innocents).[42] To the extent that civilian damage was accepted in war, it was seen as tolerable only as the unavoidable and unintended result of attacks on legitimate military targets (double effect).

Yet, given the operating premise of the realist perspective, it was perhaps unavoidable that some Catholic realists would examine how far the moral limits of armed force could be pushed. The overarching task of the Catholic realist was to provide a moral *and* practical military deterrent and defense of Western civilization. This meant that the right of self-defense had to be practically functional within the actual conditions of what war had come to be in the nuclear age. Any moral limit which denied the ability to mount a militarily practical defense was tantamount to denying the right of self-defense. While most felt that a just defense could be mounted within the limits set by the traditional understanding of the just war, a minority view arose which questioned key aspects of the traditional limits. This development is most clearly and systematically represented in the work of Dr. William V. O'Brien.[43] While considered a minority voice among Catholic realists, O'Brien's work is significant for the logical clarity and consistency with which he has attempted to push to its ultimate conclusion the realist quest to make the right of self-defense a functional reality in the conditions of modern warfare. O'Brien saw himself as consciously carrying out the task set by John Courtney Murray, to make the actual likelihood of modern war a moral possibility. Thus, the major problem uniting his work was the definition of the limits that can and must be set on war. In setting forth his operating premises, O'Brien sought to distinguish the point of differentiation between the realist position and that of its chief ideological opponents, pacifism and idealism.[44]

O'Brien argued that the major line of demarcation between realism and both pacifism and idealism was their differing evaluation of the present international arrangement and the possibilities of change within it. Pacifists, in varying degrees, rejected the present international and domestic system,[45] and idealists focused on the imperative to change the international system to eliminate the causes of war. Realists, on the other hand, accepted the continuance of the present nation-state system and the inevitability of war and revolution within it as instruments of change and conflict resolution. As such, O'Brien asserted that, as important as it was to confront the moral problem of war, it was even more important to confront the present and future problems of security. Even if the idealist dream were achieved and an international government were established, that world government would still have to deal with the use of military force to maintain order and settle disputes. Consequently, the basic question of the use of force and its moral limits would remain and only the focus would be changed. It is therefore on the problems of security and the use of force that O'Brien chose to focus. Consequently, he did not treat other economic or social factors that would be considered as part of the causes of war. He saw the inevitability of armed conflict as a feature of the international system and the ideological clash of Western culture and the "Gulag Society." The question of the use of armed conflict, therefore, had to be considered apart from other questions of world economic development.[46]

In addressing the problem of armed force and security, O'Brien rejected what he saw as one of the major assumptions of both the idealist and the pacifist positions, that is, the assumption that there is or should be a code of moral principles above and divorced from the facts, problems, and attitudes of empirical reality which, once determined, resolve all moral problems. On the contrary, O'Brien argued, normative principles are formed dialectically in the interchange of the material facts of a moral issue with the abstract principles relating to that particular moral subject matter. Abstract norms dealing with war only become meaningful when discussed in terms of the concrete political and technical problems that constitute the phenomenon of war today.[47]

Rejecting the tendency of many intellectuals to declare the Cold War over, O'Brien maintained that there is more than one cold war. The ideological struggle between Western society and communism continued and with it the likelihood of armed conflict, if not directly between the superpowers, then between their surrogates. Consequently, the maintenance of a balance of power remained a prime consideration. In the contest of this continuing global ideological struggle, O'Brien argued, it was essential to examine the current state of the just war theory in light of the actual conditions of war and security in the present era, in order to determine the morally binding limits on the use of armed force.[48]

O'Brien was distressed with the trend of much contemporary Catholic teaching on the issue of war. He saw himself as increasingly less appreciated in a Church where official teaching was dominated by an idealist approach, and within which there had been an increasing rise of pacifist sentiment in the few years following Vatican II.[49] Early in the debates over *Gaudium et Spes*, O'Brien maintained that most of those seeking condemnation of modern war were pacifists. He feared that the Church would be pushed to make pronouncements on war based on abstracted moral principles, without attempting to relate them to an analysis of the historical trends of the world ideological conflict and to the probable future of the Church under each competing regime.[50]

Taking issue with those who saw in *Pacem in Terris* a departure from traditional teaching, O'Brien interpreted the encyclical as a basic reiteration of the teaching of Pius XII. It in no way proscribed the right of self-defense, even in the use of nuclear weapons. Yet O'Brien lamented that the encyclical's call for trust and conciliation with communist regimes reflected a false optimism about the decline of ideological conflict and the likelihood of armed confrontation. Similarly, he criticized the encyclical's call for the creation of a world authority as unrealistically disregarding the means and the difficulty of obtaining such a goal. O'Brien lamented that the encyclical revealed how traditional scholasticism had become a haven for "fuzzy one worlders."[51]

The final draft of *Gaudium et Spes* was unsatisfying to O'Brien because of the ambiguity he saw in its treatment of the issue of war. He had argued early in the sixties that the Church could not speak meaningfully on war without clearly coming to terms with the reality of strategic nuclear deterrence as setting the ground rules for all limited wars in the modern world.[52] He stressed that American defense policies were very clear on this. The United States was committed to a policy of appropriate retaliation to any strike against itself or its allies. This included the policy of limiting any necessary use of nuclear weapons to counterforce strikes, yet reserving counter-city nuclear warfare as retaliation in kind for such attacks on American cities and to deter further such attacks. Furthermore, American policy was clearly committed to the belief that any credible deterrent must be based on the willingness to do what is threatened, even if it means executing the threat of the total destruction of an adversary's society (the MAD doctrine).[53]

In contrast, O'Brien saw Vatican II as reiterating the Church's teaching against "total war" by means of instruments of mass destruction that escape human control. This clearly would prohibit counter-city nuclear strikes, and even a conventional defense of Europe if "total war" were interpreted in terms of its historic meaning in World War II, which included obliteration bombing. Yet the council also upheld the right of self-defense, even in the nuclear age. Thus, O'Brien concluded, the Council still visualized the possibility of a limited just war of defense

which was subject in its execution to the traditional principles
of the immunity of non-combatants from direct intentional attacks, and also to the general principle of proportionality.[54]

While the conciliar teaching is thus sufficiently vague to
allow discussion of a just limited war in the nuclear age, it also
contains assertions of principles that are at odds with the premises of Western deterrent and defense policies. He concluded:

> If the modern teaching of the Church on just war were as clear as
> United States defense doctrine, it is likely that there would be a head-
> on collision between the two. American Catholics who wanted to be
> both good Americans and good Catholics would suffer from that col-
> lision. The teaching of the Church on this subject is still sufficiently
> vague and incomplete so that such a collision is not immediately
> imminent. But no one who wants to avoid a collision without partic-
> ipating in hypocrisy and deception should have any doubt about the
> urgency of the problem of determining the moral limits of just defense
> and deterrence.[55]

This statement clearly illustrates the motivation of the realist
position, which O'Brien represents, to avoid a clash between
the Church and American society, and to allow the Church to
morally support the necessary means of defending that society
against its ideological adversaries. Yet it is precisely here that
O'Brien also carried the realist position beyond where most of
his fellow Catholic realists would go.

The point of departure is over the interpretation of the principle of non-combatant immunity as an absolute moral norm.[56]
From the beginning of the conciliar debates, O'Brien contended
that this principle lay at the heart of the problem of a just
defense in modern war.[57] The central principle from which
O'Brien argued was that the right of self-defense, which Church
teaching has consistently upheld, must be practically functional within the actual necessities of contemporary warfare if
it is to remain an actual, that is, functional, right. His contention was that to make the right of self-defense meaningful
today, it was necessary to change one's understanding of the
normativeness of non-combatant immunity.

In viewing the history and practice of the principle of non-
combatant immunity, O'Brien concluded that, rather than being

a self-evident principle of natural law, the principle did not explicitly appear until the sixteenth or seventeenth centuries, and then as a customary principle of municipal and international law. It was from this forum of secular legal thinking that it entered into the moral categories of the just war theory. O'Brien contended that there is no explicit reference to the principle as such in papal teaching, and even the conciliar prohibition of weapons of mass destruction (as with Pius XII's interdiction of weapons beyond human control) does not make it clear if the reasoning for the prohibition is based on the principle of proportionality or the principle of non-combatant immunity. Furthermore, even though international law formally adopted the principle, the actual practice of war in the twentieth century reflects that the principle is no longer operative within the legal and moral consensus of the world's nations.[58] He concluded:

In contrast to the state of military technology and science when the customary law principle of non-combatant immunity was introduced, continued application of the principle in its strict form (including the concept of "intent" herein rejected) would not only preclude most forseeable nuclear wars, but also almost any conceivable type of major defensive war in populated portions of the earth.[59]

O'Brien further rejected any attempts to deal with this problem by using the principle of "double-effect" to justify the "unintended, indirect" destruction of non-combatants as a result of attacks on legitimate military targets, even though such destruction should be known in advance. He states:

When a belligerent unleashes many large nuclear weapons, even though they be directed at military targets, the inevitable result will be death, injury and contamination for large numbers of non-combatants.... These non-combatant deaths may not be *desired* but they are certainly *intended*. To pretend otherwise is to add neither higher morality, clarity, or dignity to an attempt to meet our moral dilemma.[60]

Thus, O'Brien was led by the military necessities of actually mounting a defensive deterrent and war to conclude that, while non-combatant immunity is a preferred goal and is to be respected, it cannot be held to be an absolute norm. This did not mean that all restrictions were off, but that since a strict interpretation of the principle would eliminate any possible defense, the principle must be modified to allow for a successful defense policy. In specifying what would constitute an appropriate moral deterrence posture, O'Brien rejected any deterrence based solely on MAD or a rapid escalation to the level of strategic nuclear exchange. He listed the following principles which should be adopted: 1) no first use of nuclear weapons;[61] 2) graduated deterrence—begin with limited counterforce use of nuclear weapons in response to such use by an adversary; 3) prohibition of counter-city warfare, except as a last resort against its use by an enemy—even here it must not be indiscriminate, but against those cities of essential military significance; 4) necessity of arms control talks.[62]

Thus, while deeply concerned to limit war, O'Brien was willing to allow the direct attack on civilian population centers to the degree that it was demanded by the military necessity of mounting a realistic deterrence or defensive war. Likewise, he was willing to accept the strategic exchange of nuclear weapons against cities as the "bottom line" in modern military deterrence and the ultimate threat which could keep any outbreak of armed conflict within limits. In rejecting the absolute normative character of non-combatant immunity, O'Brien went beyond where most Catholic realists would go in interpreting those "limit principles" laid down by official Church teaching.

To those critics who accused him of subordinating morality to the exigencies of military technology, he responded that the material facts relevant to the morality of war are the facts about the necessary requirements for mounting a successful military defense in the modern world. He stated:

If on their face the requirements contravene absolute moral principles there can be no moral defense. But the church, well aware of the character of modern war, has affirmed the continued existence of the right of defense. We are left, therefore, with the question whether the good of saving one's society through legitimate defense is in some circumstances sufficient reason for the killing of non-combatants which must inevitably accompany such defense.[63]

In answering this question in the affirmative, O'Brien felt himself to be more consistent than official Church teaching in carrying out the logical implications of continuing to uphold the right of self-defense. In so doing, he was consciously motivated by the desire to avoid the head-on collision of the Church and the American defense establishment that would occur if the former were ever to become clear and consistent in applying the principle of non-combatant immunity to the means of self-defense.

Ironically, O'Brien's analysis of the inconsistency of the Church's reiteration of the principles of proportionality and non-combatant immunity along with the right of self-defense in the nuclear age, brings him very close to the type of argument used by pacifist critics. Both O'Brien and his pacifist critics would recognize the incompatibility of modern warfare and non-combatant immunity, and both would reject the use of the "double effect" argument to morally justify it. Yet where the pacifists would move to conclude that modern war is no longer morally just, O'Brien moved to challenge the normativeness of the principle of non-combatant immunity. The overriding principle of judgment remained the realist demand that a practical defense be made a moral possibility, although O'Brien's position also stressed that a moral defense must be a practical one. The thrust of O'Brien's reasoning, and the limits of the Catholic realist perspective which he represents, is evident in two other significant points which he treats.

The first is his recognition of the implications of the concept of limited war in the nuclear age. The contemporary international context of contending nuclear powers has given rise to the specifically modern concept of "limited war" as a type of war fought as a result of the ideological clash of the major powers, but in a way designed to avoid a direct confrontation between those powers. O'Brien would agree with the statement of Paul Ramsey that:

"Modern war" is not nuclear war. Instead, the possibility of nuclear war has made the world safe for wars of insurgency. The balance of terror, which some foolishly thought would compel peace, produces instead a multiplication of wars. The military strength of the nation-

state, which we thought made it impossible ever again to have a
successful revolution, has led instead to an era of revolutionary wars....
The fact that it would be nonsense for nations ever to fight the "central" war, or all the war they are today technically capable of fighting,
produces "peripheral" wars.[64]

These "peripheral" wars of insurgency/counter-insurgency, in
which the superpowers seek to contend with each other through
their surrogates, are the major form which armed conflict will
take in our era. Therefore, O'Brien argued, the United States
must develop the capacity and will to fight this form of limited
war.[65]

To fight this type of war requires the subordination of military necessity to clear political policy. Thus, the object of such
war is not victory in the traditional sense, but the attainment
of limited political and military ends, the definition of which
is the job of the political authority. O'Brien maintained that
the ability to fight such a war required the willingness, on both
the military and the home front, to fight a protracted and costly
struggle, without employing an all-out effort to "win and bring
the boys home." Furthermore, it required the willingness to
give up in an ultimate political solution what was won militarily. Vietnam was viewed by O'Brien as a clear example of
this type of conflict.[66]

The problem of fighting this type of war, O'Brien recognized,
was that it went against the traditional American attitude
toward war. He recognized that for Americans war was either
a crime or a crusade. It was to be avoided at all costs, but once
engaged in, no limits were to be observed in winning it as
quickly as possible.[67] To engage in modern insurgency/counter-
insurgency warfare, which O'Brien saw as an inescapable element in defending the West from communist expansion, would
thus require a willingness for Americans to develop a new
attitude toward war that was commensurate with the realities
of the "new rules" for armed conflict in the nuclear era.

Furthermore, against the critics of American involvement
in Vietnam, O'Brien argued that such a war had to be viewed
as an instrument of a broader political conflict. It could not be
morally judged by abstract moral principles separate from the

morality of the larger political struggle of which it was a part.[68]
O'Brien saw the strongest rationale for the Vietnam war to lie,
not in any good being done for the Vietnamese people, but in
the fact that this war would prevent the spread of similar conflicts elsewhere in Southeast Asia.[69] Thus, for O'Brien, the moral
focus on the unique problem of limited war in the nuclear era
remains where the realist perspective consistently placed it,
namely, on the global ideological struggle between communism
and liberal Western democracy. The exigencies of this struggle
provided the determinative consideration in the application of
all moral principles.

The second point which O'Brien stressed in his treatment of
insurgency/counter-insurgency warfare involved an extension
of his previous position on the principle of non-combatant immunity. He contended that the key to fighting such a war is
not, as many argued, to win the hearts and minds of the people.
Rather, it is to show that you have the will and means to outlast
the struggle, and make reforms where possible. The question
is again one of security, and the same rules governing international conflict are seen as applying here as well. O'Brien reasoned that the harsh measures usually associated with such
warfare (deprivation of civil rights, harsh population relocation
and control, torture) are endemic to this type of war, and their
acceptance is an inescapable part of the decision to wage it. He
contended that in the exercise of such warfare, the situation
makes it extremely difficult to make the distinction between
combatant and non-combatant, and would, therefore, require
the maximum extension of combatant status to the population.[70]

Furthermore, O'Brien held that the absolute prohibition of
torture, like the absolute adherence to non-combatant immunity, would make it practically impossible to wage a revolutionary or counter-insurgency struggle. Here O'Brien again
goes beyond most Catholic realists as he did with his earlier
questioning of the normativeness of non-combatant immunity.
His logic is the same: the prohibition of torture and reprisals
is so widely ignored in the actual conduct of nations that O'Brien
questions its continued validity as a legal prohibition. If international law is what is stated in formal conventions, torture
is illegal. If it is what states and revolutionary forces are doing

on a universal level without guilt, then, O'Brien argues, a legal-
moral case could be made for torture in extreme cases.[71]
   The conditions O'Brien lays down for the justified resort to
torture are: 1) it must be done at the direction of the competent
authorities; 2) the means must not be intrinsically inhuman—
that is, they must not produce lasting physical or psychological
damage; 3) it must be justified by the genuine necessity of
obtaining vital military information.[72] O'Brien is again following here the logical conclusion of his starting point; that is,
making morally possible and practically effective what the legitimate right of self-defense demands for its feasible exercise.
   O'Brien was particularly critical of those left-wing Christians whom he saw advocating a theology of revolution while
not facing the realities of what waging a revolutionary struggle
entails, and thus making no moral guidelines for doing what
they would have to do to wage such a war successfully. O'Brien
put the question with polemical bluntness:

Will the priest-guerrillas of Latin America find "gentle means" of
torturing their enemies to obtain information which may be the difference between survival and annihilation by the counter-insurgents?
Or will they take a walk and say some prayers while a tough leftist
rebel does the job?[73]

   In defending his position, O'Brien contended that the radical
revolutionaries, like the pacifists and idealists, did not take
seriously the moral requisites for guiding and limiting the necessary use of force. By so doing, all of them help to create a
moral vacuum with no sense of limits in those situations where
armed conflict becomes inevitable. He asserted that he was not
trying to do away with the prohibition of torture any more than
with the principle of non-combatant immunity. Rather, O'Brien
saw the absolutizing of either principle as vitiating any realistic use of armed force in a just international war, or a just
revolution or counter-insurgency struggle.[74]
   O'Brien was also critical of Church teaching for failing to
keep up with the reality of the problems posed by revolutionary
wars, and failing to apply the just war tradition to them. He
contended that it has been demonstrated that force is usually

the only means of achieving significant social change in a situation dominated by elites with every incentive to preserve the *status quo*. It was also clear, he argued, that the success of a revolution primarily depends on the willingness of the revolutionaries to persist indefinitely and to use all means necessary to upset the existing order. To fail to provide realistic moral guidelines to the actualities of this form of struggle is to leave the Church mute in the face of the form which war is most likely to take in our day. To insist on the strict moral application of non-combatant immunity and the prohibition of torture would, on the other hand, eliminate any right to a just revolutionary struggle. O'Brien contended it would also undermine the moral grounds for a meaningful counter-insurgency struggle and would require surrender to communist rebels.[75]

O'Brien judged Paul VI's 1965 encyclical *Mense Maio* and his Easter message of the same year to be the only modern papal attempt to address the question of subconventional war. While the Pope left open the possibility of violent revolution in the most extreme circumstances, he was vague in defining what these circumstances could be. Rather, Paul VI condemned guerrilla warfare and all but excluded the actual possibility of a violent and moral revolution.[76]

In general, O'Brien remained distressed by what he saw as the contrary rationales for just war and just revolution in contemporary Catholic thought. As he stated it,

Today the just war permits international war almost solely on the basis of the right of self-defense. There is a conspicuous absence of references to justice.... In the case of violent revolution, however, the rationale is the necessary use of armed force to secure justice. Whereas, both international law and modern Catholic thought consider the dangers of war disproportionate to the possible achievement of justice, proponents of violent revolution apparently contend that virtually all dangers are proportionate and justifiable in pursuit of the rights of those who are denied them by oppressive or indifferent regimes.[77]

In both cases O'Brien saw the contemporary failure of the Church to address the specific concern of how the legitimate use of force can be employed in the actual conditions of the modern world.

Thus far can be seen the spectrum of thought which constituted the Catholic realist perspective on the issue of war from 1960 through the end of the seventies. In John Courtney Murray and William V. O'Brien can be found the two poles demarcating the limits of that perspective. Despite certain internal differences over the moral limits of the use of armed force, Catholic realists represented a distinct unified perspective on the issue of war. They were in agreement on the necessity of approaching the issue within the context of the global ideological struggle between communism and Western liberal democracy, which was seen as giving international relations their shape and meaning. Within this context, their central concern was to provide liberal democracy with a moral and effective defense.

It was also precisely the concentration on this question of security which brought about the major division within the realist camp over the moral limits which must be imposed in the use of armed force in a just war. While some critics would have O'Brien and those who agree with him (for example, James E. Dougherty and William V. Kennedy) appear outside the Catholic realist perspective, symbolized in John Courtney Murray, they are nevertheless self-conscious heirs and developers of the political-moral task set forth by Murray. If Murray and the majority of Catholic realists focused on the insistence that the defense of the West can and must be within the traditional limits of the just war teaching, O'Brien and others stressed that any meaningful just defense must also be practically effective within the conditions in which war is actually fought today. Their movement beyond Murray on questions such as the principle of non-combatant immunity and the prohibition of torture reflect the need to keep practically operative the realist moral emphasis on self-defense in the struggle against communism. Perhaps the shift of focus seen in realists like O'Brien and Dougherty is in large measure due to the fact that they are not primarily moral theologians but political analysts and students of international law.

Within the unifying framework of the realist school of thought there was also a common ecclesiological concern for the place and role of the Church within Western society, which they all sought to defend. In their common concern to find a middle ground between pacifism and bellicism, Catholic realists sought to affirm the traditional American Catholic contention that it was possible to be both a good Catholic and a good American. That is, it was possible to preserve the traditional Catholic teaching on war and still accommodate the stated necessities of American foreign and defense policies. The deep concern that the minority position of O'Brien has for the practical meaningfulness of a just defense doctrine, itself reflects the equally deep concern that any moral prohibition which is not in conformity with the practical necessities of fighting war today would, if followed, remove Catholics from the business of defense. Obviously, if Catholics were so removed from the business of defense, the proposition that one could be both a good Catholic and a good American would become questionable, at least in the sense that American Catholics have always understood it.

Consequently, while most Catholic realists did not address the ecclesiological dimension of their position in the same manner and extent as Murray did, all were in agreement in resisting the sectarian implications of any Catholic inability to provide an adequate and moral military defense of America. O'Brien voiced the feelings of all Catholic realists in consciously seeking to head off the confrontation of Church and government which any such inability would imply. Beneath the question of American defense policies there was always the deeper and larger question of Catholic participation in shaping American society.

Thus in focusing on the problem of providing an adequate and moral defense of America and the West, American Catholic realists brought together both their chief political and their chief religious concerns. Their political presupposition of the priority of preserving Western liberal society was easily wedded to their ecclesiological priority of preserving Catholicism as a significant part of that society. In blending their Americanism and Catholicism in this way, Catholic realists preserved part of the intellectual heritage of the CAIP, while they rejected

another significant part of it in their rejection of internationalist idealism. Their break with internationalism created tension between most Catholic realists and the thrust of most
official Church teaching, which still strongly upheld internationalist goals. It also created tension between Catholic realists
and other American Catholics who sought to continue to blend
their Americanism with internationalism, and who took a different view of defense issues.

NOTES

1. Brian Wicker, *First the Political Kingdom: A Personal Appraisal of the Catholic Left in Britain* (Notre Dame: The University
of Notre Dame Press, 1968), p. 3.
2. Patricia F. McNeal, *The American Catholic Peace Movement* (New
York: Arno Press, 1968), pp. 124–125; Charles DeBenedetti, "The
Peace Opposition in Cold War America, 1955–1965," unpublished paper originally prepared for the 1981 annual meeting of the Organization of American Historians, and later submitted as part of the
Historians' Project of the World without War Council, Seattle, Washington, 1982.
3. This summary of the just war criteria follows that given in
William V. O'Brien, *Nuclear War, Deterrence and Morality* (Westminster, Maryland: Newman Press, 1967), pp. 22–27. Other more
systematic treatments of the just war criteria are found in James F.
Childress, "Just War Theories: The Bases, Interrelations, Priorities,
and Functions of Their Criteria," *Theological Studies* 39 (September
1978): 427–445; Ralph B. Potter, "The Moral Logic of War," *Mc-
Cormick Quarterly* 23 (May, 1970): 203–223; and J. T. Johnson, *Just
War Tradition and the Restraint of War: A Moral and Historical In-
quiry* (Princeton: Princeton University Press, 1981).
4. Ibid., p. 34. In this action Pius XII did not act in a vacuum.
The U.N. charter had already culminated a trend in international
law by limiting justifiable use of armed force to defensive war. For a
treatment of the interaction of theological and secular influences in the
development of modern just war doctrine see James Turner Johnson,
*Ideology, Reason and the Limitation of War: Religious and Secular
Concepts 1200–1740* (Princeton: Princeton University Press, 1975).
5. Treatment of the role of double effect can be found in Paul
Ramsey, *The Just War: Force and Political Responsibility* (New York:
Charles Scribner's Sons, 1968) pp. 150, 287, 315–317; relationship of
discrimination and proportionality, 347–355.

6. For a sample of the view of this school of realism see Reinhold Niebuhr, *Christianity and Power Politics* (New York: Charles Scribner's Sons, 1940) and *Christian Realism and Political Problems* (New York: Scribner, 1953). Hans J. Morganthau, *Politics Among Nations*, 4th ed. (New York: Knopf, 1967; 4th ed., rev., 1975). *N.B.* In treating the differing positions here and throughout the entire study the terms "idealism" and "internationalism" are used interchangeably.

7. John Courtney Murray, "Remarks on the Moral Problem of War," *Theological Studies* 20 (March 1959): 40–61; also his *Morality and Modern War* (New York: Council on Religion and International Affairs, 1959). The substance of this article also appeared in Murray's book, *We Hold These Truths* (New York: Sheed and Ward, 1960), as well as in William J. Nagle, ed., *Morality and Modern Warfare* (Baltimore: Helicon Press, 1960), pp. 69–90. *N.B.* While Murray is identified here as a representative of realist thought in Catholic circles, this is not meant to imply a complete agreement between Murray and Protestant realists, such as Reinhold Niebuhr. Murray strongly attacked Protestant moralists for creating false dilemmas in relating foreign policy and morality by their rejection of the tradition of natural law teaching, which Murray upheld as the foundation of the "American proposition" (*Truths*, chap. 12). Yet despite their radical differences in moral methodology, Murray's stances on specific policy questions were often in accord with those of his Protestant counterparts. Thus, the parallel drawn here between Catholic realists and Protestant and secular realists is meant to refer to their unanimity in attitudes towards internationalism and the struggle with communism, and their stances on particular policy issues, but is not meant to infer a unanimity of moral presuppositions and methodologies.

8. Murray, *Truths*, pp. 9–10.

9. Ibid., pp. 12–23.

10. Ibid., p. 221; pp. 293 ff.—Murray provides a treatment of the Catholic understanding of natural law as opposed to false modern conceptions of it.

11. Murray, "Remarks on the Moral Problem of War," p. 42.

12. Murray, *Truths*, pp. 223–227; also p. 229 ff.—Murray gives his interpretation of the post-World War II history of the Soviet Union.

13. Ibid., pp. 232–234.

14. John Courtney Murray, "Things Old and New in Pacem in Terris," *America* 108 (April 17, 1963): 612–614; Reinhold Niebuhr, "Pacem in Terris: Two Views," *Christianity and Crisis* 23 (May 13, 1983): 81–83.

15. Murray, *Truths*, pp. 232–233, 235.
16. Ibid., pp. 236–238.
17. Ibid., pp. 239–241.
18. John Courtney Murray, "War and Conscience," in James Finn, ed. *A Conflict of Loyalties: The Case for Selective Conscientious Objection* (New York: Pegasus, 1968), p. 20.
19. Murray, *Truths*, pp. 244–245. Murray is referring here to the doctrine of "massive retaliation" announced by Secretary of State John Foster Dulles in 1954.
20. Murray, *Truths*, pp. 237–239.
21. Murray, "The Moral Problem of War," p. 58.
22. Murray, *Truths*, p. 246.
23. Ibid., p. 247; also Murray in Nagle, *Morality and Modern Warfare*, pp. 88–89—Murray cites the work of Henry Kissinger, *Nuclear Arms and Foreign Policy* (New York: Harper, 1957), and the Rockefeller Fund Report, *New York Times* (January 6, 1958), p. 20 to support his contention that United States strategic concepts lag behind its technological development.
24. Ibid., pp. 75–79.
25. Ibid., pp. 85–86. Murray cites as an example of such policies that should have been condemned the decision of the allies in World War II to press for unconditional surrender; this violated the criterion of right intention.
26. Murray, "Remarks on the Moral Problem of War," p. 61.
27. John A. Coleman, S.J., "A Possible Role for Biblical Religion," in David Hollenbach, S.J., ed., "Theology and Philosophy in Public: A Symposium on John Courtney Murray's Unfinished Agenda," *Theological Studies* 40 (December 1979): 704–705.
28. Cited in Note 7, above. In a later article, "Where are the Theologians?" *Commonweal* 76 (May 18, 1962): 203–206, Nagle lamented that even though the United States had resumed nuclear testing one year after his book appeared, there had as yet been a quite insufficient response on the part of Catholic theologians to the issue of war.
29. Charles S. Thompson, ed., *Morals and Missiles: Catholic Essays on the Problem of War Today*, with an introduction by Michael De La Bedoyere (London: James Clarke and Company, Ltd., 1959). Another good example of the contrast of approach between English and American Catholics can be found in Walter Stein, ed., *Nuclear Weapons: A Catholic Response*, with a Foreward by T.D. Roberts, S.J. (New York: Sheed and Ward, 1962).
30. Nagle, *Morality and Modern Warfare*, pp. 7–8.
31. Ramsey's major works on the morality of war during the sixties

were: *War and the Christian Conscience: How Shall Modern War Be Conducted Justly?* (Durham, N.C.: Duke University Press, 1961); *The Limits of Nuclear War: Thinking About the Do-Able and the Un-Doable* (New York: Council on Religion and International Affairs, 1963); *Again, The Justice of Deterrence* (New York: Council on Religion and International Affairs, 1965); *The Just War: Force and Political Responsibility* (New York: Charles Scribner's Sons, 1968). For a general assessment of the influence and import of Ramsey's work see James T. Johnson and David H. Smith, eds., *Love and Society: Essays in the Ethics of Paul Ramsey* (Missoula, Montana: The American Academy of Religion and Scholars Press, 1974).

32. James E. Dougherty, "The Political Context," in Nagle, *Morality and Modern Warfare*, pp. 13–18. Dougherty continued to be one of the more prominent spokesmen for the Catholic realist perspective throughout the sixties and seventies. Typical of the sentiment orienting the realist perspective is his statement:

But our human reason … tells us that we must resist the spread of Communism; for if that system triumphs, or rather where it triumphs, Christian or any other spiritual tradition as such is erased, and a new, purely materialistic interpretation of the meaning of life on earth is substituted. Christians should occasionally remind themselves of this brutal fact before passing adverse judgments on the defense policies of Western nations. Western governments may deserve criticism for the form in which they have cast their defense policies, but not for their preoccupation with the problem itself (p.18).

33. Ibid., pp. 18–29.

34. Thomas E. Murray, "Morality and Security—The Forgotten Equation," in Nagle, *Morality and Modern Warfare*, p. 63; Murray was appointed to the Atomic Energy Commission in 1950 and was an influential voice in shaping American Catholic realism in the early sixties. His views were further set forth in his book, *Nuclear Policy for War and Peace* (Cleveland: The World Publishing Company, 1960).

35. A good example of a strict application of the just war tradition to modern war that would be typical of the mainline Catholic realist outlook can be found in Joseph C. McKenna S.J., "Ethics and War: A Catholic View," *American Political Scientist Review* 54 (September 1960): 647–658.

36. *Gaudium et Spes*, par. 77–82, in Joseph Gremillion, ed., *The Gospel of Peace and Justice: Catholic Social Teaching since Pope John* (New York: Orbis Books, 1976), pp. 313–319.

37. James E. Dougherty, "The Christian and Nuclear Pacifism," *Catholic World* 198 (March 1964): 336–346. At the time of this article

Dougherty was an associate of the Foreign Policy Research Institute of the University of Pennsylvania and chairman of the Arms Control Committee of the CAIP.

38. Discrimination here refers to the just war principle of only targeting legitimate military targets.

39. William V. Kennedy, "The Morality of American Nuclear Policy," *Catholic World* 198 (September 1964): 363–370. Kennedy is a military analyst who was a prominent advocate of Catholic realist thought during these years.

40. In defending a pre-emptive nuclear first strike Kennedy would not be in accord with the majority of American Catholic realists who interpret the application of the just war theory differently.

41. It is somewhat ironic that McNamara's name is so closely associated with the MAD nuclear deterrent policy. In 1962 at the University of Michigan he advocated the need to move away from a total reliance on MAD and to develop a flexible counterforce deterrent, that is, a deterrent focusing on a limited strike against enemy military targets. This idea, however, was not taken up again with great seriousness by the government until the early seventies.

42. A good example of this can be found in Sylvester Theisen, "Man and Nuclear Weapons," *American Benedictine Review* 14 (September 1963): 365–390.

43. O'Brien served as president of the CAIP from 1961 to 1962 and again from 1966 to 1968.

44. William V. O'Brien, *War and/or Survival* (Garden City: Doubleday and Company, Inc., 1969), pp. 5–10. O'Brien also lists here what he calls the crusade position such as that held by advocates of a "Pax Americana" like Edward Teller and General Curtis LeMay. The concern of the crusade mentality is not so much to limit the use of force as to insure that the right side wins. This position is not dealt with here, as O'Brien himself quickly dismissed it as outside the boundaries of serious moral consideration.

45. O'Brien recognized that among pacifists there were differences between those who urged a purely negative withdrawal from society and others, like Gordon Zahn, who felt it was possible to effect change in the social system.

46. O'Brien, *War and/or Survival*, pp. 11–12.

47. Ibid., pp. 12–13.

48. William V. O'Brien, "Just War and Just Revolution," *World Justice* 9 (March 1968): 341.

49. Ibid., p. 334.

50. William V. O'Brien, "War, Peace and the American Catholic,"

Catholic World 202 (March 1966): 3332; also O'Brien, "After Nineteen Years Let Us Begin," in James Finn, ed., *Peace, the Churches and the Bomb* (New York: The Council on Religion and International Affairs, 1965), p. 28.

51. O'Brien, *War and/or Survival*, p. 18.; *Nuclear War*, pp. 42–47; "Just War/Revolution," p. 18.

52. O'Brien, in Finn, *Peace, the Churches and the Bomb*, p. 29.

53. O'Brien, *Nuclear War*, pp. 74–75. The term counterforce is used to designate nuclear strikes against military targets rather than population centers, even though those military targets may be located in or near civilian population centers.

54. Ibid., p. 78.

55. Ibid., pp. 80–81.

56. The term non-combatant immunity is a legal one from international law and not used in official church teaching, which generally refers to the rights of "innocents." Here these terms are used interchangeably.

57. O'Brien, "War, Peace and the American Catholic," p. 332.

58. O'Brien, *Nuclear War*, pp. 82–83: O'Brien's claim here is supported by the work of Richard S. Hartigen, "Noncombatant Immunity: Reflections on Its Origins and Present Status," *The Review of Politics* 29 (April 1967): 204–220; also "Non-Combatant Immunity: Its Scope and Development," *Continuum* 3 (Autumn 1965): 300–314. For treatment of the principle of non-combatant immunity see also Ramsey, *Just War* and Johnson, *Ideology, Reason and the Limitation of War*. Both authors treat various aspects of the principle and its development throughout these works.

59. Ibid., p. 82.

60. Ibid., p. 82–83.

61. O'Brien, *War and/or Survival*, p. 127–130. O'Brien stated that his stance on no first use of nuclear weapons was a change of position for him. He previously allowed a first use to bolster the American conventional deterrent.

62. It is important to realize here that when O'Brien and other realists speak of arms control, they do not mean disarmament as others often do. The conception of arms control accepted by Catholic realists was that developed in the late fifties by such figures as Henry Kissinger and Herman Kahn, and the RAND think-tank. According to this conception the prospects for genuine disarmament are quite meager. The object of arms control is to control the arms competition between the superpowers so as to maintain a stabilized balance of power. Thus arms control and national military strategy would be the same thing.

82 The Cross, The Flag, and The Bomb

63. O'Brien, *Nuclear War*, pp. 83–84.

64. Paul Ramsey, *The Just War: Force and Political Responsibility* (New York: Charles Scribner's Sons, 1968), p. 427. For O'Brien's evaluation of Ramsey's thought on the just war theory see "Morality and War: The Contribution of Paul Ramsey," in Johnson and Smith, eds., *Love and Society*, pp. 163–184.

65. O'Brien, *War and/or Survival*, pp. 61–63. While he was Secretary of Defense Robert McNamara wrote: "The greatest contribution Vietnam is making—right or wrong beside the point—is that it is developing an ability in the United States to fight a limited war, to go to war without the necessity of arousing the public ire. In that sense, Vietnam is almost a necessity in our history because that is the kind of war we'll most likely be facing for the next fifty years." Cited in Finn, *Conflict of Loyalties*, p. xii. This treatment of O'Brien's thought on the nature of limited and just war focuses on his work during the debates of the sixties and seventies. O'Brien's thinking on the subject has been summarized and updated with practical assessments of specific wars in his latest work, *The Conduct of Just and Limited War* (New York: Praeger, 1981).

66. Ibid., pp. 63–65.

67. Interview held with William O'Brien at the Bishops and Scholars Colloquium on the Church and Nuclear Arms, September 24, 1982, in Washington, D.C.

68. An example of this reasoning is also found in "War, Peace and the Christian Tradition," *Jubilee* 13 (March 1966): 36–41. In the exchange of views within this article James E. Dougherty defended the American intervention in Vietnam on the basis of its role as part of a larger global strategy to contain communism. In contrast James Forrest rejected the war precisely because it was only a tool for implementing larger political designs.

69. O'Brien, *War and/or Survival*, p. 213. O'Brien also was quick to point out that, while he defended United States intervention in Vietnam to fight off a communist incursion into the South, he would not defend the United States intervention in the Dominican Republic. He argued that Vietnam cannot be used as a model to deal with Latin America.

70. Ibid., pp. 198–206; 212.

71. Ibid., pp. 224, 232.

72. Ibid., pp. 228–231.

73. Ibid., p. 213.

74. Ibid., pp. 248–249.

75. O'Brien, "Just War/Revolution," pp. 352–353; O'Brien in James

Finn, *Protest: Pacifism and Politics* (New York: Random House, 1967),
pp. 413–414.

   76. O'Brien, *Nuclear War*, pp. 48–49.

   77. O'Brien, "Just War/Revolution", p. 354.

3

Catholic Americanism: Nuclear Pacifist and Idealist

One of the major charges which Catholic realists made against their fellow Catholics, who claimed a position of relative pacifism in rejecting the use of nuclear weapons, was that those who claimed such nuclear pacifism were really total pacifists who were either not honest, or had not thought out their position far enough. In effect, they denied the validity of a nonpacifist position which rejected the deterrent and actual usage of nuclear weapons. This was based on the realist's conviction that to deny the use of nuclear weapons was to deny the possibility of a feasible moral defense and, therefore, to move into *de facto* pacifism.

It is true that many of the most prominent Catholic antinuclear critics did move into total pacifism and a more radical critique of American society. There were, however, significant elements of the American Catholic community which accepted the realist definition of the ideological conflict defining international relations, and the superiority of Western liberal society in its struggle with communism. Yet they differed with the realists by their use of the just war tradition to reject nuclear weapons, and in their opposition to certain immediate features of American foreign policy, such as the war in Vietnam. In its most systematic expression, the perspective of these Catholics reveals an effort to maintain the union of Americanism and internationalism seen in the CAIP. In its less systematic expressions it articulates an attempt to reject certain American policies (for example, the Vietnam intervention) in the name of the prevailing American and Western value system, which these policies were seen as contradicting, and consequently undermining the ability of the West to oppose communism.

Thus, the term nuclear pacifism is adequate, in one sense, to designate the perspective treated here, in that it identifies the major issues with which these American Catholics were concerned. It is, however, somewhat misleading in expressing the full scope and focus of their interests. Yet it is legitimate to use the term here, as it was accepted by many of the proponents of the outlook treated in this section, as well as by their critics.

In many ways, the intellectual perspective of Catholic nuclear pacifists parallels that of the secular movement for nuclear pacifism as found in the organization SANE (Committee for a Sane Nuclear Policy).[1] During the sixties, SANE attempted to articulate a middle line of dissent from American defense and foreign policies without getting into the more radical elements of the anti-war movement.

Similarly, the term nuclear pacifism here designates the attempt of Catholics to articulate a dissent from American foreign and defense policies that is still within the confines of Catholic Americanism. Despite their criticism of governmental policy, they continued to adhere to the need for an adequate military defense and deterrent. Their retention of internationalist ideals reflected their desire to reorient American policy in line with their own optimism about the possibility of transforming the international order. Their opposition to communism, while as adamant as that of the realists, placed its emphasis on the non-military aspects of opposing communism, thus preserving the moral *raison d'être* of the West.

While Catholic nuclear pacifists and internationalists were no more monolithic in their views than Catholic realists, there can be discerned among them a distinct intellectual perspective, which was one of the major ways in which American Catholics approached the issue of war in the past two decades. In one sense this school of thought can be seen as a middle ground between Catholic realists and more radical Catholic pacifists and political dissenters. In another sense, this position and realism together can be seen as constituting two polarities within the overarching perspective of Catholic Americanism. The most significant and systematically developed expression of the perspective of Catholic nuclear pacifism and internationalism in the sixties was to be found in the work of Justus George Lawler and his fellow editors of the journal *Continuum*. In 1963 Lawler co-edited a book entitled *The Challenge of Mater et Magistra*, which was designed as an American response to Pope John's encyclical.[2] In his contribution to this volume Lawler expressed some of the guiding perspectives of his thought.

Lawler heard in *Mater et Magistra* the voice of Teilhard de Chardin. He termed it the first encyclical "to see the world as no longer a heterogeneous assemblage of separate and self-sufficient nations, but as a single entity moving more and more, save for one great obstacle, toward a deeper sense of co-operation and community. And it is the first encyclical to discuss in detail what Teilhard called, 'the divinization of human action.' "[3] Against its critics, Lawler contended that the encyclical's call to Christianize the economic and social sectors of the temporal order was not a call for the ecclesiastical domination of society, but a call to bring society into conformity with the principles of justice and brotherhood espoused in the gospel. He further argued that those conservatives who opposed *Mater et Magistra* as too socialistic would not be able to undo a half century of economic progress in America, which Lawler identified with the Christianization process spoken of in the encyclical. Lawler viewed domestic economic problems as on the way to being solved, and, while defending the basic goodness of American society, indicated that the chief areas where Americans would have to respond to the challenge of *Mater et Magistra* were the problems of racism and international relations. Yet he stressed that the implementation of *Mater et Magistra* could only be done by American Catholics within the framework of our pluralistic society and its traditions of freedom and constitutionalism.[4]

In the face of the widespread perversion of human values, which *Mater et Magistra* deplored, Lawler saw no justification for the constantly growing expenditure of vast sums of money for armaments to defend the free world. For Lawler, there could be no such thing as the free world unless there is the affirmation of a code of morality which the encyclical described as "transcendent, absolute, universal and equally binding on all." He argued that the "free world" had already mortgaged its freedom by acquiescing in the obliteration bombing of World War II. While retaining certain peripheral liberties, it has, in fact, become utterly enslaved in its inner spiritual depths by embracing as a matter of policy the military doctrine of destructive threat to the enemy's cities.[5]

In this article, Lawler thus set forth two contentions which he worked out in most of his writing on the issues of war and peace. First, whereas the realist viewed international relations from the perspective of the East-West conflict and the need to provide security for the West, Lawler viewed international conflict from the perspective of its "Teilhardian framework," that is, from the perspective of the evolving unity of the human race, which John XXIII was credited as being the first pope to explicitly recognize. In Lawler's view, the fostering of this evolving world unity must be the chief objective of American foreign policy. Lawler even saw one positive aspect to nuclear weapons in their leading men toward this greater unity by threatening them with unparalleled catastrophe.[6] Secondly, while not denying the prime significance of the West's conflict with communism, Lawler stressed, not the need for security, but the reasons why the "free world" was worth keeping secure by military means, and of its need to stand for a transcendent code of morality. He stated that the chief difference between himself and his realist opponents was that, while they both had the same idea of the just war, they differed on their approach to the larger, overarching policy of containing communism, and what this policy could be used to justify. Realists used this larger political vision to justify nuclear deterrence, the use of nuclear weapons, and the United States' intervention in Vietnam. In contrast, Lawler chose to focus on the immediate violations of a moral code, for which no grand strategy can be a justification.[7]

From this quite different starting point Lawler and his fellow editors of *Continuum* set forth to counter the realist position, and, in their own way, attempt to find a middle ground between pacifism and bellicism. Lawler emerged in the debates of 1962–1964 over the proposed drafts of *Gaudium et Spes* as a leading advocate of the Catholic nuclear pacifist position. If the realists held that nuclear weapons present no qualitatively new problem in the use of force within the just war categories, Lawler argued the opposite. Nuclear weapons presented a qualitatively different situation because they could not be subsumed into the just war presumption to limit the use of armed force within moral boundaries. Furthermore, he argued that, if the use of nuclear weapons was wrong, so was the threat to use them in the present defense policy of nuclear deterrence. In this Lawler was in agreement with his realist opponents that the issue at hand was the rational control of war, but he insisted that nuclear weapons eliminated all such rational limits.[8]

Lawler stressed that he was not an absolute pacifist, and what he wanted the Vatican Council to condemn was not all nuclear weapons as such, but weapons of mass destruction. He granted that theoretically it was possible to conceive of usable nuclear weapons that could be targeted against strictly military targets. His position, however, was that it was an intellectual *cul-de-sac* to engage in such abstracted arguments over such theoretically limited usage of nuclear weapons. More importantly, Lawler sought to attack nuclear weapons as an aggregate in their overkill capacity, and the national policy to use them that way, which was the actual reality with which we are faced.[9]

In this effort to confront the historical reality of nuclear weapons and nuclear war, Lawler concluded that while certain individual weapons could be called moral, it is still possible to declare any nuclear war to be immoral.[10] Regarding just war theorists who argued that limited nuclear war could be waged within the boundaries of moral limits (for example, John Courtney Murray, Paul Ramsey, William O'Brien), Lawler placed such people under the judgment of Cardinal Newman, who charged that logicians are usually more interested in arguing rightly than in right conclusions. Against these theoretical constructions of the possibility of a just, limited nuclear war, Lawler placed what he held to be his own historically more realistic moral certitude:

I would base my own total denial of the morality of any nuclear war not on strict logic, but on the certitude flowing from the converging probabilities created by the history of all recent major wars, by the exorbitant potential of the weapons themselves, by the consequences of the psychological strain induced by more than a decade of living on the edge of a volcano, by the fact that even in limited engagements where our vital interests are not at stake—as in Vietnam—war has been prosecuted through immoral means: on the basis of the convergence of all these probabilities and a score of others in the individual judgment, I would conclude with what is certitude for me to the immorality of any nuclear war.[11]

With this conviction, Lawler and the editorial staff of *Continuum* constantly criticized much of the American debate over nuclear deterrence and strategy as hopelessly removed from reality. This attitude can be seen in their reaction to the debates in the early and mid-sixties over counter-city versus counterforce nuclear deterrence.

In 1962 Secretary of Defense Robert McNamara, in an address at the University of Michigan, called for a move away from a nuclear deterrence focused on the doctrine of mutually assured destruction (MAD—counter-city retaliation) to a more flexible nuclear deterrence capable of fighting a limited nuclear war focused on military targets (counterforce). The eminent Protestant moral theologian, Paul Ramsey (recognized as the most systematic expositor of modern just war theory, whose views would generally accord with the majority of Catholic realists) welcomed McNamara's speech. Ramsey saw it as a positive step toward the creation of a morally usable nuclear deterrent.[12]

Lawler scathingly retorted that Ramsey's assumption that such a policy would force the U.S. and the U.S.S.R. into a classic weapon-to-weapon war and away from counter-city warfare ignored the fact that Russian numerical inferiority in nuclear weapons would not allow them to cooperate in this. Furthermore, the Russians were on record as believing the whole idea of a limited nuclear war was absurd. Also, any presumption of the controllability of war conveniently ignores the fact that in World War II we already demonstrated our unwillingness to be so confined. Lawler asked why, if the United States was serious about moving to a counterforce deterrent, it was concentrating on building the Polaris submarine missile, which was useful mainly as a terror weapon against cities.[13] Lawler judged the concept of a counterforce nuclear strategy as actually constituting an attempt to prepare the American people for war, by wedding the conception of the evilness of the communist enemy to the myth of having a nuclear arsenal that can morally be used against them. Lawler feared that the reality of this danger found expression in an article of the *National Review* in 1963, which justified a pre-emptive nuclear first strike against the Soviet Union, if the United States possessed a "controllable" counterforce capacity. *Continuum* also rejected the counterforce strategy of McNamara as only suitable for an offensive first strike.[14] Lawler confessed that it strained his faith in the cause of the West to believe that it would justify placing ourselves in a position of irrationally destroying the planet.[15]

Lawler viewed the development of a counterforce nuclear strategy as part of an insidious attempt to reduce nuclear war in the popular mind to a conventional and comprehensible engagement. One of Lawler's most frequent targets was what he saw as the "cult of the expert," which stifled most public discussion on the issue. For Lawler, much of what was wrong with the "expert strategists" who dominated contemporary consideration of the issues of nuclear war was embodied in the person of the physicist Herman Kahn. Kahn's influential and controversial books, *On Thermonuclear War* and *Thinking the Unthinkable*, focused on the problems of how to conduct and survive a nuclear war.[16] Lawler saw in Kahn the strategist's tragic search for an all-encompassing body of rules and techniques which would guide us in "controlling" and coping with every conceivable situation. It was typical of such "crack-pot realists,"[17] said Lawler, to show little awareness of history and little appreciation of the irrationality of the forces unleashed in war.

Lawler was especially critical of Catholic realists, such as Dougherty, Kennedy, and O'Brien, and accused them of playing to the "higher knowledge" of the technical expert, only to muddle the moral issues at stake and deny the capacity of the layman to exercise moral discernment. He charged that their

lumping together of nuclear pacifists and total pacifists was a
refusal to concede that, in fact, many use the just war theory
to arrive at a condemnation of nuclear weapons.[18]

Lawler's most vehement invective was directed at their rejection of the normative status of the principle of non-combatant immunity, and accused them of departing from the tradition
of Murray and Ramsey, who were at one with the pacifists in
accepting the principle. He saw them as standing alone in following the course of expediency and a non-critical approach to
government.[19]

In contrast, Lawler saw his position and that of most Catholic
nuclear pacifists as focusing on a program of four points:

1. unilateral initiatives by the United States to reduce tension in its
   relationship with the Soviet Union;[20]

2. a United States declaration of no first use of nuclear weapons;

3. gradual reduction of Strategic Air Command (SAC) bases;

4. greater government research on the subject of conflict resolution.

In response to the charges of the realists, Lawler argued that
such a program of immediate action would not threaten the
ability of America to defend itself, or in any way dangerously
destabilize the balance of power. He particularly resented the
attempts to picture nuclear pacifists as calling for unilateral
disarmament, and insisted that the program they were calling
for in no way entailed such a demand.[21]

Yet, if nuclear war and the present nuclear deterrent were
immoral and if unilateral disarmament was not the appropriate response, how was the Christian nuclear pacifist to respond
in the present situation? Lawler and the editors of *Continuum*
declared that the Christian attitude toward the "Deterrence
State" *as such* must be that of the early Christians. By this,
however, they did not mean that the Christian should go into
the kind of sectarian withdrawal and rejection of society that
many radical pacifists advocated. They conceded that the system of nuclear deterrence is responsible for the present mode
of world stability, as fragile and impermanent as that is. Consequently, the Christian, Lawler argued, must take advantage

of this period of quasi-international stability and work to educate people and inform them of the facts of nuclear war. The last thing Lawler ever envisioned for the Christian was retreat into an apocalyptic withdrawal or what he called a "sterile jeremiad of protest." What was needed was not demonstrations, but formation; that is, the implementation of the long-range program of *Mater et Magistra* and *Pacem in Terris*.[22]

In this regard Lawler cautioned the peace movement on its tendency to transpose the tactics of the civil rights movement to the peace movement. He argued that the civil rights demonstrations worked because they applied pressure in a situation where there already existed a moral consensus that was being violated in practice. On the war issue, however, no such moral consensus existed. Consequently, Lawler feared that many of the protests of the peace movement, especially the more provocative forms like draft card burning, were only adding to national polarization, and not to the most vital task of forming an enlightened public opinion.[23]

Crucial to the Catholic role in creating this enlightened moral climate was the role of the hierarchy. Lawler contended that if the bishops had spoken out against obliteration bombing during the last war, perhaps Hiroshima would not have happened. He credited the encyclical *Pacem in Terris* with helping to create the climate which allowed John Kennedy to attempt to put a new, less tense accent on American-Soviet relations. In general, however, Lawler's hopes for American episcopal leadership were muted by his seeing in the bishops the same divisions and lack of moral consensus present in the community at large. Nevertheless, he was optimistic that the Vatican Council had set in motion a discussion among Catholics which would move the Church toward a clearer understanding of the issue of war and peace.[24]

Throughout their articulation of educational goals that Catholics should work for within American society, Lawler and the editors of *Continuum* strongly upheld the internationalist ideals of the CAIP and modern papal teaching. One of the main criticisms they leveled at realists like Murray and O'Brien was that, while they showed great confidence in the power of human reason to control war, they abdicated that same confidence in rejecting the world federalism called for in *Pacem in Terris*. Lawler asked, if reason and the good will of statesmen could control the irrational forces unleashed in war, why could they not work to establish a world authority to eliminate the need for war? He questioned whether the rejection of this possibility by the realists was rooted in their theological presuppositions or in their political ones.[25]

Lawler was convinced that all past civilizations were a rehearsal for this present moment in history, in which as never before the human race is faced with determining the possibilities of its own survival. In such an historical moment the choice, he argued, is not between being red or dead, as many envisioned it. Rather, the choice is between embracing the feasibility of mutual disarmament and the establishment of a world authority, or preparing for an inevitable and unparalleled holocaust.[26]

Writing in 1965, Lawler stated that the two most pressing problems threatening global war were Berlin and Vietnam. These problems, he felt, were created by our tendency to raise political slogans to the level of absolute political-moral values. In the case of Berlin, Lawler contended that the West itself created the problem when it broke the four-power agreement on the division of Germany and created the state of West Germany. At this point, the Soviets logically concluded that Berlin, whose special status was part of the four-power agreement, now reverted to being a city belonging to East Germany. Lawler felt that the Western attitude toward West Berlin reflected an unrealistic identification of Berlin's interests with the interests of America and the West. The potentially explosive confrontation which occurred at the time of the Berlin blockade was, in Lawler's view, an example of the disastrous potentialities of absolutizing the value of political symbols.[27]

Even more disastrous was the United States involvement in Vietnam. Lawler insisted that the "domino theory" was a myth, and all of Southeast Asia would not fall to the communists if Saigon did. He argued that the United States was conducting a counter-insurgency war by means which showed no regard for non-combatant immunity and which were immorally disproportionate in their destructiveness. Unlike the realists,

Lawler held that no larger political objective could justify this violation of moral principles. Furthermore, the use of the Strategic Air Command was seen by him as an ominous sign of how this war threatened to expand to global proportions.[28]

Thus in Lawler and the journal *Continuum* can be found a perspective quite at odds with the realist conception of the issue of war. Rather than focus on the question of security, they stressed that force was not the best or chief means of containing communism. Consequently, where realists would chose to focus on the questions of the moral use of armed force, nuclear pacifists and internationalists insisted that the question of war was not separable from the need for world economic development and the creation of international structures to adjudicate conflict. Where the realist saw the ultimate task of America to be the defense of the free world, the nuclear pacifists saw that task to be the validation of the free world's moral reason for existence in the fostering of a greater world unity. Yet, despite their differences with the realists, the perspective of Lawler and *Continuum* is still clearly within the Americanism of the CAIP tradition.

During the latter years of the sixties the negative judgments which many American Catholic liberals made on the war in Vietnam reflect a view in many ways similar to that found in Lawler. While many of these Catholics could not be said to fit within Lawler's total internationalist perspective, they do reflect an attempt by Catholics to dissent from American policy in the name of America, that is, to condemn American involvement in Vietnam as against American interests as well as a violation of the Catholic understanding of the moral use of force.

David O'Brien has judged that Catholic liberals tended to support American intervention until 1965, when the introduction of large numbers of American troops changed the war from a Vietnamese to an American campaign.[29] In the judgments they made, Catholic liberals reflected the strain between their failing confidence in the American cause, as explained by the administration, and their desire not to blame America for the war. When they did judge the war to be immoral, they sought to call the nation away from it in the name of what America was seen as morally standing for, that is, to preserve the moral code which Lawler saw as giving the free world its meaning, and which was seen as the true character of American society. An example of this phenomenon can be found in a debate between Father George Tavard and Michael Novak, which appeared in the pages of the *National Catholic Reporter* (*NCR*) in 1965. Tavard complained that the moral issues surrounding the war had been clouded by the pacifists, and the entire anti-war opposition was in danger of being absorbed by the pacifist position. He argued that without accepting pacifism, the war must be rejected. The United States had an obligation not to use Vietnam for its own interests, but to foster the development of the Vietnamese people. By Americanizing the war Tavard saw the United States as simply taking over in order to fight its own war there.[30]

Novak initially replied by rejecting Tavard's position. He argued that it was proper for America to intervene on behalf of a global strategy of containing communist plans for expansion. Yet Novak did not deny that the United States was responsible for engaging in terror and brutality in Vietnam and must accept responsibility for that. This, however, was not seen as negating the justice of the cause.[31]

Two years later, Novak had changed his mind. He concluded that the Saigon government had failed to win the loyalty of its own people, and that it was impossible for the United States to fight their war for them. Furthermore, the strategies for fighting the war, which involved torture and non-combatant destruction, were out of proportion to any value being defended there. The neglect of domestic issues which the war had caused only added to the fact that the war could no longer be held to be in the interests of America.[32]

The editorial position of the *NCR* itself reflects a similar evolution of judgment. Initially the *NCR* supported the government's intervention in the hope that military force would bring the communists to a negotiated settlement. From 1965 to 1967 its editorials expressed a growing concern that American strategy and tactics were growing out of proportion to that goal. They feared that technology and not moral purpose was directing the country's conduct in the war. The indiscriminate killing that the editors saw as part of United States strategy reflected to them an American determination to destroy Vietnam rather than admit defeat.[33] Finally in January of 1967 the editors denounced the war as immoral on the grounds that the ends for which America was fighting could not be achieved, except by the nearly total destruction of the enemy in both north and south Vietnam. The rationale of this judgment made clear that not only were the editors invoking the Catholic just war teaching, but also the American tradition. As they claimed: "We are casting away a heritage. We are changing the meaning of America. The very sound and symbolism of the word; we are destroying the trust and hope it inspired, we are dissipating the influence America might otherwise wield in the building of a just and stable world order."[34]

Following this conclusion the *NCR* became increasingly favorable to efforts to resist the war. Yet the weekly's conclusion did not represent a change in political perspective on the world ideological conflict, nor in its belief in the need to fight and to contain communism. Neither did it represent a move toward pacifism, or a change in the editors' understanding of American cultural ideals. Rather, the *NCR*'s stance represented a sense of America's ideals being betrayed by its own government, and the use of the just war criteria to judge the means by which the war was being prosecuted to be immoral.

In the same year *Commonweal* and *U.S. Catholic* also used the just war criteria to declare American involvement in Vietnam immoral.[35] While not all Catholic papers which came out against the war demanded immediate withdrawal, as the *NCR* did, they at least demanded a graduated withdrawal and an end as soon as was feasible. The Catholic liberal rejection of the war continued to reflect a growing disbelief in the government's honesty and the fear of a larger expansion of the war, as well as constant reassertion of betrayed American ideals.[36] Michael Novak argued that in the struggle against communism, the real enemy was poverty and disease. Rather than focus on the ideological clash, the United States, he asserted, must address itself to needed social, economic, and political revolution, which is the source of communist appeal in most parts of the world. He feared that forgetting this larger context of the struggle against communism had led to making Vietnam akin to the Spanish Civil War, in being a testing ground for military technology and tactics and a rehearsal for future conflicts.[37]

Thus, in this sampling of the American Catholic liberal rejection of the Vietnam war can be seen an attempt similar to the early efforts of Justus George Lawler to delineate a middle position between the realists, who would justify such wars in the name of a wider global strategy, and the pacifists, who would reject all use of arms and even America's global role. From the mid-sixties until its termination in 1975 the American involvement in Vietnam became the nearly exclusive focus of discussion on war for Catholics as well as for the nation at large. This entailed a shift of concern away from the question of nuclear weapons and deterrence, which had been the initial focus of the issue of war, to an "examination of conscience" over the meaning of Vietnam for the moral quality and goals of American society.

In the course of this examination, Catholic liberals who rejected the war on grounds such as those stated above were, in a significant sense, closer to their realist opponents than they were to their pacifist and radical fellow dissenters in refusing to interpret Vietnam as a symptom of a radical cultural degeneracy in American society. Their protest remained a defense of the liberal Western state, not a rejection of it. They continued to hold to the liberal optimism that mistakes in American policy could be changed through effective communication, dialogue, public education, and direct political action. Yet perhaps it is significant that this optimism regarding change in the political system did not continue to focus as much on the internationalist ideals which earlier had been a more prominent feature of Lawler's work. By the end of the Vietnam war, the internationalism which had been a prominent feature of the program of earlier Catholic advocates of nuclear pacifism had become submerged in the acrimonious debates over the moral quality of America's role in the world. The resurgence of the issue of nuclear weapons and deterrence in the post-war years to become again the focus of debates in the evolving Catholic analysis of war and peace will be the subject of a later chapter.

SUMMARY

As can be seen in the first chapter, the intellectual perspective which the CAIP brought to the issue of war prior to 1960 held together various elements which were in tension with one another. Its Americanism and internationalism attempted to combine a strong anti-communism and a demand for an adequate military defense with a call to transcend the current world ideological conflict in the establishment of international structures and mutual world economic and social development. Within the Americanism of the CAIP was a strong defense of contemporary Western culture as the product and hope of Christian civilization, and also a profound concern that the greatest threat to the West was its own materialism and moral confusion.

In the differing perspectives of realism and nuclear pacifism which emerged among Catholics in the sixties, there can be seen the elements which constituted the intellectual tradition of the CAIP, but which could no longer be held together in a single synthesis. The tensions inherent in the CAIP tradition had produced a split between two similar yet opposing camps. The strain between the dual emphasis of defending the West against a nemesis culture of communism and the call to transform the international order and create a world federal government caused a severing of the two.

In focusing on the unappeasable nature of the competing social order of communism, Catholic realists could not entertain much hope of joining with communist powers in new international structures. The only possibility for a new world order lay in the transformation of the communist world to be in conformity with the social traditions of the pluralistic West. Only then could there be a common truth on which to formulate a conception of an international common good. Consequently, the development of the Catholic realist perspective focused on the question of security apart from and primary to other questions of world economic development, which were the focus of discussion for the internationalist CAIP.

To the extent that Catholic nuclear pacifists tried to hold

onto the internationalist ideals of the CAIP and modern papal teaching, they necessarily had to place their emphasis not on the problems of security, but on the call to lessen international tensions and move toward a restructuring of the international order. This implicity entailed a less monolithic conception of communism, and a greater optimism about the ability to find common ground without a prior "defeat" of the communist adversary.

In pursuing their major concern for security and reconciling American defense policy with Catholic moral teaching, Catholic realists found themselves in tension with the thrust of contemporary official Church pronouncements on war. In following their own interpretation of Catholic just war teaching and internationalist ideals, Catholic nuclear pacifists found themselves in tension with the stated needs of contemporary American defense doctrine. Yet both were clearly committed to defending the proposition that one could be both a good American and a good Catholic.

The Americanism of the CAIP tradition united these two schools of thought, which were otherwise vitriolic opponents in their differing attempts to balance the need both to defend Western culture and to keep the world from the disaster of global war. While the nuclear pacifists and internationalists like Lawler reflected more mixed feelings about American society, their criticisms were never close to making a radical break with the American social system, and were informed by an optimism that related issues such as economic and racial problems were on the way to being solved. Though divided in their beliefs concerning the possibility of change in the international system, Catholic realists and nuclear pacifists/internationalists were one in their understanding of the ideological schism dividing the world, and in their confidence of the positive role America had to play within it.

The Americanism of both perspectives is also reflected in their common view of the relation of the Church to society. Catholic realists were quite clear that the ultimate issue in reconciling Catholic teaching with the practical needs of American defense policy was the meaningful participation of Catholics in American political life. If Catholics could not participate in providing what was necessary for a practical military defense in the nuclear age, they would have no option but a total pacifism and withdrawal from political life.

While nuclear pacifists like Lawler took a stand which the realists saw as tantamount to running Catholics out of the American defense establishment, they also strongly rejected any sectarian interpretation of their position. While their rejection of nuclear weapons placed them outside the stated needs of American defense policy, their commitment to American society and culture prohibited embracing any sectarian withdrawal or anti-state posture. They chose to walk a line between dissent and total pacifism or rebellion, and saw themselves as akin to John Courtney Murray in seeking to create a climate of enlightened moral opinion, through which America could be re-grounded on its own true heritage of values.

Thus for both Catholic realists and nuclear pacifists, the issue of war was still the issue of culture in the same way as it was for the CAIP. For the realist it was a matter of providing security for America and Western civilization. For the nuclear pacifist it was a matter of calling that civilization to fulfill its moral role in transforming the present international order. Beneath their debates there was still a common understanding of what that civilization was and the place of the Church within it. Consequently, despite the frequent tendency to see these two perspectives as radically separate, it would be more correct to see them as two polarities within Catholic Americanism. Together, they continued into the sixties and seventies the elements of the intellectual heritage which the CAIP tradition bequeathed to the American Catholic understanding of war. They also reflect how the constitutive elements of that heritage could no longer be held together by American Catholics in a workable synthesis. The interrelation of these two schools of thought becomes even more apparent when considering the perspectives of more radical Catholic pacifists and dissenters, who present quite different assumptions about the meaning of war as a social issue in America.

NOTES

1. Milton S. Katz, "Nuclear Pacifism in Cold War America: The National Committee for a Sane Nuclear Policy," unpublished paper

submitted to the *Historians' Project* of the World Without War Council, Seattle, Washington, 1982.

2. Joseph N. Moody and Justus George Lawler, eds., *The Challenge of Mater et Magistra* (New York: Herder and Herder, 1963).

3. Ibid., p. 5.

4. Ibid., pp. 6–8. An example of Lawler's view of Catholics failing to recognize the pluralistic nature of American society is his charge that Catholics working to enforce Sunday "blue laws" or place Christian symbols *qua* Christian symbols in public buildings were confusing a society based on values in accord with the Christian tradition with a society that was officially Christian.

5. Ibid., p. 10.

6. Justus George Lawler, *Nuclear War: The Ethic, The Rhetoric, The Reality* (Westminster, Maryland: Newman Press, 1965), p. 3.; also idem, "Catholics and the Arms Race, *Commonweal* 76 (May 18, 1962): 199–203.

7. James Finn, *Protest: Pacifism and Politics* (New York: Random House, 1967), pp. 84–86; 92–93.

8. Lawler, *Nuclear War*, p. 30.

9. Lawler, "The Council Must Speak," in Finn, *Peace, The Churches and the Bomb*, p. 33; *Nuclear War*, p. 30.

10. Lawler, *Nuclear War*, p. 41; "Moral Issues and Nuclear Pacifism," in James Finn, ed., *Peace, the Churches and the Bomb* (New York: Council on Religion and International Affairs, 1965), p. 93.

11. Ibid. p. 93.

12. Paul Ramsey, *The Limits of Nuclear War* (New York: The Council on Religion and International Affairs, 1963), pp. 7–9.

13. "Nuclear Strategy and Christian Morality," editorial, *Continuum* 1 (Summer 1963): 198–201; Lawler, *Nuclear War*, p. 75.

14. Justus George Lawler, "Balancing the Terror," *Continuum* 1 (Summer 1963): 105–107. Lawler here reviewed Richard Fryklund's book *100 Million Lives* (1962), in which he saw Fryklund's thought as representing the deterrent strategy operative in the government; "The Folly of a No-Cities Nuclear Strategy," editorial, *Continuum* 1 (Spring 1963): 99–100.

15. "Nuclear Strategy and Christian Morality," p. 203.

16. Herman Kahn, *On Thermonuclear War*, 2nd ed. (Princeton: Princeton University Press, 1961), *Thinking the Unthinkable* (New York: Horizon Press, 1962): Lawler, *Nuclear War*, pp. 80–81; "Balancing the Terror," pp. 107–109.

17. The term "crack-pot realist" was coined by the sociologist C. Wright Mills in 1958 in his volume, *The Cause of World War Three* (New York: Simon and Schuster).

18. Lawler, *Nuclear War*, pp. 126–145.

19. Justus George Lawler, "Charity and Nuclear Nonsense," *Continuum* 4 (Summer 1966): 308–309. *N.B.* While O'Brien was the most systematic in developing his rejection of the interpretation of the principle of non-combatant immunity followed by such mainline just war theorists as Paul Ramsey, he would be joined in much of his critique by others such as James Dougherty and William Kennedy.

20. The type of initiatives which Catholic liberals advocated were similar to the program advanced by Charles E. Osgood. A summary of his views are in James Roosevelt, ed., *The Liberal Papers* (Chicago: Quadrangle Books, Inc., 1962), pp. 155–228.

21. "The Direction of the Peace Movement," editorial, *Continuum* 1 (Summer 1963): 225–227.

22. "Nuclear Strategy and Christian Morality," pp. 209–210; Lawler, *Nuclear War*, p. 179. Lawler cited the work of Prof. Louis B. Sohn as a constructive example of a program for relaxing cold war tensions. Louis B. Sohn, "Creating a Favorable World Opinion of American Foreign Policy," *The Annals of the American Academy of Political and Social Science* 330 (July 1960): 11–21.

23. "Direction of the Peace Movement", pp. 276–277; Lawler, *Nuclear War*, p. 176; Finn, *Protest*, pp. 88, 90–91.

24. Finn, *Protest*, pp. 90–91; Lawler, *Nuclear War*, p. 178.

25. "Nuclear Strategy and Christian Morality," p. 199; Lawler, *Nuclear War*, pp. 175–176.

26. Lawler, *Nuclear War*, pp. 175–176; "Catholics and the Arms Race," p. 203.

27. Lawler, *Nuclear War*, pp. 118–119.

28. Ibid., p. 121; Finn, *Protest*, p. 86–87.

29. David J. O'Brien, "American Catholic Opposition to the Vietnam War: A Preliminary Assessment," in Thomas A. Shannon, ed., *War or Peace: The Search for New Answers* (Maryknoll, New York: Orbis Books, 1980), p. 132.

30. Rev. George Tavard, "A Theologian's Question," *National Catholic Reporter*, August 11, 1965, p. 3.

31. Michael Novak, "Our Terror, Our Brutality," *National Catholic Reporter*, August 18, 1967, p. 3.

32. "Novak Calls War Immoral," *National Catholic Reporter* 4, January 1967, p. 5.

33. Examples of this developing editorial opinion in the *NCR* are: "The New Morality in Guerilla Warfare," September 1, 1965, p. 6; "On the Limits of War," August 25, 1965, p. 3; "Ends and Means in War," January 25, 1966, p. 3; "More Bombs More Doubts," July 6, 1966, p. 6.

34. "You Make a Desert and Call It Peace," *National Catholic Reporter*, January 3, 1967, p. 1.

35. "Just War," *Commonweal* 87 (December 22, 1967): 321–322.

36. Finn, "War, Peace and the Christian Tradition," *Jubilee* 13 (March 1966): 36–41; "Nuclear Weapons Next?" *Commonweal* 93 (February 26, 1971): 507.

37. Michael Novak, Robert McAfee Brown, and Abraham J. Heschel, *Vietnam: Crisis of Conscience* (New York: Herder and Herder, 1967), pp. 7–46.

4

Catholic Pacifism and Resistance

The events of the late fifties and early sixties which gave rise to a revival of concern among many Americans over the issues of war and nuclear weapons also spurred a revival of a more radical pacifist movement in American society. In the same year (1957) that SANE was formed to promote a nuclear pacifist position reflected in Catholic liberals such as Justus George Lawler, radical American pacifists like A. J. Muste joined to form the Committee for Non-Violent Action (CNVA). Whereas SANE attempted to work for change within the political system, the CNVA dedicated itself to the development of tactics of direct non-violent confrontation and disruption. The radical pacifists organized around CNVA identified themselves as non-violent social revolutionaries, convinced that the establishment of world peace required a revolutionary alteration in the cultural values and the distribution of wealth and power within all of the nations involved in the Cold War.[1]

These radicals sought to go beyond the traditional pacifism of individual objection to war, and to create an organized pacifist movement committed to the realization of peace and justice within American society and capable of "jamming the gears of the war machine." As these efforts developed during the sixties, their goals expanded beyond the protesting of bomb tests and the construction of nuclear weapons, to visionary demands for unilateral disarmament and efforts to link the peace and civil rights movements into a common effort to transform society.[2]

Within the American Catholic community, the Catholic

Worker remained the chief and lonely voice of pacifism up to 1960. The Worker movement also played a significant role in the revival of the American radical pacifist movement with its campaign of organized civil disobedience in protest against the civil defense drills in New York City during the closing years of the fifties.[3]

In the early sixties American Catholic pacifists received great encouragement from the encyclical *Pacem in Terris* of John XXIII, but found their most significant breakthrough in the acceptance of pacifism as a legitimate moral option by the Second Vatican Council. Particularly under the influence of the war in Vietnam, pacifists experienced in the sixties and seventies an unprecedented rise in acceptance and prominence within the American Catholic community, without ever losing their minority status.

While not all of those associated with the development and articulation of radical Catholic pacifism during these years were part of the Catholic Worker movement, it was still the Catholic Worker tradition which provided the basic intellectual heritage for these developments, as well as their organizational womb. In 1962 members of the Catholic Worker, under the leadership of Eileen Eagan, reactivated the American branch of PAX in affiliation with the English Catholic peace movement by the same name. PAX concentrated on working for change within the institutional Church, and actively lobbied for the pacifist position at the Second Vatican Council. In 1964 Catholic Workers James Forrest, Thomas Cornell, and Martin Corbin joined with Philip Berrigan, S.S.J., to form the Catholic Peace Fellowship (CPF), in affiliation with the Protestant organization, the Fellowship of Reconciliation. The CPF sought to integrate Catholic peace activities into the wider American peace movement, as well as to continue the Catholic Worker tradition of civil disobedience and non-violent resistance to war. Thus by 1964 the Catholic Worker, PAX, and the CPF constituted the organizational backbone of the first viable American Catholic peace movement.[4]

As this movement developed, those who articulated the social perspectives of Catholic pacifism and radicalism did not constitute a monolithic group, any more than did their Catholic realist and idealist counterparts. Yet, while there were differences among them, they were united in their rejection of the Americanist presuppositions with which both realists and idealists approached the issue of war. Radical Catholic pacifists presented a quite different definition of the conflict defining international relations, as well as a more radical and negative critique of American society and the place of the Church within it. As they sought to challenge American values and governmental policy, they had to explore nonviolence as a philosophy and method for both offering an alternative to war and seeking social change. This chapter and the next will consider those individuals most representative of the worldview that emerged in American Catholicism from 1960 to 1980 under the banner of Catholic pacifism and resistance.

CATHOLIC PACIFISM

In an examination of the development of American Catholic pacifist thought in the sixties and seventies, three men emerge as its most prominent and systematic expositors, Gordon Zahn, Thomas Merton, and James Douglass. In the similarity of themes treated by these men, as well as in the differences of emphasis and nuance of their perspectives, can be found the major presuppositions and judgments defining the worldview of radical Catholic pacifism in its latest period of development.

Gordon Zahn and Milieu Catholicism

Gordon Zahn has been recognized by many as one of the people most responsible for the rise in status and respectability that pacifism has acquired within the American Catholic community in the past twenty years. Zahn was himself one of the handful of American Catholic conscientious objectors during the Second World War. As a sociologist, he gained recognition in the early sixties for his study of German Catholics under the Nazi regime, *German Catholics and Hitler's Wars.*[5] This work, in which he analyzed the German Church's failure to resist the Nazi government, served as a background for much of Zahn's analysis of the contemporary American Church. Sub-

titled *A Study in Social Control*, the book showed the focus of
Zahn's concern to be the manner in which the Church's relationship to the modern state has reduced it to the role of preparing individuals to serve the interests of the state, rather
than bearing prophetic witness against the state. For Zahn,
the crucial question was whether the Church would function
as a supra-national society of faith, fostering the peaceful unity
of the human race, or as a nationalistically confined church
subservient to the needs of national interests.

As stated earlier, Zahn was the sole contributor to William
Nagle's volume in 1960 who represented a pacifist position. His
lone position here reflected both the status of pacifism within
the Catholic community and his own early emergence as one
of the chief spokesmen for this position within the Church.
Zahn's contribution to this volume showed the beginnings of
what in the sixties would become a major reassessment, on the
part of the growing Catholic peace movement, of what John
Courtney Murray called the conflict defining international relations today.[6]

Zahn set forth one of the major contentions of radical Catholic
social criticism in the sixties and seventies. That is, in the
present era the Church must reassess its traditional understanding of its relationship to the state, and must return to the
suspicion of the state which was characteristic of the early
Church prior to Constantine. In rejecting the trust which the
medieval Church placed in the "Christian Prince," Zahn argued
that there is no longer (if there ever was) any reason to assume
that the demands of the secular ruler will even meet the minimal standards of Christian morality.

For Zahn, the anti-Christian and anti-human character of
the modern state is most manifest in the problem of war. The
modern state has been built upon the reliance on ever greater
force to achieve security. Yet the result has only been ever
more destructive wars and the ultimate insecurity of living
under the threat of nuclear holocaust. The inhumanity produced by the cult of force lay at the heart of the corruption of
modern civilization and was much more fundamental than the
ideological conflicts of East and West.

At the root of the moral collapse of modern society Zahn saw an exaggerated idea of the authority of the state and a correlatively restricted conception of the moral competency and responsibility of the individual. In effect, modern society had destroyed the moral autonomy of the individual, and the maintenance of the modern state depended upon the effectiveness of this moral lobotomy. For Zahn, therefore, a prerequisite for any true social reform was a revival of the personal and cultural sense of the competency and responsibility of the individual conscience.[7]

In facing this task Zahn referred to his work on the German Church as an historical case in point illustrating how the Church becomes ensnared in nationalism and unable to stand against the dominant currents of the secular environment. In such a state the task of the Church to morally form the individual becomes a function of social conformity to the dominant cultural milieu. The result is a "milieu Catholicism," incapable of prophetic witness, whose social orientation is the preservation of its own status and privileges within the *status quo.* As an illustration of the dynamics of milieu Catholicism, Zahn used his book on the Austrian peasant Franz Jägerstätter, who was executed in 1943 for refusing to serve in the German army and participate in what he judged to be an unjust war.[8] Jägerstätter had to stand alone, not only against the authority of the state, but also against the German Church, which refused to recognize the validity of his conscientious objection while it supported the duty of Catholics to serve in the military.

Zahn contended that the failure of the German Church to support resistance to Nazi policies reflected the same condition present among American Catholics. He argued that since World War II Americans had gone from blaming all Germans for the war to the opposite extreme of denying the very principle of corporate responsibility. The American attitude tended to view the individual as helpless before the state and dissent as psychologically aberrant.[9]

Despite its compromises, Zahn still laid upon the Church the principal responsibility for resurrecting the rights and role of individual conscience, especially since he saw it as the only institution left in modern society with the potential for doing this. As a sociologist Zahn recognized the importance of a cul-

tural context supporting the individual in the formation and
exercise of conscience. Just as milieu Catholicism in Nazi Germany and contemporary America conditioned the individual
to conformity, so too the ability of the individual Christian to
stand against social evil required an equally strong and supportive counter-cultural community.[10]

The problem, as Zahn analyzed it, was that most of the institutions normally responsible for the formation of individuals, such as the family and school, have been subverted in their
ability to provide a context in which to stand against the state,
or else have been co-opted into serving as instruments for teaching conformity. Thus, the Church remains the only institution
with the potential to provide a counter-cultural context which
can exist within and yet still apart from the complex of our
current attachments and obligations to the larger society, and
thus be able to support individuals in a culturally "deviant"
stance. Only by being able to take a stance of social deviance
that is still in conformity with a religious community will most
individuals be able to "stand apart" in the manner of a Franz
Jägerstätter.

In effect, Zahn was calling on the Church to create a new
version of the "inner directed" person written of by sociologist
David Riesman. Zahn recognized, however, that attempting
this could drive the Church back to the catacombs. Consequently, the Church must reject its desire to maintain a com-
fortable position within society and return to the ideal of the
"Church of the Martyrs." This would mean rejecting the myth
that the Church cannot place burdens upon its people that
would require martyrdom of them. Zahn quoted an unnamed
expert at the Second Vatican Council as having said, "We don't
encourage martyrdom. To prevent this, the Church will make
almost any adjustment."[11] It was just such adjustments which
Zahn credited with having robbed the Church of its prophetic
vitality.

The prime example for Zahn of the type of adjustment which
milieu Catholicism had made to modern society was the just
war theory. More precisely, Zahn saw the problem as the manner in which the just war theory was used to abdicate the
Church's moral judgment to the state, rather than using the

just war criteria to seriously criticize government policies. Zahn argued that the case of the German Church in the last world war only illustrated the experience of the last couple of centuries, which showed that the just war criteria are actually irrelevant to the fact of war today. This conviction was only further reinforced by the use of the just war theory by realist thinkers to justify nuclear warfare. Even if the just war theory were strictly adhered to, Zahn could see it only as a good pagan morality.[12]

In effect, Zahn interpreted the essence of the tradition of just war thinking to be a history and practice of the casuistry of accommodation, which began when Christians wrongfully assumed responsibility for the state at the time of Constantine. For Zahn, as for Dorothy Day, the Christian commitment of faith required the rejection of violent force, and the willingness to die rather than violate respect for even the life of an unjust aggressor. Thus, even the normal uses of force inherent in the maintenance of the state are forbidden to the Christian. For Zahn, the idea of a Christian policeman or soldier is a contradiction in terms.[13]

The worst effect of the Church's adherence to the just war theory was, in Zahn's view, the Christian's participation in what he called the "inhumanity quotient" of modern man, that is, the ability of the human mind to develop a justification for an ever increasing degree of violence, finally culminating in such events as Auschwitz and Hiroshima. For Zahn, any mind which can justify such wholesale liquidation of humanity is corrupt, and today such corruption is general.[14]

While Zahn rejected the validity of the just war tradition, he did not hesitate to embrace it as a tool of argumentation. This was because of his conviction that, even if the just war categories were accepted and strictly interpreted, no actual modern war could meet their requirements for discrimination and proportionalty, as World War II demonstrated.[15] Zahn pointed to the example of the Second Lateran Council which outlawed the crossbow because "by reason of the very perfection of their mechanism they had become too efficiently murderous." He contrasted this willingness of the medieval Church to address the morality of specific weapons with the absence of any episcopal statement in 1963 on proposed plans to develop the neutron bomb. Zahn likewise contrasted the obvious sense of proportion used by the Second Lateran Council in judging the destructiveness of war with the modern Church's accommodation to the development and use of weapons designed to kill millions. He questioned whether any real sense of moral proportion would not also demand the condemnation of modern weapons, especially nuclear ones, "because by the perfection of their mechanisms, they had become too efficiently murderous."[16]

Zahn did not posit the problem of the Church's official teaching in lack of Roman leadership, but rather in the general nature of that teaching which allowed interpretations which undercut the very principles the teaching sought to uphold. In Zahn's interpretation of modern papal and conciliar teaching can be seen the different way in which pacifists like himself read the same documents as the nuclear realists to support quite different conclusions.[17]

Zahn stressed that all modern popes condemned modern war and the inordinate destructiveness of modern weapons technology. He recognized that Pius XII upheld the right of self-defense in the nuclear age, but Zahn pointed out that the Pope did not say that any modern war actually met the just war criteria. More importantly, Zahn interpreted *Pacem in Terris* as the most significant modern papal teaching. Whereas the nuclear realists argued that John XXIII did not rescind Pius XII's recognition of the right of national self-defense, Zahn focused on the statement of the encyclical declaring war not to be a rational option in the nuclear age. Zahn also contended that the condemnation of total war in both *Pacem in Terris* and *Gaudium et Spes* effectively outlawed any modern war, since he argued that modern war by its very nature was total war.[18]

Zahn actually sounded like his nemesis William O'Brien in contending that American Catholics were grossly undereducated in the actual principles of Church teaching on war and equally uninformed about the actual policies of the United States on the deterrent threat and planned usage of nuclear weapons. If the two were ever clearly stated side by side, their mutual contradiction would be unavoidably clear. Whereas, however, O'Brien moved to align Church teaching with defense needs, Zahn condemned such a move as an immoral accommodation to avoid a rupture between the Church and the government.[19]

Zahn argued that the realist use of the just war theory to defend a "limited nuclear war" was only possible by engaging in an abstract conversation on the theoretical usages of such weapons, while never really confronting their actual planned use and effects.[20] Similarly, Zahn spoke out against Vietnam, condemning Catholic justifications of it as a fearful parallel of the moral capitulation of German Catholics to the Nazis. He insisted Vietnam could not meet any of the criteria of the just war, and was only a proving ground for military technology. Even more insidiously, the furor over Vietnam had taken attention away from the threat of a still escalating nuclear arms buildup, so that the conclusion of the Vietnam conflict could actually leave us closer than ever before to global disaster.[21]

Zahn's conclusion was that there was no moral alternative for the United States except to move toward a rejection of the use and possession of nuclear weapons and the development of a non-violent alternative to war. Zahn was clearly aware that such a conclusion necessitated a radical change in the present Church-state relationship which in effect rejected the realist contention that one could be both a good Catholic and a good American within the present context of American policy. Yet, for Zahn, this radical cleavage in Church-state relations was not to mean a sectarian withdrawal of the Church into apocalyptic obscurity. The Church was to be the leaven for a new social order, not withdrawing from the state and society, but rather constantly engaging it in non-violent confrontation with the challenge to replace its commitment to violence with a commitment to a new moral force. Only when this moral basis of individual and social action is changed can meaningful structural change occur, such as the establishment of a world authority. In this sense Zahn was also at odds with those nuclear pacifists and idealists who advocated internationalist solutions to the problem of war. In Zahn's view they missed the deeper level of moral revolution which must occur before nations surrender reliance on the violence by which they now defend their sovereignty.[22]

Thus, Zahn's call for a radical transformation of the Church's relation to the state was understood by him as necessitating a rejection of what he saw as the false dichotomy of the traditional conceptions of Church-state relations. This traditional view, he felt, allowed only for either a sectarian withdrawal from society or the Church's acceptance of responsibility for supporting the state. Zahn hoped that the changes occurring in Catholic thought would lead to transcending this false dichotomy so that the withdrawal of the Church from one form of participation in society (military defense) could be replaced with an active and even aggressive reentry into society in another form.[23] The nature of this new form of Christian participation in society is contained in Zahn's understanding of nonviolence.

Zahn was not particularly happy with the negative term nonviolence and preferred a more positive term like Gandhi's use of the word Satyagraha, which means truth force. Zahn, like most American Catholic pacifists, greatly admired Gandhi and viewed him as the most significant figure of the twentieth century witnessing to the possibility and the necessity of a moral revolution in the operation of society.[24]

Zahn argued that total violence, as embodied in nuclear deterrence, had failed to provide the security that was used to justify its creation. It was necessary to create an alternative means of defense that did not further the disintegration of humanity that violence had brought about. That meant a means of self-defense and resistance to evil that maintained a respect for humanity, including the enemy, precisely because he is human. In this Zahn echoed John XXIII's call in *Mater et Magistra* to respect the dignity of individual human beings as the foundation and end of society.[25]

Zahn thus clearly called for more than a traditional pacifism of witness by non-participation in war, and insisted on a pacifism of active resistance to evil and oppression. As mentioned earlier, the development of this new style of pacifism of resistance had been underway in American radical pacifist circles since the late fifties. Under the influence of Ammon Hennacy, the Catholic Worker movement had helped pioneer the employment of Gandhian-style civil disobedience in an American pacifist program.[26] Zahn's writings in the early sixties were a continuation of this earlier effort of the Catholic Worker, in which he sought to give to non-violence a political significance, rather than allowing it to be merely an a-political withdrawal from society into a utopian dream.

In 1963 Zahn set forth his belief that a non-violent defense and deterrent could be developed for use by a nation in place of military force. Such a defense posture, Zahn argued, would have two strengths. First, it would eliminate the exaggerated tensions between nations, and thus allow the eventual establishment of new relations built on trust. Secondly, it would confront a potential invader with the prospect of having to cope with a population prepared to resist them with massive organized civil disobedience and non-violence.[27]

Zahn recognized that the ultimate premise of such a non-violent defense is the willingness to accept the suffering of massive brutality and killing. The strategy of such a non-violent defense is based on the belief that even in the most totalitarian aggressor there is a "breaking point" beyond which the aggressor could not accept the inhumanity he would have to inflict, or at which he would realize that the destruction he would have to inflict would leave him nothing worth having. To mount such a defense would require a social training and discipline and cultural support at least equal to what society presently provides for the formation of individuals into soldiers. As a final refutation of those who would reject the price of such a non-violent defense as unthinkable, Zahn insisted that the price in suffering and death could not be any higher than that which would be inflicted by a nuclear war. In the end, such a non-violent strategy offered the only kind of defense in which the world and the humanity of those in conflict would not be destroyed.[28]

To uphold the ideal of a nation such as the United States actually embracing a non-violent means of defense, was to require a revolutionary change of present value orientations. Such a revolution would require a trust in the ability of the individual conscience to be formed in such a non-violent outlook and to embody it in action and suffering. Fundamental to such a revolution, Zahn contended, was the leadership of Christians. Such Christian leadership required a return to the early Christian awareness that political freedom and personal survival are not ultimate goods and must be subordinated to the welfare of all people, including the enemy.

Thus, Zahn comes full circle in calling the Church to renounce its enslavement to its cultural and political milieu and to embrace the prophetic and ascetic ideal of the age of the martyrs. The greatest obstacle to this is not the weakness of individuals, but two self-imposed restraints of the Church in modern society: the separation of spiritual and temporal concerns, and the unwillingness of the Church to place too great a burden on its members. Zahn pointed out that the first temporal victory of the Church over the Roman Empire was won by centuries of non-violently suffering persecution. He speculated that the "re-conquest" of the modern world would require the willingness to pay an equal price.[29]

Thomas Merton and the Christian Diaspora

Because of his status as a monk and his reputation as a spiritual writer, Thomas Merton was recognized by many as the most prestigious spokesman for the Catholic peace movement in the sixties, and was responsible for winning the movement a wider hearing within the Catholic community. In the late fifties Merton had become aware of the moral and spiritual significance of contemporary social issues, and until his death in 1968 devoted much of his writing to the task of blending spiritual contemplation with social criticism and action.[30]

Unlike Gordon Zahn or James Douglass, Merton was not an ideological pacifist, and consistently refused to accept that term as descriptive of himself. Merton's concern was not to work out the implications of any preconceived theory of pacifism or the delineation of the limits of the exercise of the right of self-defense. Rather, he sought to describe the existential condition of modern society and the concrete requirements for justice and human survival in the modern era. In doing this Merton crit-

ically examined the limitations of most of the ideological and
tactical positions assumed by American Catholics on the issue
of war, and thus emerged as perhaps the most comprehensive
American Catholic writer on the subject. Yet in the practical
conclusions he reached on the requirements of peace and justice
in the modern world, Merton was clearly in the pacifist camp.
While he theoretically admitted the possibility of a just recourse to armed force, Merton's judgment on the actuality of
violence in modern society placed him together with Gordon
Zahn, Dorothy Day, James Douglass, and other representative
figures of American Catholic pacifism.[31]

Most basic to Merton's assessment of the social context in
which the Christian must deal with the issue of war and peace
is that the world in which we now live is a post-Christian one.
Merton accepted Karl Rahner's description of the Christian's
position in the twentieth century to be that of a diaspora situation in which the medieval cultural-religious synthesis, which
was the ideal of Peter Maurin and the early CAIP tradition,
no longer existed and could not be expected to be revived.[32]

The diaspora situation is one in which the faith and vision
of the Church are not only no longer culturally normative, but
are even despised and actively attacked. In such a condition
the Christian vocation becomes ever more a desperate wager
because the Church is hindered in its apostolic activity by secular powers, and access to the sacraments can become restricted. The clergy will become more and more a despised and
unappreciated class, and the faith of the individual Christian
will be constantly menaced and insecure.

Merton argued that acceptance of this diaspora condition is
a prerequisite to any meaningful consideration of Christian
action in the modern world. To continue to be guided by the
model of medieval Christendom, and for the Church to continue
to seek its institutional privileges and autonomy in the secular
world, would be to invite greater calamity.

Even in the worst conditions of the diaspora, Merton contended, the Church must and will continue its missionary activity, but in radically new forms, in which the purity of
individual witness will take precedence over everything else.
Thus, while agreeing with Zahn that the Church's mode of

presence in the modern world cannot be a sectarian withdrawal, Merton seemed more pessimistic on the ability to provide a counter-cultural institutional context to support
individuals in a "deviant" social stance. Merton felt it may be
necessary to rely on the heroic witness of individual Christians
as the norm of faith in the new age of the diaspora.

Another fundamental feature of the modern Christian diaspora is what Merton termed the eschatological vision which
Christians must assume. It is necessary, he argued, to have
the correct interpretation of the conflict between the Church and
the world. In this conflict faith demands both the expectation of
persecution and trust in the promise of Christ that the Church
will endure. Most especially, it demands that Christians understand that the victory of Christianity will not be the fruit
of imminent development and progressive leavening of the
world, but will be the act of God coming in judgment to gather
up world history into an unexpected end. Thus, the Christian
cannot work for a temporal revolution which will transform
the secular world overnight into the city of God. Rather, the
Christian must enter into the diaspora in a positive and truly
apostolic effort to meet the non-Christian on his own ground
and witness to the Gospel in a way he can understand and
accept. If necessary, this witness must be one of non-violent,
suffering love upholding the cross as a sign of contradiction
until the final act of God brings the drama of history to its
conclusion.

Merton's understanding of the diaspora condition of the
Christian also had obvious implications for a re-evaluation of
the conflict defining contemporary international relations. Merton agreed with Zahn that the Christian attitude toward the
state must entail the same suspicion as that held by the early
Church toward Rome.[33] Merton was far more systematic than
Zahn in developing this theme.

In the present critical moment of history, Merton argued, a
twofold task confronts the human race, but especially the citizens of the great power blocs which hold the fate of the other
nations in their hands. "On the one hand we have to defend
and foster the highest human values: The right of man to live
freely and develop his life in a way worthy of his moral great-

ness. On the other hand we have to protect man against the criminal abuse of the enormous destructive power which he has acquired."[34]

Merton stated that for most Americans and Western Europeans this dual task was reduced in practice to a struggle against totalitarian dictatorship (communism) and against war. He contended that to truly understand the challenge before them, Americans and Western Europeans must see that the struggle against totalitarianism is directed not only against communism as an external enemy, but also against our own tendencies toward fascism and totalist aberrations. Likewise, the struggle against war is directed not only against the bellicosity of communist nations, but also against our own violence, fanaticism, and greed. Merton branded as the greatest heresy the tendency of the Church to identify itself with the cause of the West in the international power struggle. He argued that the Christian responsibility was not to one side or the other in this power struggle, but to God and truth, and the whole of mankind.[35]

Merton used the images of the twins Gog and Magog from the book of Ezekiel to describe the conflict between the United States and the Soviet Union. Both were giants with great power and little sanity, living on the lies that each told with great conviction. Gog, the East, is a lover of power, and Magog, the West, is a lover of money, and while their opposing idolatries seem quite different, they are in fact two faces of the same inhumanity. Both claim to care about humanity, but in both societies life depends on everything except what you are, and both societies ignore the needs of humanity as they arm themselves for Armageddon.[36]

Yet Merton's criticism of the United States (Magog) was somewhat mitigated, in that he recognized that Magog was willing to allow him a degree of freedom that Gog was not. Under the surface of American materialism Merton sensed that a certain idealism still lived, and at times he seemed to hope that this underlying idealism could still be appealed to as a humanizing force. Yet Merton was as critical of Americanism as the free world's ideological alternative to communism, as he was of communism itself. The Christianity of Magog, he claimed, was willing to fight the atheistic communism of Gog, but not the money changers of Magog. In the end Magog would tolerate only a useful Christ. Both communism and Americanism, Merton argued, had betrayed their original ideals and locked themselves in a cold war which threatened to destroy the world. Communism had long ago abandoned its ideals and imitated the hated Nazi, and America, Merton feared, was on the verge of doing the same. In order to win its struggle with Gog, Merton was afraid that America would set aside the last vestiges of humanity and values and become a fascist state, complete with concentration camps, and prepared to liquidate "inferior peoples" and to engage Gog in a final cataclysmic war. In the end, it seemed likely that Gog and Magog would destroy each other, leaving the earth to the peoples of the Southern Hemisphere, if perchance they survived.[37]

At this point it is important to see that a vital element in Merton's criticism of American society was the problem of race. Merton feared the results of Western racism almost as much as nuclear war and saw the two issues as intimately interrelated as the two major manifestations of the dynamic of violence which underlay American society. Among American Catholic pacifists, Merton was the most systematic writer on the race question and its interrelation with the issue of war, and it is here that his pessimism regarding the future prospects of American society was most apparent.

Merton pointed to the fact that, while American defense policies are founded on the claim to defend human rights and freedom, our domestic treatment of black people contradicted any real commitment to those realities. To some extent Merton paralleled the views of the early Marx in saying that in American society people had value only in so far as they could be seen as objects in the market place. He argued that we had become alienated from our true selves because we believed not in ourselves but only in money. Merton contended that the civil rights movement became a real issue only when it began to threaten economic interests, and that even the material advances made by some blacks did not eliminate the underlying status of the black man in American culture as less than human.[38]

Merton clearly saw the "Negro problem" to be in reality a white problem rooted in the hearts of white people. In "Ishi: A Meditation," Merton reflected on the genocide practiced against the American Indian. He indicated that, while many view genocide as a new problem since World War II, it is in fact not new at all, but is an intimate part of the history of America and the West. Genocide is the ultimate conclusion of declaring certain groups of people to be sub-human. Likewise, slavery and the present status of black people in American society are also the products of the cultural denial of our common humanity. Merton concluded that the inner realization of this is the reason why white people cannot really listen to black people. If they did, they might have to admit that their property and wealth are ill-gotten gains. To act seriously on such a realization could mean the dislocation of the entire American economic and political system.[39]

Merton saw a parallel between the war in Vietnam and earlier American wars of extermination against the Indians. Both reflected the violent power of the myth of the diabolical enemy against whom any destructive act could be justified. Merton saw in Vietnam another sign that the United States had become a warfare state, a nation controlled by fear and economic interests. He warned that we should not be surprised if our involvement in Vietnam led to a harvest of violence in our own cities. Merton was convinced that the urban racial violence that erupted in the late sixties was directly related to the escalation in Vietnam, and reflected black people's acceptance of America's enshrinement of violence.[40]

Merton's most scathing criticism was reserved for white liberals, who hypocritically missed the whole point of the black movement in America. He did not hesitate to term the black struggle for full equality a revolution because Merton knew that to give the black man full acceptance in American society would require a radical revision of that society. Merton saw white liberals, however, as really committed to preserving their material privileges, while giving support to the civil rights movement in the illusion that American society could grant justice to black people without jeopardizing the conduct of business as usual. Merton charged that blacks saw through the white liberal, and knew that he would betray them when his own white liberal position was threatened.[41]

Furthermore, Merton argued, liberalism suffered under the illusion that blacks wanted only assimilation into white society and to become like whites. He contended that to seek integration of others into a supposedly "superior" white culture was a travesty of truth. Contradicting the early CAIP position, Merton did not view the Latin American pattern of race relations as a model, for it still reflected the dominance of white European culture. Merton argued that social salvation could only come when both blacks and whites saw each other and each other's culture and character as correlative and necessary to each other. White atonement must involve a willingness to completely reform the social-economic system in partnership with black people, whose providential time had come.[42]

Merton's final thoughts on the racial problem in 1968 reflected a profound pessimism that a solution would be achieved. He felt 1962 and 1963 had been moments of truth for America which passed without being seized. The failure of whites to respond to the deeper challenges of the civil rights struggle and the escalation of the Vietnam conflict had caused the black movement to turn from its commitment to non-violence, which Merton feared would lead to a non-redemptive and nihilistic assault on the existing order. He feared democracy had become discredited and all efforts for reform would only be seen as further attempts at control. Merton saw the American black revolution as part of a worldwide rejection of colonial Western civilization and the compromised white Christianity which blessed it. This world movement was messianic and eschatological in its dimensions and intentions, and Merton feared that the refusal of American and European whites to see it as the spawn of their own violence only insured that movement's violent and cataclysmic consummation. Though he feared that the black movement in America was falling victim to the same racist delusion that ensnared whites, and was becoming an orgy of hopeless frustration, Merton's sympathy was still clearly with the struggle of black people. In the end his pessimism reflected his sense of apocalyptic judgment that was befalling

America because of its pathology of violence. The hope he continued to express was not the hope of political solutions, but the eschatological hope of the Christian, who witnesses to truth in the midst of darkness and the apparent triumph of evil.[43]

In his analysis of the dehumanization process of modern civilization, which reflects itself in racism and war, Merton designated the insidious effect of this destruction to be the elimination of the sense of personal responsibility. Technological society creates a social climate of moral passivity in which moral obligations have become meaningless. Therefore, he concluded, "There is no control over the arbitrary and belligerent self-determination of the great nations ruled over by managerial power elites concerned chiefly with their own self-interests."[44] Consequently, Merton argued, it was imperative to restore a climate of rationality to domestic and international affairs and to establish a sense of our ability to control the forces determining our social, political, and economic lives.

In this Merton was in complete agreement with Zahn's stress on affirming the competency and responsibility of the individual conscience. The sense of cultural despair which welled up in the face of the challenges of racism and war were attributed by Merton to the myth that these issues were too great for the average person to grasp. The result was a fatalistic submission to economic and social forces and an unquestioning belief in machines and processes which characterizes the mass mind. In the face of this fatalism Merton continued to assert that history is ours to make.[45]

This sense of moral paralysis and blindness which modern society imposes on its citizens was also at the heart of Merton's attack on the tradition of just war teaching among Catholics. As stated earlier, Merton was not an ideological pacifist and did not reject the just war theory as such. The problem, Merton argued, was not so much the just war principles themselves but the state of mind with which most contemporary thinkers applied them. Merton contended that most debates on modern warfare were conducted on such an abstracted plane of principles that they never really dealt with the concrete condition of modern war.[46]

Thus, in attacking the position of nuclear realists like Her-

man Kahn or William O'Brien, Merton argued that it is easy
to appeal to norms of justice and law to arrive at logical conclusions about the possibility of just and limited nuclear wars.
The very plausibility of these conclusions, however, is most
dangerous if we forget that, while they may be based on premises which we take as axiomatic, those premises have, in fact,
been invalidated by modern weapons technology. Merton acknowledged the distinctions and qualifications made by realist
thinkers who used the just war theory to provide a rationale
for nuclear deterrence and even limited use. He charged, however, that their qualifications were irrelevant to the fact that
they were being used to justify the military policies of Washington which recognized no real limitation. The military mind,
Merton noted, does not employ the distinctions of the just war
theorist. While there was no official American policy to wage
"total war," Merton argued that the actual effects of the strategies we do have amount to precisely that. Talk of counterforce
strategy seemed especially ominous to Merton because of its
movement closer to a first strike use of nuclear weapons. In
the end, the sheer destructiveness of modern weapons and the
present inability of the political situation to control their use
invalidates, in Merton's view, the premise of the nuclear realists that a just and limited use of nuclear weapons was possible.[47]

Merton was particularly frightened by the new generation
of realist experts represented by Herman Kahn, because he felt
they corrupted everyone's thoughts by making the unthinkable
thinkable. In a reflection on Adolf Eichmann, Merton stated
that, contrary to the fear of many that a madman will get
control of "the bomb," the real danger lies not in any alleged
madmen but in "sane" men like Eichmann, who can rationalize
the most horrendous evil and carry it out in obedience to their
orders. The rationality of the realists, in Merton's judgment,
produced the moral climate that made phenomena like Eichmann, Auschwitz, and Hiroshima possible. He concluded that
in a world where another Hitler or Stalin is likely to appear,
the existence of nuclear weapons along with the moral paralysis of leaders and the passivity of the masses constitutes the
gravest problem in the whole history of mankind.[48]

While not as identified with the debates over *Gaudium et*

Spes as other figures such as James Douglass and Gordon Zahn, Thomas Merton urged and welcomed the Vatican Council's condemnation of total war. Prior to the Council, Merton had already argued that a specific condemnation by the Church of nuclear war was not necessary to see that the teaching of Pius XII and John XXIII against total war already eliminated the possibility of nuclear war. Merton also cited the work of Cardinal Alfredo Ottaviani and Father Franziskus Strattmann, O.P., as examples of non-pacifists whose application of traditional Church teaching led them to conclude that war can no longer be a moral means of solving international conflict. While rejecting inadequate solutions such as unilateral disarmament, Merton concluded that there was no alternative to seeking other means of defense.[49]

In this, Merton was completely in accord with Gordon Zahn in stressing that beyond a purely negative condemnation of war, Christianity had a more positive avenue for addressing society in the development of non-violent alternatives to armed force in the defense of justice. Merton probably was also most responsible for getting non-violence a wider hearing among American Catholics, who, like most of their countrymen, viewed pacifism as a weak and aberrant philosophy. Much of Merton's writing on the subject stressed the difference between an individualistic pacifism which did not resist evil, and the pacifism of resistance which Merton endorsed. He considered Gandhi as the best twentieth-century example of employing non-violence for political action and social transformation. With Gandhi, Merton agreed than it was better to resist evil with violence than not to resist it at all.[50]

Merton insisted that his non-violence was ideological, not merely tactical. He felt it was the only form of social-political action which fulfilled the ideals of democracy and Christianity in being able to insist on one's rights while still respecting the humanity of others. Merton was keenly sensitive to the mental climate of fear which pervaded modern society and believed that only non-violent tactics of protest on the Gandhian model could avoid further polarization and dehumanization. For Merton, what distinguished the non-violent resister from the mere revolutionary was precisely his willingness to suffer and accept punishment at the hands of the unjust. The non-violent resister placed his hopes not on success but on witnessing to the truth and the power of the truth to transform the human heart.[51]

Writing near the end of his life in 1968, Merton felt that the loss of faith in non-violence among many within the peace movement as well as the civil rights movement did not bode well for the possibilities of meaningful social and cultural change in the United States.[52] Yet his pessimism on American society continued to be balanced by his faith in the eschatological fulfillment of Christian hope and witness. Beneath growing clouds of apocalyptic gloom he concluded, "We seem to be assisting in the unwrapping of the mysteriously vivid symbols of the last book of the New Testament. In their nakedness they reveal to us our own selves as the men whose lot it is to live in a time of ultimate decision."[53] For Merton, non-violent Christian witness remained the only source of light revealing the true nature of that ultimate decision, and the only voice expressing the faith that even at the brink of Armageddon humanity still had the power to choose to turn back.

James Douglass and the Cross of Non-violence

While he did not write as much as Zahn or Merton, James Douglass's *The Non-Violent Cross*, published in 1966, was regarded as one of the most systematic and influential expositions of a theology of non-violence produced during the sixties and seventies. Together with the thought of Merton and Zahn, Douglass's theological treatment of non-violence provides the basic parameters of the analytical perspective of radical Catholic pacifism during this period.

Douglass characterized the present historical situation of the human race as one in which the pursuit of security has produced eschatological weapons capable of providing only the ultimate insecurity. "To see reality in our time," he stated, "is to see the world as crucifixion." The event which revealed the essence of this era of crucifixion was the atomic bombing of Hiroshima. For this event inaugurated a new era in the history of humanity which revealed the emergence of a global scale of violent power equivalent to the human moral capacity for self-destruction.[54]

In Douglass's vision the apocalyptic power of modern weapons forms one arm of the global cross marking the fate of modern society. The second arm of this cross is formed by the major consequence of the arms race, which is what Douglass called the sustenance gap. That is the poverty and lack of human development caused by the usurpation of resources by military priorities. He concluded, "The growing mass of hunger alongside the growing affluence of military states emphasizes the impotence of destructive power to effect any truly human change in the world and the guilt of those who choose impotence."[55]

The primary theological question which the precarious state of humanity raises is the question of power itself. Referring to humanity's present capacity for global destruction Douglass concludes:

The possession of such power renders man impotent because he cannot survive its use, yet remains committed to it in principle through a mythology of power relations. The only genuine power which eschatological weapons have for man is the power to provoke in him a complete re-examination of the nature of power itself.... Man has developed what he thought was power to the point where its emergent reality as self-destruction has rendered him impotent, and where only a repudiation of the illusion of power and a committed search for its true existence elsewhere can deliver him from himself.[56]

Thus, to understand the destructive reality of a world shaped by the cult of power is, for Douglass, to commit oneself to resistance and revolution for the transformation of the world.

Yet any revolution which employs violence would destroy the very essence of the revolution which the world needs. Douglass attributed the failure of the Russian revolution and most mass movements precisely to their subordination of life to ideological conceptions of life, and the consequent rationalization of life-destroying violence as a means of imposing their ideology. All of the dominant world ideologies were judged by Douglass as equally murderous, so that neither East nor West was able to deliver humanity from its global agony.[57]

The revolution which Douglass deemed necessary is a non-violent one, which seeks to transform politics by the transformation of political man. A non-violent revolution was one in which the spiritual and the political revolution were understood to be the same thing. In this, Douglass was reflecting the same theme as Merton and Zahn in looking to the Gandhian notion of Satyagraha as the only human way to transform people and their society by the suffering witness to the truth.[58]

For Douglass such a non-violent revolution is of particular relevance to both the condition of post-Christian secular society and the struggle of the world's oppressed peoples against power of unprecedented genocidal capabilities. Accepting the image of the secular city, as popularized by the Protestant theologian Harvey Cox to designate post-Christian society, Douglass maintained that the chief idiom through which the divine presence can be communicated in the secular city is the political rather than the metaphysical. Yet he criticized those who sought to provide a naive theological celebration of the secular city as an era of new maturity for the human race. Rather, Douglass argued, it was necessary to address modern people where they most meet God in the secular city, in suffering and injustice.[59]

The problem with the secular city, as Douglass described it, was not so much its secularity as its technology. It was technology which provided the secular city with its sustaining power and which created the peril of our times. If secularity has given humanity a spiritual sense of absolute autonomy, technology has given it the power to press this autonomy into experiments with inconceivable effects on human life and psyche. In speaking of technology in this way Douglass relied on the work of the French theologian Jacques Ellul, who described the role of technology in modern society as involving more than the use of machines. It is a state of mind that creates a single, all-embracing civilization marked by the domination of people by machines, of standardization over spontaneity, and means over ends. Technological civilization is essentially a civilization of means without any true or human ends.[60]

Douglass argued that the fatal weakness of the technological mentality of the secular city is that, while it pretends to be pragmatic, it is just the opposite. It doubles back on man with a plurality of systems of technique whose cumulative effect is totalitarian. When measured against humanity and its aspirations for justice and peace, the overwhelming power of technology has coincided with moral impotence. The perfect example of this for Douglass were nuclear realists like Herman Kahn. The tragedy of one like Kahn, in Douglass's view, was that he succumbed to the illusion that the problems of war and peace are subject to technical solutions. The technical rationality of realists like Kahn can only divert us from the search for true power and into a further and ultimate destruction.[61]

In the midst of this moral and psychic collapse of the secular city, Douglass saw the only hope for human change to lie in the nonviolent revolution embodied in Gandhi. He considered Gandhi's experiments in truth to be the most effective events of our age, in staking out a genuine hope for the correction of injustice through the power of the truth. The insight behind Gandhi's revolution was the realization that means are end-creating. The means of revolution must correspond to the end of truth which the revolution seeks. As the means of technology have ensnared modern humanity in the embrace of power which it cannot control or direct to human ends, so only the means of a revolution of non-violent suffering love and witness to truth can open to modern humanity the possibility of a new personal and social existence.[62]

Douglass also saw a nonviolent revolution as most pertinent to the struggle of the so-called Third World against Western imperialism. He felt that the struggle of the Viet Cong against American strength in Southeast Asia refuted the logic of modern war, which was to change the enemy's mind by making him suffer. That logic did not work on the Vietnamese, nor did Douglass see it working on any likely enemy of the United States. He argued that the power of the Vietnamese to continue struggling came precisely from their poverty and suffering, which destroyed the logic of corrupt power which Douglass saw motivating the American intervention.

Yet Douglass saw the resistance of the Viet Cong to be compromised by their use of violence. He argued that when the oppressed wage war with the weapons of the oppressor they compromise the truth which their suffering witnesses to, and only justify the oppressor's resort to greater and more efficient power, which can threaten genocide. Douglass believed that the violent revolution of the Viet Cong had effectively submerged the more promising non-violent Buddhist movement in Vietnam, and caused the Vietnamese struggle for justice to become swallowed up in the rhetoric and categories of the East-West conflict.[63] Douglass argued that the nonviolent campaign of Gandhi's disciple Venoba Bhave for land reform and a similar effort for reform by Danilo Dolci in Sicily were far better examples of a struggle for true justice than the Vietnamese civil war. The contrast between modern Marxists and Christians and men like Venoba Bhave and Danilo Dolci demonstrated for Douglass that both Marxist and Christian messianism had lost faith in the ability to change people through the power of truth. Both modern Christians and Marxists were blind to the fact that Gandhi's greatest act of liberation was not of India but of the British.[64]

In his criticism of the failure of the Church to witness to the truth of the modern world's dilemma, Douglass paralleled Zahn's critique of milieu Catholicism. He saw present American Catholicism to be an "incarnational heresy" which dogmatically preserved the truth of Jesus Christ in its teaching, but compromised it in practice by accommodating itself to the expectations of society. As a prime example of this compromise Douglass focused on the tradition of just war teaching, which he evaluated in light of his interpretation of the thrust of modern papal and conciliar teaching. Most radical Catholic pacifists interpreted modern Church teaching on war in light of its pacifist implications or applicability, but Douglass went the farthest in claiming a pacifist intention behind this teaching.[65]

Along with Gandhi, Douglass saw John XXIII as the great symbol of the revolution needed in humanity's perception of itself, and in *Pacem in Terris* he found one of the most realistic perceptions of the reality of power and social change in the modern world. Douglass argued that the Johannine vision, as expressed in this encyclical, viewed non-violence as a natural law imperative and the only means of settling disputes that was in accord with the dignity of the human person. Thus, while the Pope did not explicitly repudiate Pius XII's teaching on the just war, Douglass saw in *Pacem in Terris* a definite pacifist view of the present evolutionary stage of human development. This pacifist intention he also claimed lay behind the teaching of Vatican II.[66]

Douglass was one of several American Catholic pacifists who went to Rome during the Council debates on *Gaudium et Spes* to lobby for a condemnation of modern war and nuclear weapons. Referring to his personal contact with bishops involved in the construction of the document, Douglass argued that in condemning the use of indiscriminate weapons to wage total war the Council Fathers' condemnation also was meant to include the threat to wage such total war. The reason why the Council did not explicitly condemn the possession of nuclear weapons for deterrence purposes was, according to Douglass, their hesitancy to judge the actual intentions of statesmen, which they felt a condemnation of deterrence as such would imply. Douglass argued that the clear interpretation of the document accepted beforehand by the Council was that the intent to wage war unjustly is itself unjust. He concluded that with this understanding the Council teaching would have to be seen as condemnatory of the actual policies of deterrence, which Douglass argued contained at least a conditional intention to carry out the threat to use what the Council had clearly condemned as indiscriminate weapons. Douglass concluded that those who used the conciliar text to justify present deterrence policies violated the first rule of exegesis that a document must be interpreted in light of the intentions of the author. The problem, however, was, as Douglass conceded, that the background of the document was never made clear to most people.[67]

In this interpretation Douglass stands almost alone, since it is based mainly on his personal contacts with bishops at the Council. Also, his principle of exegesis is not above challenge, for the actual rule for interpreting the normative content of conciliar statements is that they must be judged as saying what they actually say. The ideological agenda or the intentions of the Council Fathers who got the statement passed cannot be seen as part of the official content of the text unless explicitly expressed within it. Thus, the conciliar text stands as it has

been read even by most pacifists as stopping short of a condemnation of possessing nuclear weapons for deterrence
purposes.

Yet apart from this question of interpretation Douglass insisted that the real question was not the abstract distinction
between the mere possession of nuclear weapons and the intent
to use them, but rather the actual preparations for total war
going on among the world's major powers. He felt that the
Council's clear condemnation of total war and the arms race
provided a substantial basis on which to stand against the
actual military policies and preparations of these nations.[68]

Furthermore, Douglass argued that the desire of the Council
to treat the issue of war with an entirely new attitude and in
the context of humanity's evolving unity and the threat of
global destruction required a rejection of the traditional use of
the just war theory. Douglass pointed to Paul Ramsey as the
chief exemplar of the contemporary usage of the just war theory. He noted that in 1960 Ramsey called for the maintenance
of the United States nuclear deterrent within the range of lower
scale kiloton weapons, even though by 1960 multimegaton
weapons had already become the norm. In 1963, however, Ramsey had moved to accept the use of multi-megaton weapons and
thus became "relevant" to the sixties. Douglass argued that
this was an example of what had been the historical legacy of
just war thinking, which was forced to accommodate itself to
the military necessity of ever greater degrees of destruction.
The only escape from this logic of accommodation, he contended, was to reject the theology of just war, and to replace
it with a theology of just resistance. In so doing war would be
rejected as no longer a form of resistance to evil that is recon-
cilable with justice.[69]

The rejection of the just war and the demand for non-violent
resistance obviously has serious consequences for the Christian's relation to the state as the wielder of the sword of temporal power. Douglass, while taking the same attitude toward
the state as Zahn, provided a more developed theological rationale for the Christian's resistance to the state.

Because Jesus was crucified as a Zealot rebel against Rome,
Douglass asserted, the problem of church and state is at the

heart of the New Testament. He argued that the person and
teaching of Jesus constituted a revolution against Caesar's authority which made insignificant the violent revolt of the Zealots. The Zealots were crushed by the sword they took up and
brought on the final elimination of the Jewish state, but Christianity conquered Rome after three centuries of non-violent,
suffering resistance.[70]

Douglass maintained that in the person of Christ can be seen
that the proper Christian attitude toward the state is one of
indifference. Essentially it is a matter of indifference to the
Christian *qua* Christian whether the regime he lives under is
capitalist or communist. The Christian does not object to living
within a state as such, but rather opposes the totalitarian claims
of the state, without seeking its violent overthrow.[71]

The state in Douglass's theology remains a basically negative
force. His interpretation of Romans 13 is that the Christian is
called to submit to the governing authority even though by
wielding the sword the state does what the Christian could
never do. The state can be seen as God's servant only in the
sense that even sin is subject to the lordship of Christ and can
be used by Him as an instrument of judgment. The essence of
the state as a power, in Douglass's interpretation, is constantly
to seek to assert its independence of God and absolutize itself.
The ultimate fulfillment of the state's ambition is found in the
image of the Beast in the Book of the Apocalypse. Here cosmic
powers converge in a totalitarian state for the final and complete idolatrous rebellion against God. Thus, the struggle of
the Church with the state is a constant repetition of the drama
of the cross, in which, without taking up the sword of the state,
Christ rejected its claim to authority.[72]

Thus, the Christian responsibility for the world cannot be
translated into assuming responsibility for the state and me-
diating Christian responsibility through the force exercised by
the state. To reject responsibility for the state is also to reject
the natural law ethic by which the Church historically sought
to accomplish the translation of the Gospel vision into an ethic
for a Christian social order, and of which the just war theory
was the classic expression. Thus Douglass rejected the whole
attempt to formulate a natural law social philosophy based on

Christian truth, as embodied by John Courtney Murray. Instead, he argued with scripture scholar John McKenzie that the Church can only speak to society from an explicitly evangelical basis of faith.[73]

Douglass agreed completely with Zahn and Merton that the false dichotomy of the traditional models of church-state relations must be rejected. The choice is not between controlling the social order or withdrawing from it. He likewise rejected the ethical dichotomy of Max Weber, which was adopted by Reinhold Neibuhr and other Christian realists. This ethical typology distinguishes between an ethic of responsibility, which is concerned with the forseeable political results of any action, and an ethic of ultimate ends, which is concerned with strictly upholding principles regardless of the social or political consequences. Douglass saw Gandhi as having refuted the validity of this dichotomy, in having shown the ethic of ultimate ends to be the only responsible political ethic. He argued that Gandhi transcended Weber's categories in his establishment of a politics of protest rather than a politics of rule, to wage a struggle within the state, but against its power.[74]

Theoretically Douglass allowed the possibility of a new type of state which, through a revolution of values and structure, would make a non-violent politics of rule possible. He did not, however, clarify what this would concretely mean, nor did he address how this could be possible in light of his contention that the state was inherently a force at odds with God and the Christian way of life. Instead he focused on the need to break the nationalistic nexus of politics and work to establish a global institution such as the United Nations which could eliminate war. Here again, however, he did not address how a new international structure would escape the problems which he attributed to the state power on the national level.[75]

In the end the Christian seems to remain in an unresolvable struggle with the state. The Christian must confront the state with a non-violent witness to a quality of human relationships which does not admit to the coercive force that is the foundation of the state, and a witness to the sovereignty of God which negates the state's claim to totalitarian self-sufficiency. While the state is thus challenged to transform itself, in Douglass's vision, it cannot accept the witness of the Church without ceasing to exist. The search for resolution to the tension within Douglass's theological vision would seem only to lead one to the eschatological plane, where a resolution is found only in God's decisive resolution of history itself, in the vanquishing of the Beast which is the ultimate totalitarian state.

SUMMARY

In the similarity and differences presented here of the thought of Gordon Zahn, Thomas Merton, and James Douglass can be found the parameters of the social vision which guided radical American Catholic pacifism from 1960 to 1980. There are several clear themes which they continue from the earlier Catholic Worker heritage. First, they reject the conventional definition of the East-West conflict and view both capitalist and communist systems as reflecting the same dehumanization of modern technological society. Secondly, they reject as inadequate, or as a fundamental compromise of Christian faith, the tradition of just war teaching. All, however, argue that in the terms of that very tradition no modern war could be justified. Thirdly, all insist on the primary necessity of reestablishing the sense of the responsibility and competency of the individual conscience. Fourthly, they all seek to redefine the Christian's relationship to the state in a way that transcends the either-or dichotomy of sectarian withdrawal or the establishment of a Christian state. At the heart of this effort to redefine the relation of the Christian community to the state was the effort to articulate in the context of American society a pacifism of resistance— that is, a pacifism that went beyond individualistic non-participation in war to an active, non-violent, communally based resistance to injustice, and which offered an alternative means to armed force for national self-defense. Before further comment on this endeavor of Catholic pacifists, it is necessary to examine the most radical expression to which the Catholic antiwar movement gave rise.

NOTES

1. Charles DeBenedetti, "The Peace Opposition in Cold War America, 1955–1965." Paper prepared for the 1981 annual meeting of the

Organization of American Historians and later submitted to the Historians' Project of the World Without War Council, Seattle, Washington, 1981, p. 10,

2. Neil Katz, "Citizens Efforts for Peace: The Contribution and Influence of Post World War II American Radical Pacifists," a paper presented at the symposium on "Citizen Peace Efforts Since 1980," World without War Council, New York City, December 10, 1980, p. 11; Nat Hentoff, "By Common Dissent," *Commonweal* 75 (January 19, 1962): 433–435.

3. Patricia F. McNeal, *American Catholic Peace Movement* (New York: Arno Press, 1968) pp. 183–187.

4. Ibid., pp. 191–193; James H. Forest, "No Longer Alone: The Catholic Peace Movement," in Thomas E. Quigley, ed., *American Catholics and Vietnam* (Grand Rapids, Michigan: William B. Eerdmans Publishing Co., 1968), pp. 145–146.

5. Gordon Zahn, *German Catholics and Hitler's Wars: A Study in Social Control* (New York: Sheed and Ward, 1962). James Finn, *Protest: Pacifism and Politics* (New York: Random House, 1967), p. 59. Zahn stated here his debt to the sociologist C. Wright Mills, who argued that it was the task of the sociologist to make value judgments. He also stated that he would accept the term "absolute religious pacifist" as descriptive of himself (p.62).

6. Gordon Zahn, "Social Science and the Theology of War," in William J. Nagle, *Morality of Modern Warfare: The State of the Question* (Baltimore: Helicon Press, 1960), pp. 104–125. Much of the same article was also presented in "The Case for Christian Dissent," in Thoma Merton, ed., *Breakthrough to Peace* (Norfolk, Conn.: New Directions, 1962), pp. 117–138.

7. Gordon Zahn, "The Church as a Source of Dissent," *Continuum* 1 (Summer 1963): 156.

8. Gordon Zahn, *In Solitary Witness: The Life and Death of Franz Jägerstätter* (New York: Holt, Rhinehart and Winston, 1965).

9. Gordon Zahn, "The Private Conscience and Legitimate Authority," *Commonweal* 76 (March 10, 1962): 9–13.

10. Zahn, "The Church as a Source of Dissent," p. 163.

11. Ibid., p. 164.

12. Finn, *Protest*, p. 67.

13. Gordon Zahn, "The Problems of a Practical Pacifist in a Nation at War," *National Catholic Reporter*, June 26, 1966, p. 7.

14. Gordon Zahn, *War, Conscience and Dissent* (New York: Hawthorne Books, Inc., 1967), pp. 79–80.

15. Ibid., p. 57. Zahn also used the just war theory to urge the

bishops to oppose what he called the government's discrimination in not recognizing selective conscientious objection for draft deferments, since such selective objection was a part of the Catholic just war teaching (Forword by Gordon Zahn in Thomas E. Quigley, ed., *American Catholics and Vietnam* (Grand Rapids, Michigan: William B. Eerdmans Publishing Co., 1968), p. 15.

16. Zahn, *War, Conscience and Dissent*, pp. 66, 71, 82.

17. Ibid., p. 67; idem, "The Scandal of Silence," *Commonweal* 5 (October 22, 1971): 79–85. Zahn here criticized the teaching of the American bishops for being locked in tentative generalities.

18. Zahn, *War, Conscience and Dissent*, pp. 57, 14–15.

19. Ibid., pp. 68, 70–71.

20. Gordon Zahn, *An Alternative to War* (New York: The Council on Religion and International Affairs, 1963), pp. 28–32. Zahn stressed that a deterrent, to be real, must involve an actual intent to use it. He argued that the experience of the Cuban missile crisis showed that the United States' deterrent is based on a real intent to use. Moreover, he could not conceive of any actual war remaining limited.

21. Gordon Zahn, "American Catholics and the Attack on North Vietnam," *Continuum* 3 (Spring 1965): 118–120.

22. Zahn, *War, Conscience and Dissent*, p. 27.

23. Gordon Zahn, "The Threat of Militarization," *Continuum* 7 (Autumn 1969): 438–442. Here Zahn rejected the Troeltschian church vs. sect models of ecclesial organization as too constricted for understanding the dynamics of church-state relations.

24. Zahn, *Alternative to War*, p. 9.

25. Ibid.

26. McNeal, *American Catholic Peace Movement*, pp. 183–191.

27. Zahn, *Alternative to War*, p. 13.

28. Ibid., pp. 14–16, 21.

29. Ibid., pp. 26–27.

30. Gordon Zahn, "The Peacemaker," *Continuum* 7 (Summer 1969): 265–273. A good biography of Merton can be found in Monica Furlong, *Merton: A Biography* (San Francisco: Harper and Row, Publishers, 1980); see also James Thomas Baker, "The Social Catalyst," *Continuum* 7 (Summer 1969): 255–264.

31. Thomas Merton, "Peace and Protest," in *Thomas Merton on Peace*, edited and with an introduction by Gordon Zahn (New York: McCall Publishing Co., 1971), pp. 67–68; Gordon Zahn, "Original Child Monk," in *Merton on Peace*, pp. ix, xxvii-xxix.

32. Thomas Merton, *Seeds of Destruction* (New York: Farrar, Straus, Giroux, 1964), pp. 184–199. The following account of Merton's view of the diaspora situation of Christians is taken from this book.

33. Thomas Merton, *Faith and Violence: Christian Teaching and Christian Practice* (Notre Dame: University of Notre Dame Press, 1968), p. 48. Merton stated that the culture of Christendom in which the tradition of church-state relations was developed no longer exists.

34. Merton, *Seeds of Destruction*, p. 97.

35. Ibid., pp. 97–98; Merton, "Peace: A Religious Responsibility," in *Breakthrough to Peace*, p. 91.

36. James Thomas Baker, *Thomas Merton: Social Critic* (Lexington, Kentucky: The University of Kentucky Press, 1971), p. 74; Merton, *Faith and Violence*, pp. 3–4.

37. Baker, *Thomas Merton*, pp. 72–76; Thomas Merton, "Spirituality for the Age of Overkill," *Continuum* 1 (Spring 1963): 11; Merton, *Faith and Violence*, pp. 51, 175.

38. Thomas Merton, "The Black Revolution," *Ramparts* 2 (Christmas 1963): 5–8. This article is also reproduced as "Letters to a White Liberal", in *Seeds of Destruction*, pp. 3–71.

39. Merton, "Ishi: A Meditation," in *Merton on Peace*, pp. 248–253; Merton, "Letters to a White Liberal," pp. 16–48.

40. Merton, *Faith and Violence*, p. 166; "Vietnam: An Overwhelming Atrocity," in *Merton on Peace*, pp. 186–191.

41. Merton, "The Black Revolution," pp. 11–12.

42. Ibid., pp. 19–22.

43. Merton, *Faith and Violence*, pp. 167–175.

44. Merton, *Breakthrough to Peace*, p. 91.

45. Merton, *Breakthrough to Peace*, pp. 10–12. Merton used the example of Alfred Delp, S.J., as a paradigm of the type of spirituality and witness that was required of the Christian in the diaspora of the nuclear age. Delp was a German priest who was executed for anti-Nazi activities; Merton used his example in the same manner as Gordon Zahn used that of Franz Jägerstätter (Merton, "Spirituality for the Age of Overkill," pp. 9–21).

46. Ibid., pp. 12–13. In criticizing the just war tradition as it originated in St. Augustine, Merton stated that Augustine's theory had two major weaknesses: 1) Its stress on subjective purity of intention which can be doctored and manipulated with apparent sincerity; 2) its tendency to pessimism about human nature and the world, which is now used as a justification for recourse to violence (*Seeds of Destruction*. pp. 150–151).

47. Ibid., pp. 12–13; Merton, "Christianity and Defense in the Nuclear Age," in *Merton on Peace*, pp. 88–93. Merton stated here that he believed war would be inevitable within a decade under present policies and attitudes; also "Peace and Religious Responsibility," in

Merton on Peace, pp. 107–128. As an example of the gross illusion of the technical conceptions of nuclear realists, Merton noted that by their standards a "tactical" nuclear weapon could include the twenty-kiloton bomb dropped on Hiroshima. He claimed that it was absurd to think that a smaller force being beaten would not resort to larger nuclear weapons. Therefore, all talk of limited war was absurd.

48. Thomas Merton, "A Devout Meditation in Memory of Adolf Eichmann," in *Merton on Peace*, pp. 160–162; "Peace: A Religious Responsibility," p. 111.

49. Thomas Merton, "Christian Ethics and War," in *Merton on Peace*, pp. 83–87; "Christianity and Defense in the Nuclear Age," pp. 90–91.

50. McNeal, *American Catholic Peace Movement*, pp. 138–140; Merton, "A Tribute to Gandhi," in *Merton on Peace*, pp. 178–184.

51. Merton, *Faith and Violence*, pp. 31–36.

52. Ibid., pp. 42–46.

53. Merton, "Peace and Religious Responsibility," in *Merton on Peace*, p. 111.

54. James W. Douglass, *The Non-Violent Cross: A Theology of Revolution and Peace* (New York: The Macmillan Co., 1968), pp. 3–5. This book was Douglass' major expression of his theology of non-violence and serves as the main source of this presentation.

55. Ibid., pp. 6–7.

56. Ibid., p. 6.

57. Ibid., pp. 9–11.

58. Ibid., p. 22.

59. Ibid., p. 331; Cox's book was *The Secular City* (New York: Macmillan, 1965).

60. Ibid., p. 28; Jacques Ellul, *The Technological Society* (New York: Vintage Books, 1964).

61. Ibid., p. 41.

62. Ibid., pp. 21, 41–42; idem, "Catholicism, Power and Vietnamese Suffering," in Quigley, *American Catholics and Vietnam*, pp. 99–108.

63. Douglass, *Non-Violent Cross*, pp. 13–14; idem, *Resistance and Contemplation* (Garden City, New York: Doubleday and Co., 1972), pp. 31–33.

64. Douglass, *Non-Violent Cross*, pp. 17, 20–23.

65. Ibid., pp. 49–50, 81–82; idem, "A Non-Violent Christology," *Commonweal* 87 (November 24, 1967): 259–264.

66. Ibid., pp. 23, 86.

67. Ibid., pp. 102–122.

68. Ibid., pp. 112, 120–123.

69. Ibid., pp. 157–176.; idem, "Peace and the Overkill Strategists,"

Cross Currents 14 (Winter 1964): 87–103; idem, "War and Peace Beyond Niebuhr and Murray," *Cross Currents* 17 (Winter 1967): 107–114.

70. Douglass, *Non-Violent Cross*, pp. 182–183.
71. Ibid., pp. 188–192.
72. Ibid., pp. 194–196.
73. Ibid., pp. 205–207.
74. Ibid., pp. 202–204, 262–266.
75. Ibid., p. 270.

5

The Catholic
Resistance Movement

In chapter 2 it was seen that the realist attempt to support the
United States in its struggle with the communist world and to
provide a moral and practical possibility of self-defense produced tension within this school of thought over the limits of
violence that could be accepted within a just war framework.
In the case of radical Catholic pacifism a similar tension developed over the limits of non-violence and the mode of seeking
radical change in American society. The radical Catholic desire
to link the rejection of war with active non-violent resistance
to injustice, and a growing sense of the systemic nature of
injustice in American society, would lead some into more extreme experiments to explore the meaning of a non-violent
revolution. These efforts would issue forth what became known
as the "Catholic Left" or the Catholic resistance movment.
   The chief architects of this movement were two brothers,
Daniel Berrigan, S.J., and Philip Berrigan, S.S.J., who on May
7, 1968 led seven associates into the Catonsville, Maryland,
draft board, took Selective Service files outside, and burned
them with homemade napalm. The group became known as
the "Catonsville Nine." Philip Berrigan had earlier led the
"Baltimore Four" in a similar action, in which he and three
companions poured blood on draft files in the Baltimore Cus-
toms House. The term "Catholic Left" or Catholic resistance
movement was the label applied to the activities of the Berrigan
brothers and a growing following of peace activists who engaged in similar acts of disruptive civil disobedience, from the

Catonsville action in 1968 to the trial of the "Harrisburg Seven" in 1972. In this trial Philip Berrigan and six others were charged with conspiracy to kidnap Henry Kissinger and destroy heating tunnels for government buildings in Washington, D.C. In the sixties the draft had become the chief target for concretizing anti-war sentiment. Members of the Catholic Worker had already been committed to helping people resist the draft when in October, 1965, Catholic Worker David Miller became the first man to publicly burn his draft card after such actions had been made illegal. This act marked the high point of Catholic Worker protest against the draft. By 1968 a deep sense of frustration had grown within the American peace movement over failure to stop the Vietnam war, and within Catholic anti-war groups over failure to even get a condemnation of the war from the institutional Church.[1]

The "Catonsville Nine" action marked a new phase in the anti-war movement and a dramatic shift in Catholic efforts to resist the war and commit themselves to non-violent revolution for American society and the Church. The major analytical judgments behind this movement and the questions which its development raised, for those within it as well as for other Catholic pacifists, are vital to understanding the radical Catholic perspective on war during these years.

The chief ideological force behind the movement were the Berrigans. Both came by different routes to the decision to inaugurate a new phase in non-violent resistance. Daniel was influenced by exposure to the worker priest movement in France and by work among the poor in America. Philip, as a Josephite, worked among American blacks and was deeply affected by the civil rights movement and the black struggle for justice.[2]

The decision for the Catonsville action reflected a complete disillusionment with American and Western society, and a deep sense of the systemic character of injustice in America as well as a negative view of American influence in the world. The movement which the Catonsville action inaugurated most forcefully applied the traditional Catholic pacifist critique of modern technological society to the United States, as the chief embodiment of that civilization in the world today. With the

Catholic resistance movement, the Catholic pacifist critique of power becomes most specifically the critique and rejection of American power. The sense of this judgment is strongly set forth in the beginning of Philip Berrigan's book, A *Punishment for Peace*:

Western society, under the guise of evolving and ennobling benefactor, stands today as the enemy of man. It has effectively suspended freedom, making man both victim and operating cog.... Western society has become both idol and dictator, hope and inflexible director of life.... America's power can neither accept its blacks, nor succor its poor, nor assure its peace, nor answer the starvation of millions abroad.... America's power is, finally, a threat that keeps the world unnerved and aghast, that has in large measure defined the course of the cold war and nuclear brinksmanship, and that may in all probability bring mankind to the final idiocy of World War III.[3]

In analyzing American society Berrigan acknowledged his debt to Herbert Marcuse and Carl Oglesby, whose analysis he reflects.[4] Berrigan saw the American national establishment as inherently resistant to significant change in its value system, rationale, and operation. Because any genuinely humanistic change would be at odds with its vested interests, the social power structure could only give lip service to anti-poverty programs, co-opt human rights movements, and oppose the establishment of peace.[5]

Following Marcuse, Berrigan viewed modern technological society as perfecting the scientific control of man, not so much by overt repression as by the creation and manipulation of appetites and needs. Society requires the formation of the individual into conformity to the needs of the technocracy and therefore cannot allow the development of critical reason among its citizens, thus creating what Marcuse called one-dimensional man. It was the effectiveness of this scientific control that led Berrigan to conclude that Merton's fear of America becoming a fascist state was in process of fulfillment.[6]

Berrigan argued that the real functional value system of America was identical with and expressed in its national policies and purposes. Beneath the propaganda about protecting freedom, that real value system of America was revealed to be its economy. It is the capitalist system, Berrigan contended, that has always been the motive force of American history, and has given to that history an expansionist and racist theme.[7]

In this assessment Berrigan obviously was in absolute opposition to the liberal Americanist criticism of United States foreign and military policies. He argued that the problem was not that America was betraying its ideals, but that it was in fact living out what were always its values. Because of its support of free enterprise, he contended, America had always followed the road to empire and economic world colonization. Berrigan charged that it was not possible for the United States to have gained control of one-half of the world's wealth without great injustice. The essential drive of American history as interpreted by Philip Berrigan was well summarized by Carl Ogelsby, whose account of American history Berrigan closely adheres to:

There is nothing more common in our economic mentality, nothing more constant in our foreign policy, than this conviction that the basic problem of the American business system is domestically undistributed wealth, and that the basic solution to that problem . . . lies in our penetration of foreign markets—most especially, the markets of those lands we now think of as underdeveloped. . . .

For us, peace finally exists when the world is finally safe for American businessmen to carry on their business, on terms as favorable as they can be made, in settings managed preferably by native middle-class governments, but if need be, by oligarchic and repressive ones, by the old foreign grads of Fort Bragg, or if the panic hits in a pivotal place, by our own Marines.[8]

It was this desire for global control and management that in Berrigan's estimate produced the wars in which the United States has been involved, and was presently the basis of the Cold War. It was also this vision of America's role in the world that led James Douglass (who in 1972 became active in the resistance movement) to conclude: "In most parts of the world today, most obviously in Vietnam but no less murderously in Latin America, the liberator's blood is being shed in resistance to the United States of America, and specifically in resistance to its policy of forcibly managing the economies of other states and peoples." Berrigan himself concluded that under American influence the hope of being human is almost destroyed.[9] The racist dimension of American imperialism in subjugating the non-white peoples of the world was understood by Berrigan to be a reflection of the racism in the American soul. Berrigan and the resistance movement linked the issues of race and war more clearly and forcefully than most Catholic radical pacifists, with the exception of Thomas Merton. Merton credited Philip Berrigan with offering one of the best analyses of the race problem in print. Berrigan had himself publicly joined the race and war issue a year before Martin Luther King had done so.[10]

Berrigan argued that the commercial culture which established the American colonies combined its commercial mentality with a fundamentalist Calvinistic form of Christianity to create a racial mythology for the justification of slavery, which was essential to its economy. The present racial conceptions of Western society are the product of four hundred years of creating and maintaining a myth of race to both hold the black man in slavery and keep him unassimilable after emancipation.[11]

This history, Berrigan contended, could not be shrugged off as only belonging to the past. It was the formative reality of America's racist dilemma and remains at the heart of the Western world's problem of relating to the so-called Third World. Berrigan argued that domestic segregation was a crucial element in creating the moral climate where a massive reliance on nuclear weapons may flourish. The two were related because they both concretize our cultural refusal to accept others as fully human. In this context Berrigan saw the black struggle as raising the issue of democracy more than anything else in American history. It drew into question the historical reality of the nation's dream of equality and showed that there was still the possibility of revolution in America.[12]

Berrigan directed a polemic against American liberals that was more trenchant than that of Thomas Merton. He complained that liberals always asked what is right about America, not what is wrong, and always insisted on seeing the evil in

the context of a larger mitigating package of good. Consequently, they could not see the institutionalized racism in
American society or the technological-economic imperative behind involvements like Vietnam. Liberals failed to contribute
to meaningful social change, Berrigan argued, because they
refused to admit the radical level of change that would be
necessary for America to be able to accept and benefit from
those who historically have been its victims.[13]

For this reason Berrigan came to reject the civil rights movement as a liberal attempt to buy off black people with laws
that would not fundamentally change their status in society.
Similarly, he rejected the "war on poverty" as a farce, claiming
that black poverty was a reflection of black people's status in
the white mind. Daniel Berrigan also wrote on his experience
working with poverty programs which he felt were not really
designed to change anything. These programs, he argued, were
finally undercut by the Vietnam War, and the contradiction of
pretending to help the poor at home while bombing them abroad.
Philip Berrigan strongly agreed with Merton that the focus of
attempts to deal with the race problem should not be on urban
problems or programs to equip blacks to fit into white civilization, but on the hearts of whites where the problem of race
was rooted.[14]

Because of the rise of the Black Power movement and their
own analysis which so closely linked the race and war issues,
Philip Berrigan and other members of the resistance movement, who had previously worked in the area of the racial
struggle, shifted their focus to the issue of war. Together with
this shift, and after years of working with those in power, Philip
Berrigan concluded that working within the system only compromised integrity and justice. To focus on the issue of war was
to join a criticism of domestic and foreign policy into a revolution against all that America really was. As Daniel Berrigan
explained the meaning of the decision to do the Catonsville
action,

one misses the point entirely if he sees the Catonsville act as merely
a protest against this or that aspect of American life.... Our act was
aimed ... at every major presupposition underlying American life

today.... We were denying that any major structure of American life was responding seriously on behalf of the needs of young people, of black people, of poor people, of working people, of church people, of passionate people—as such men scrutinized their institutions, rightly expecting decent performances of them.[15]

The non-violent revolution that was needed was, according to Philip Berrigan, not possible without Christians. The problem, however, was that the Church was as much a part of technological society as any other institution. Berrigan charged that religion had become the servant of society, functioning as an ethical management system and providing the moral sanction which the system needed. Thus, the revolution called for was as much for the Church as against society.[16]

Berrigan contended that rather than seeking to transform society the Church had only fought to protect a Catholic precinct within it. He recognized the fear of communism, which had been a dominant motivation in the Church's identification with the Western political structure, but argued that the real problem was our own failure to address the needs and suffering of the world. Our secularism had created a vacuum where communistic materialism could counter our own. In the end, the Church must accept as its own the judgment that must be passed on American and Western civilization.[17]

The Berrigans became quite critical of attempts at renewal in the Church following the Second Vatican Council. They argued that much of the concern with liturgy and internal ecclesial reform was as much a liberal "cop-out" as civil rights and poverty programs, for it ignored the Church's primary challenge to address the deeper crisis of society. Philip Berrigan contended that the lethargy and confusion in the Church was a direct result of its having decided to function as an institution within capitalist society. As long as it continued to do so, it could not possibly be a Christian community. He concluded that no reform within the Church would be meaningful unless Catholics understood that the Church cannot survive without embracing the issues of human survival which vexed the world today.[18]

The same disillusionment that led the Berrigans outside the

political system also reflected itself in their attitude toward the institutional Church. They saw as good the disaffection from the institutional Church of those who were seeking to involve themselves in social issues. The Berrigans hoped that this would give rise to new Christian communities small and poor by choice, with a revolutionary passion for justice and a desire to identify with the victims of human greed. They envisioned the Church of the first three centuries as composed of such Christian communities, and felt that expecting the present institutional Church to move in this direction was as hopeless as expecting the United States government to genuinely work for peace and justice.[19]

In moving to a new level of non-violent confrontation, the resistance movement also gave rise to the first sign of serious tension within the Catholic peace movement, and for the first time Catholic peace activists found themselves attacked from within the Left.[20] Dorothy Day, Thomas Merton, and Gordon Zahn were very sympathetic but fearful over the implications of this new step in disruptive civil disobedience. Day felt that the destruction of property was not in accord with non-violence, and remembered that fascists had caused such disruption at peace movement meetings.[21]

Merton was perhaps the most disturbed because of his stated concern that protest be communicative and not increase the fear and polarization of society. Merton questioned whether this new form of protest was making social headway toward a new attitude toward war, or was it just an outlet for the irrational frustration of those who saw no hope for change? He feared that these actions bordered on violence and reflected a desire for quick results and using the media for making a dramatic impact, rather than being concerned with the true effects of that impact. Ironically, he lamented, it was the same desire for quick results which led Americans to accept the war as reasonable. Merton argued that an act of protest should by its nature give a clear and reasonable account of itself, and help sincere minds accept an alternative to war without surrendering the genuine interests of our own national community. The destruction of draft records, he felt, was an ambiguous act which seemed to seek only to shock and horrify and thus dispensed from the need for serious thought.[22]

Another difficulty arose when the continuing series of draft board actions changed their style in no longer being "stand-by" actions, in which the participants would openly commit civil disobedience and await arrest on the scene. Instead, draft boards were surreptitiously invaded and the participants would publicly "surface" at another time and place to claim responsibility. The secrecy involved in this further dismayed Dorothy Day and others in the Catholic Worker, who felt this to be a deviation from the necessary openness of the non-violent tradition. In April of 1970 Philip and Daniel Berrigan carried this tactic a step further by refusing to surrender to begin their prison terms, and choosing instead to "go underground." James Douglass argued that this was not a rejection of the traditional willingness of the non-violent tradition of accepting punishment. Rather, it was postponing the punishment by continuing the protest in a refusal to co-operate with the legal process. He argued that the very public way in which Daniel Berrigan conducted his underground stay showed that he did not entertain a serious intention of permanently fleeing. Gordon Zahn also came to accept the legitimacy of this tactic and said he felt Merton would have also, had he lived.[23]

Despite criticism, the Catholic resistance movement continued to see its methods as the best means to mount a non-violent resistance to the war-making process and to offer an alternative to violence within the American anti-war movement. Its actions reflected the dual motivation of seeking to maintain a sense of personal integrity and authenticity, and of expressing a deep revulsion for liberal reformism. Philip Berrigan stated that the only reason he was alive today was that his conscience did not allow self-immolation such as practiced by the Buddhist movement in Vietnam. Yet in the face of the witness of young draft resisters and the dying of the Vietnamese, he had to do something of comparable personal risk to put "his own life on the line" in solidarity with them. Daniel Berrigan similarly described his participation in the Catonsville action as relieving him of a deep burden of guilt.[24]

Criticism of the Catholic resistance by the wider peace movement was countered with the Catholic resistance's critique of
the peace movement. Philip Berrigan quit his association with
organizations such as the Catholic Peace Fellowship, which he
helped found, and Clergy and Laity Concerned. He viewed these
organizations as caught in the trap of liberalism, trying to
orchestrate a movement but unwilling to take the risk of disrupting the system. Daniel Berrigan charged that in one sense
there never really was a real peace movement, because those
in it felt the war could be opposed while carrying on business
as usual. He argued that they were unwilling to pay the price
of genuine resistance. The Berrigans, therefore, claimed that
there was no alternative but to dissociate themselves from a
compromised movement which played into the ability of technological society to contain dissent.[25]

Daniel Berrigan insisted that a major difference between the
Catholic resistance and the rest of the peace movement was
the rejection by the Catholic resistance of the obsession with
results. He termed this obsession diabolical and a product of
modern society that only breeds violence. Berrigan argued that
the Catholic resistance movement witnessed to the need to
change ourselves if we want society to change. In this spirit
he wrote a message in 1970 to the underground Weathermen
organization calling them away from the use of violence. He
argued then that the revolution must avoid the plague it seeks
to heal.[26]

While many who initially formed the resistance movement
came from or were influenced by the Catholic Worker, the resistance movement differed from the Catholic Worker in focusing on the issue of peace apart from the Houses of Hospitality,
which Dorothy Day considered the distinguishing characteristic of the Catholic Worker. Yet the resistance movement
clearly continued the Catholic Worker's traditional emphasis
on the primacy of personal witness and the concomitant refusal
to fit into the institutional structure of American society, even
as an agency of dissent. In a very real sense Maurin's vision
of a counter-cultural movement to "create the new in the shell
of the old" was very much alive in the Catholic resistance
movement, only now the "seed of the new" had become the

"action communities of risk." The emphasis of these new communities would not be on servicing the victims of the system
but on disrupting the system itself.

A final feature of the Catholic resistance movement which
must be noted is the degree to which it maintained or valued
its specifically Catholic identity, and the success it had in maintaining a political analysis which allowed it to continue as a
coherent movement. In the Catonsville action all the participants were Catholic and consciously spoke as such to their
Church and society. All were committed philosophically to a
non-violent revolution.

The action of the "D.C. 9" in March, 1969, marked the beginning of a noticeable change in ideology among elements
attracted to the resistance movement. The action itself showed
a broadening of tactics by including corporation offices as targets. Beyond that, however, a more leftist-militant ideology
was evident among some members of the group, for whom non-
violence was a political tactic and not a philosophical or religious commitment. In the "Chicago 15" action in May of the
same year eleven out of the fifteen were Catholic. The statement they issued was secular enough in its tone to cause seven
of the Catholic members to issue a separate statement stressing
the religious convictions motivating their actions.[27]

With these actions it became clear that while the media may
have given the impression of the movement as more ideologically coherent, it was increasingly not so. Furthermore, while
labeled the Catholic resistance movement, it was increasingly
clear that religious motivation or explicit Christian faith was
not a condition of adherence. The focal point of the action communities became the action itself, and the degree of political
analysis required for participation was to be opposed to the war
and willing to "act."

This inability of the Catholic resistance movement to maintain a clear Catholic identity is perhaps clear evidence of the
very *American* character of the movement and its desire to be
part of a wider movement for revolution in America. As previously stated, Philip Berrigan's initial involvement in the formation of the Catholic Peace Fellowship was part of a deliberate
effort to move away from the Catholic Worker's tradition of

avoiding organizational links with other non-Catholic groups precisely to preserve its Catholic identity. The purpose of the CPF was to integrate Catholic peace activities with wider non-Catholic movements and organizations like the Fellowship of Reconciliation. Similarly, the previous involvement of Berrigan and many other members of the Catholic resistance movement in inner city work and the civil rights movement had given them the experience of breaking down interfaith boundaries in forming a wider movement for social transformation. As Catholic resisters developed a more radical critique of Western society and included the Church as fully a part of the corruption of that society's institutions, many could translate that radical critique into an ideological rejection of the institutional Church. Even for many who did not outrightly reject the institutional Church, the Church could no longer serve as an organizational or ideological focus for supporting or developing the movement for radical change to which they had become committed. These radical Catholics would consequently find their support and inspiration, not from the Church, but from their association with other Americans and people in other countries who were committed to the same struggle for liberation and social change. Thus it was inevitable that the Catholic resistance movement's focus would shift, so that as it became more a part of a wider American effort at revolution, its emphasis would be less on "Catholic" and more on "resistance."

The movement's shift away from its specifically Catholic identity was in marked contrast to Dorothy Day's insistence, despite her strong criticism of the institutional Church, that the Catholic Worker remain loyal to the Church and retain its Catholic identity. In a *Commonweal* article in 1973 Gordon Zahn expressed concern over the future of the Catholic peace movement. One of his main concerns was the failure of the movement to maintain a clear Catholic identity. Zahn still held the hope of awakening Catholics to the pacifist implications of their faith, and stressed the importance of the Church as an international institution, whose influence is vital to world peace. To move the Church toward being the force for peace that it could be, Zahn insisted, it was vital to remain loyal to it. Yet

Zahn's concern seemed already left behind by many within the resistance movement.[28]

Another criticism which Zahn raised in the same article was the tendency of the Catholic peace movement to lack a clear focus. He felt that people had become so obsessed with the systemic nature of war that they were becoming involved with too many issues on too many levels and losing any clear focus on the war issue. He feared that without this focus the movement would dissipate after Vietnam, and not be able to continue to expose the political policies and economic practices which produced Vietnam. The Catholic resistance movement seemed to prove the validity of Zahn's concern in that by 1973 it had mainly dissipated.

This dissipation was obviously aided by the anarchistic nature of the movement, which it shared with its Catholic Worker predecessor. More importantly, however, having the "communal base" of the movement focused on a disruptive act of civil disobedience provided a far more limited and ephemeral grounding for a movement than the Catholic Worker enjoyed in its Houses of Hospitality. Increasingly, the action communities became a temporary tactical marriage for those seeking to "do an action," and provided no means to integrate the diverse ideological outlooks gathered together in the movement to oppose the war. With the exhaustion of this form of protest and the conclusion of the "Harrisburg Seven" trial, the Catholic resistance movement faded away as an identifiable movement.[29]

SUMMARY

The development of radical Catholic pacifism and resistance after 1960 continued the Catholic Worker tradition of adhering to a definition of the conflict determining the international order which was quite at odds with that adhered to by Catholic Americanists of either the realist or nuclear pacifist persuasion. For these more radical Catholics the conflict between the Western and communist powers was not the fundamental conflict with which the Christian was to be concerned, for both power blocs were seen as competing giants spawned by the same anti-hu-

man technological culture. In this context the obligation of the
Christian was not to the defense of Western democracy, but
rather to the defense of humanity against a technocratic civilization that was rapidly subjecting human life and freedom
to its own needs for control.

Perhaps one of the most significant features of this developing perspective was the much more pointedly anti-American
theme which emerged during these years, and which was most
forcefully expressed in the Catholic resistance movement. Particularly with the experience of the Vietnam War, which dominated these years, the traditional Catholic pacifist critique of
modern culture became a critique of American society and power
as the dominant expression of that commercial civilization which
had replaced the Catholic medieval world.

In a paper prepared for the World Without War Council, Ted
Galen Carpenter stated that in the late sixties a neo-isolation-
ist sentiment arose among many opponents to the Vietnam
War which was significantly different from traditional American isolationism. Historically American isolationist sentiment
was based on a belief in the moral superiority of American
society, and the need to keep America from being "contami-
nated" through foreign entanglements. In contrast, the neo-
isolationist sentiment of the Vietnam years called for American
withdrawal from foreign involvements not to protect America,
but to protect the world. American influence, as seen in Vietnam
and Latin America, was deemed immoral, negative, and socially destructive.[30]

Among American Catholics, the resistance movement and
many radical pacifists most clearly reflected this view of the
United States. While not minimizing the anti-human nature
of the communist system, Catholic resisters charged the United
States with the greatest blame and saw it as the greatest power
bent on economic, technological, and military control of the
world. They focused their criticism on the fact that most of the
liberation struggles in the world for national and cultural self-
determination were being fought against American influence
and power.

Together with this critique of American foreign policies was
the clear and strong linkage made by radical Catholic pacifists

and resisters between the issues of race and war. In the linkage of these two issues was most clearly exhibited the manner in which radical Catholics understood the issue of war to be the issue of culture. Both the threat of war and the domestic racial problem were seen as dual reflections of a culture built on the denial of the common humanity of all people. Thus, in focusing on the issue of war, they clearly understood themselves as focusing on the most world-threatening manifestation of a culture whose dehumanization went beyond the problems of war itself. The style of their opposition to war also reflected their belief that the problem of war would remain insoluble without a revolutionary transformation of American society and culture.

As previously stated, Gordon Zahn, while aware of the relatedness of other issues to the issue of war, was critical of the tendency of many radical Catholics to lose their focus on war and become immersed in other issues. He feared this could lead to the collapse of a Catholic anti-war movement. Yet this problem was itself a reflection of the deep sense which Catholic radicals had of the systemic nature of injustice in American society, and the difficulty which they had in maintaining a focus on the issue of war which adequately expressed their wider revolutionary objectives.

The development of Catholic pacifism and resistance after 1960 clearly continued to focus on the traditional Catholic Worker emphasis on personal witness and developing the sense of the competency and responsibility of the individual conscience. It also continued the inner tensions of this personalism and the anti-institutionalism which was always a part of it. In their critique of the American New Left of the sixties Peter Clecak and Christopher Lasch maintained:

From the beginning, the New Left defined political issues as personal issues. How does one achieve personal integrity—"authenticity"—in a mechanized, bureaucratized, dehumanized society? Because the New Left has acted out of an ideal of personal heroism rather than from analysis of the sources of tension in American society and the possibilities for change, it vacillates between existential despair and absurdly inflated estimates of its own potential.[31]

In contrast to the above description, the religious anchoring of many radical Catholic pacifists and resisters made a significant difference in their attitude toward failure (lack of immediate results), and therefore would have helped to undercut the psychic fluctuations Clecak and Lasch observed in the New Left. Nevertheless, the radical Catholic pacifist approach shared that characteristic of the American New Left to reduce political issues to personal ones of authenticity, even though their understanding of the content of that personal authenticity would differ. In this they continued to experience the difficulty of linking their personalist emphasis with a theory of society and social change that would allow them to go beyond mere personal protest to become a lasting movement for social change.

A crucial problem in this regard was providing a communal context to support individuals in the heroic witness to which Catholic radicals called them, and to provide continuity and development for a movement. As a sociologist Zahn recognized the importance of this supportive counter-cultural milieu but was not sure how it could be provided. Merton was even more pessimistic. The Catholic resistance movement found that the action communities became temporary tactical joinings and did not produce locally rooted communities with very much staying power. In the end personal witness remained the chief focus of activity without being able to consummate itself in the communal structure for which many felt the need.

A significant dimension of this dilemma was the anarchism which continued to be a dominant factor in radical Catholic personalism and the style of pacifist resistance being developed during these years. After 1960 radical Catholics increasingly stressed the need for pacifism to take the form of revolutionary resistance seeking to transform society rather than to withdraw from it. Yet many continued to hold to the traditional anarchism of the Catholic Worker which rejected the state and any exercise of force to maintain society. If anything, this anarchism received a more sophisticated theological justification during these years.

The result, however, of combining a non-violent revolutionary program to transform society with an ideological inability to actually take over that society by assuming responsibility

for its institutional functioning was to create a tension that
could only be resolved eschatologically. As Christians, Catholic
pacifists were correct in recognizing that their ideals could only
be fully realized with the consummation of history itself. As
anarchists, however, they demanded of the state a transformation which by their own definitions it could not give. Some,
such as Douglass and Zahn, admitted the possibility of a new
kind of state and non-violent politics of rule, but they never
concretized what that would mean. Similarly, the allowance
which they made for an ultimate move to international organizations to eliminate war was not complemented with a consideration of how such an international structure would avoid
the problems inherent in the state as such. Thus, radical Catholic pacifism continued within itself an unresolved and heightened tension between its own form of apocalyptic immanentism
and a desire for political relevance.

The same tension was evident in the radical Catholic conception of the role of the Church in society. The Church they
sought to create would embody the pacifism of resistance with
which they sought to confront modern society. Yet the anti-
institutionalism which marked their relationship to the state
also marked, for many, their relationship to the Church. Gordon Zahn was keenly aware of the role of the institutional
Church and felt the need to remain loyal to it and seek to
transform it. Others, especially many in the Catholic resistance
movement, felt the need to focus on new communities of faith
and risk outside the institutional Church which they saw as
hopelessly ensnared by the system they rejected. As the development of the resistance movement showed, such an attitude toward the institutional Church also raised the question
of the ability to maintain a movement that was consciously
Catholic or even Christian in its identification. Thus the anti-
institutionalism which caused problems for maintaining a
movement with a clear political focus also caused the same
difficulties in maintaining a clear religious focus.

It is interesting to note here as well a shift that occurred in
the radical Catholic vision of the historical ideal for Christian
society. The vision of Peter Maurin, which lay at the root of
the modern radical American Catholic movement, was rooted,

despite its anarchism, in the European right and looked to the medieval synthesis as its ideal. In the development of radical Catholic pacifism after 1960, that historical ideal was replaced with the ideal of the Church of the first three centuries before Constantine. None of the major expositors of radical Catholicism of this period refer to the value of the medieval synthesis, for the Church of this period was seen as part of the "post-Constantinian" Church, which was compromised by its acceptance of responsibility for the state. Only Merton stands out as somewhat mitigating this total condemnation of the post-Constantinian Church.

This shift in ideal to the pre-Constantinian Church may reflect the fact that Catholic pacifist thought in these years was rooted more in radical leftist thought than in the more traditional radical right-wing critique of modern society. With the exception of Dorothy Day, radical Catholic thought after 1960 offers no significant obeisance to the agrarian ideal of Maurin and the traditional conservative critique of modernity. The pre-Constantinian model of the Church more clearly served the pacifist and anarchistic sentiments which were much more militantly stressed in these years of opposition to the Vietnam War.

This pre-Constantinian model of the early Church could obviously be criticized as being a simplistic projection of a previous "golden age" of Christianity which never really existed as its proponents believed. Yet perhaps its adoption by radical Catholics is further evidence of the growing American character of the radical Catholic movement, which had its original inspiration in the European Catholic critique of modernity. Many adherents of the traditional American Protestant "peace churches" (Mennonites and others) had made this pre-Constantinian model of the early Church a part of their ideals and doctrine. As radical Catholics interacted with activists from these churches and sought to be a part of a wider American peace movement, the adoption of this model of the Church allowed for an interfaith link to form an American religious movement for social change and revolution. The pre-Constantinian model of the Church also, perhaps, lends itself better to the condition of an urban society in which radical Catholics, with no agrarian aspirations, sought to make their stand in the diaspora desert of the secular city.

NOTES

1. Patricia F. McNeal, *American Catholic Peace Movement* (New York: Arno Press, 1968), pp. 223–235.

2. Biographical background of the Berrigans can be found in Francine du Plessix Gray, *Divine Disobedience: Profiles in Catholic Radicalism* (New York: Vintage Books, 1970), pp. 45–94; also McNeal, *American Catholic Peace Movement*, pp. 246–264. While Daniel Berrigan was often presented as the chief spokesman for the Catholic resistance movement, Philip Berrigan was really its main ideological architect and instigator.

3. Philip Berrigan, *A Punishment for Peace* (Toronto: The Macmillan Company, 1969), pp. 2, 5.

4. The works Berrigan specifically mentioned were Herbert Marcuse, *One Dimensional Man: Studies in the Ideology of Advanced Industrial Society* (Boston: Beacon Press, 1964), and Carl Ogelsby and Richard Shaull, *Containment and Change* (New York: The Macmillan Company, 1967).

5. Berrigan, *Punishment for Peace*, pp. 3–4.

6. Ibid., pp. 6, 8.

7. Ibid., pp. 88–111.

8. Carl Ogelsby, *Containment and Change*, pp. 65–66, 70–71; Philip Berrigan, "Blood, War and Witness," in John O'Connor, ed., *American Catholic Exodus* (Washington, D.C.: Corpus Books, 1968), pp. 15–16.

9. James Douglass, *Resistance and Contemplation: The Way of Liberation* (Garden City, New York: Macmillan Co., Inc., 1972), p. 26; Philip Berrigan, *American Exodus*, p. 19.

10. Philip Berrigan, *No More Strangers*, with an introduction by Thomas Merton (Techny, Illinois: Divine Word Publications, 1965), p. xi; Gray, *Divine Disobedience*, p. 89.

11. Berrigan, *No More Strangers*, pp. 86–90; *Punishment for Peace*, p. 43.

12. Berrigan, *Punishment for Peace*, pp. 33–35, 41.

13. Ibid., pp. 6, 41–42.

14. Ibid., pp. 58–82; *No More Strangers*, pp. 112,117. Berrigan also felt the Catholic record of attempting to deal with the race problem in the Catholic Interracial Movement of John LaFarge, S.J., reflected the inadequacies of the liberal outlook which Berrigan rejected else-

where (*No More Strangers*, pp. 149–150). Daniel Berrigan, *No Bars to Manhood* (New York: Bantam Books, 1970), p. 13.
    15. Daniel Berrigan, *No Bars to Manhood*, p. 40; Philip Berrigan in *American Catholic Exodus*, p. 13; Charles A. Meconis, *With Clumsy Grace* (New York: The Seaburg Press, 1979), p. 10–11. Meconis quoted Joseph O'Rourke, a member of the "D.C. Nine":

> I really got serious about the war when I made the obvious connection that all of the domestic evils ... were really systematic problems.... One of the real reasons was a negative reason that many of us turned to the war. There really wasn't a place for us in the ghetto anymore ... so many of us were looking to face our own white racism and our connections with the power and the system that we had. The obvious issue to pick on at that point was the war.

Another perspective on the revolutionary critique of Catholic resisters is given in the account of Thomas and Marjorie Melville of their experiences as former Catholic missionaries in Latin America: *Whose Heaven, Whose Earth?* (New York: Alfred A. Knopf, 1971).
    16. Philip Berrigan, *Punishment for Peace*, p. 2.
    17. Philip Berrigan, *No More Strangers*, pp. 20, 31. Daniel Berrigan, *Absurd Convictions, Modest Hopes: Conversations After Prison with Lee Lockwood* (New York: Random House, 1972), pp. 201–202; Philip Berrigan, *Punishment for Peace*, p. 5.
    18. Philip Berrigan, *Punishment for Peace*, pp. 17–24, 165–166; *No More Strangers*, p. 156.
    19. Gray, *Divine Disobedience*, pp. 76–77. Daniel Berrigan saw the Church of the first three centuries as composed of communities such as this.
    20. Typical sentiments of sympathetic but critical Catholics on the left are found in "Reuther's Open Letter to Dan Berrigan," *National Catholic Reporter*, June 5, 1968, p. 4; "Taking Father Berrigan Seriously," *Commonweal* 92 (August 7, 1970): 379–380.
    21. Meconis, *With Clumsy Grace*, pp. 36–37; Thomas Cornell, "The Catholic Church and the Witness Against War," in Thomas A. Shannon, ed., *War or Peace? The Search for New Answers* (New York: Orbis Books, 1980), p. 210.
    22. Thomas Merton, *Faith and Violence: Christian Teaching and Christian Practice* (Notre Dame: Notre Dame University Press, 1968), pp. 42–43; "Note for Ave Maria," in Thomas Merton, *Merton on Peace*, ed. with an introduction by Gordon Zahn (New York: McCall Publishing Co., 1971), pp. 231–233. Merton also had a problem with the earlier burning of individual draft cards by Catholic Workers, but

changed his mind to accept it, Gordon Zahn, "Original Child Monk," in *Merton on Peace*, p. xxxv.

23. Cornell, "Catholic Church and the Witness Against War," in Shannon, *War or Peace?* pp. 210–211; Douglass, *Resistance and Contemplation*, p. 82; Meconis, *With Clumsy Grace*, pp. 146–148; Gordon Zahn, "Original Child Monk," in *Merton on Peace*, pp. xxxv-xxxvi.

24. Douglass, *Resistance and Contemplation*, p. 25; Gray, *Divine Disobedience*, p. 131.

25. Gray, *Divine Disobedience*, pp. 124–125; Daniel Berrigan, *Absurd Convictions*, pp. 200–201, 217–218. Berrigan rejected Fr. Robert Drinan's role as a member of Congress, saying that it was not the role of a minister to identify himself with public policy. A minister must play a prophetic role in society. Drinan's own views on war and peace can be found in *Vietnam and Armageddon* (New York: Sheed and Ward, 1970). In *Punishment for Peace*, p. 13, Philip Berrigan recounted an experience with a meeting of anti-war people in Philadelphia which included former government officials and liberal Democrats. He charged that they reacted to the war according to their own place in the power structure and not according to moral priorities. They therefore could not call for an immediate American withdrawal from Vietnam, but only for the election of a liberal Democrat and educational programs. Only those present who worked among the poor and blacks could appreciate Berrigan's point of view.

26. Daniel Berrigan, *Absurd Convictions*, pp. 34–35, 224–226, 74–76. Berrigan related the experience of David Miller, the first person arrested for burning his draft card. In prison he was driven by his experiences there to give up both his Catholicism and his pacifism. Berrigan saw this as a sign of a deep need for training and support to provide a deep philosophical rooting of belief in non-violence in the face of the violence of the system.

27. Meconis, *With Clumsy Grace*, pp. 40–49. This evaluation as well as other parts of this section on the Catholic resistance movement is also based on the author's own experience as part of the movement.

28. Gordon Zahn, "The Future of the Catholic Peace Movement," *Commonweal* 99 (December 28, 1973): 337–342.

29. Meconis, *With Clumsy Grace*, pp. 131–133. Meconis in interviewing members of the resistance identified four major ideological directions in which he found many of them moving by the middle of the seventies: 1) establishing local communities for the study and practice of non-violence; 2) Marxism; 3) community organizing on the Alinsky model; 4) feminist organizations.

30. Ted Galen Carpenter, "A Shade of Difference: American Iso-

lationism in the Post Vietnam Era," paper submitted to the *Historians' Project* of the World without War Council, January 16, 1981.

31. Peter Clecak, *Radical Paradoxes: Dilemmas of the American Left: 1945–1975* (New York: Harper and Row Publishers, 1966), p. 235.

6

Papal and Episcopal Teaching

In May, 1983, the American bishops issued a historic pastoral letter on war and peace entitled *The Challenge of Peace: God's Promise and Our Response*. At that time many American Catholics expressed a sense of surprise or bewilderment as to why the bishops were addressing this controversial political topic, and how they arrived at their stance toward nuclear weapons and deterrence. Much of the reaction to the pastoral letter reflected a lack of historical awareness among many American Catholics of the developments within modern Church teaching on the issues of war and peace. In fact the bishops' 1983 pastoral can only be properly understood if it is seen as the culmination of positions which had been developing within the hierarchy over the previous twenty years.

The decades of the sixties and seventies were a time of significant and unprecedented development in official Catholic teaching on the issues of war and peace. Papal and conciliar teaching in this period was both a stimulus and a support for American Catholics in considering anew the problem of war, and it formed a basic framework for their moral debates on the subject. Under the spur of this teaching and the domestic turmoil and internal Church division caused by the Vietnam War, the American bishops began a renewed effort to address the issues raised by American defense and foreign policies. Their attempts to address these issues in light of the principles set down by recent popes and the Second Vatican Council constitute an essential element for understanding the perspectives determining the American Catholic approach to war in these years. Historically the American bishops have cast the image of a nationalistic body, uncritical of the government's defense policies and unwilling to oppose the government in this area. Yet in their statements over the past twenty years the bishops have shown an unprecedented willingness to examine the issues of war and peace more critically in response to both the developments in papal teaching and the demands of their own constituents.

As the official stance of the American bishops, the statements dealt with here can, in a sense, be seen as reflecting the mainstream of development in American Catholic thought on war. It must be quickly added, however, that the bishops' positions did not necessarily always reflect the majority sentiment of American Catholics, whose nationalism did not always keep pace with the stated positions of their bishops. Episcopal statements of these years do not consist of a systematically thought out or articulated social analysis which could be placed into any of the particular schools of thought treated in previous chapters. Rather, episcopal teaching consisted of a more *ad hoc* approach to various issues of world peace and justice. Yet in their teaching the American bishops sought to address many of the concerns raised by the differing factions within the Catholic community, as well as to provide a middle ground to aid Catholics in forming their consciences on contemporary issues of war and peace. The development and internal tensions evident within episcopal teaching reflect both the complexity of the issues dealt with, and the difficulty of reconciling the conflicting perspectives which underlay the Catholic debate on war.

Yet episcopal teaching during these years exhibits a growing internal tension between the moral principles enunciated by the bishops and their critical implications for American foreign and defense policies. This tension would reach its most public and controversial point to date with the issuance of the 1983 pastoral on war and peace. This chapter will first present the papal and conciliar teaching which formed the framework of American episcopal declarations. The subsequent treatment of the bishops will focus on those major statements of the hierarchy which reflect the developing themes of episcopal teaching which form the background to *The Challenge of Peace.*

PAPAL AND CONCILIAR TEACHING

The immediate background for the most recent developments in Catholic teaching on war and modern society was the work of Pius XII. Pius was sufficiently horrified by the destructive dimensions of modern warfare to limit the just causes for resorting to war to that of a defense against overt armed aggression. Pius's concession of the right to defensive war, however, was predicated on the absence of an international authority with the power to adjudicate disputes and protect the rights of nations. In this sense, his granting the right of national self-defense was articulated in the context of a critique of the inadequacy of the present international order based on the unlimited sovereignty of nation states. This system Pius deemed anachronistic in the face of the increasingly global nature of the world's problems and the globally destructive potentialities of modern warfare. In Pius's vision, the need for a world authority to eliminate war went hand in hand with the need for a new world economic order to ensure the prosperity of all peoples and thus eliminate a major cause of war. Four years before the formation of the United Nations the pontiff warned against "narrow egotistical calculations tending to corner sources of economic supply and basic material to the exclusion of nations less favored by nature."[1]

It should be noted here that when Pius XII changed Catholic just war teaching to limit the *jus ad bellum* to a purely defensive war against aggression, the same trend was establishing itself in the development of international law. Article 51 of the United Nations charter limits the justifiable use of armed force (other than an enforcement action by the Security Council) to self-defense against an attack. This stipulation of the U.N. charter confirmed a trend begun under the League of Nations to curtail the rightful use of armed force. Thus, Pius was not acting in a vacuum when he moved Catholic teaching in this direction.

In applying the right of self-defense to the contemporary world situation, Pius stood as a classic expositor of the just war theory. His teaching on the use of modern ABC weapons (atomic-biological-chemical) measured their use by traditional just war standards. That is, their use was not proscribed as intrinsically evil, but their use must be so limited as to not fall under the ban on weapons whose effects go beyond the human ability to keep them within the bounds of proportionality and discrimination. Thus, the Reverend J. Bryan Hehir interprets Pius as not seeing in the use of nuclear weapons a situation qualitatively different from the use of other modern weapons. It is also true that Pius was speaking at the beginning of the nuclear era when the full effects of nuclear war had not permeated the public consciousness and the present nuclear arsenals had not been constructed.[2]

Pius XII also represented the tradition of just war thinking in making no provision for pacifism or conscientious objection. In 1956 he stated:

If therefore, a body representative of the people and the government—both having been chosen by free election in a moment of extreme danger decide, by legitimate instruments of internal and external policy, on defensive precautions, and carry out the plans which they consider necessary, they do not act immorally; so that a Catholic citizen cannot invoke his own conscience in order to refuse to serve and fulfill those duties the law imposes.[3]

While not granting the right of conscientious objection, however, Pius upheld the obligation of the individual to military service within the context of a democratic government acting in the purely defensive manner which he taught to be the only just recourse to war. Thus Pius XII stands as both a classic expositor of just war theory and an articulator of major themes to be developed by his successors: the unprecedented danger of modern war, the need to establish a world authority to eliminate the right and need to resort to war, and the reconstruction of the world economic order to ensure mutual prosperity and eliminate the major causes of war.

The teaching of John XXIII built upon that of Pius XII but

made a transition in thinking which launched the latest phase of development in Catholic teaching on war and peace. From John XXIII through the encyclicals of Paul VI there emerged six themes which have characterized universal Church teaching on these issues in the past twenty years. Together, these themes marked the parameters of an emerging vision in papal teaching which sought to challenge Catholics and all people of good will to a fundamental re-examination of their thinking on the most threatening problem of modern civilization. These themes also set the framework within which the American hierarchy would seek to fashion their own statements on the issues of war and peace.

The first theme, which was set forth most forcefully in the teaching of John XXIII, is the call to adopt a *global perspective* on issues of war and peace. In *Mater et Magistra* (1961) John argued that the consideration of questions of social justice in the present situation must be done in a global context, focusing on the development and distribution of the world's resources. The encyclical also represents a shift in tone and approach from the previous hostile or defensive attitudes of papal pronouncements on the modern world and industrial society. John welcomed the advances which the development of technology had brought, but focused on the disparity of wealth between rich and poor nations which industrialism and colonialism had wrought, and termed this the most pressing problem in the world. He also warned against the false economic development and assistance which only replaces the older political colonialism with the neocolonialism of economic control and dependency.[4]

John made his own the criticism of Pius XI (*Quadragesimo Anno*, 1931), who recognized the emergence within capitalism of a new form of managerial control of society, in which the concentration of economic power in an elite who manage the world's wealth had resulted in the substitution of economic power for the free marketplace, and even the replacement of the traditional profit motive by the unbridled ambition for domination. Consequently, even public authorities were serving the interests of these concentrations of wealth, which to some extent have achieved power over all people. For John this sit-

uation had grown worse since the time of Pius XI and required
the submission of economic interests to the necessities of the
common good of humanity.[5] John also noted the teaching of
Pius XII that the right of all to the goods of the earth necessary
to secure the common good were prior to the right of private
property so often used to justify the injustices of the capitalist
system.[6]

The socialization, or multiplication of associations, and the
consequent increase of interdependence that characterized
modern society also had the potential of creating a climate
destructive to the sense of personal moral responsibility and
initiative. John strongly stressed that modern social relations
were not the result of blind forces, but products of the human
will and must be subject to that will's determination to achieve
justice.[7]

In thus placing the Church's traditional teaching in a global
perspective, John called the world's peoples away from the ideological conflicts shaping international relations to look at the
objective requirements of their common good, and to create a
new world order to achieve this. This tone and perspective were
continued in *Pacem in Terris*, which many believe was issued
in response to the Cuban missile crisis, and has been credited
with launching a planetary Catholic peace movement.[8]

Pacem in Terris did not employ the just war method of approaching the issue, nor did it even directly apply just war
categories as such to evaluate specific weapons or policies. It
is also the only major papal document on war and peace not to
mention the right of self-defense of nations. Following the perspective of *Mater et Magistra*, the encyclical viewed the world
as evolving into an ever greater interdependency, which required a greater world unity to meet human needs. A tragic
part of this present development of the world is the technological capability for humanity's destruction. It was this historical
awareness of the potential destructiveness of modern war which
led John to conclude, "It is hardly possible to imagine that in
the atomic era war could be used as an instrument of justice."[9]

As previously demonstrated, this statement, as well as the
whole tenor and approach of *Pacem in Terris*, became the stimulus for much debate among the representatives of the conflict-

ing schools of American Catholic thought on war and peace. Even though *Pacem in Terris* did not explicitly repudiate the tradition of just war teaching, many pacifists like James Douglass interpreted the encyclical as giving a definite pacifist view of the present state of world development. This pacifist interpretation, however, does not seem at all warranted. In *Pacem in Terris* John presupposed the just war teaching of the Church and Pius XII's continued recognition of the right of self-defense. Rather, John sought to speak on a different level to the reality of war in the modern world, as something which that world could no longer afford to countenance. Bryan Hehir would seem correct in interpreting John XXIII as differing from Pius XII in making the substantive judgment that nuclear weapons present a qualitatively new reality. In the face of this reality, John's emphasis was not to seek to apply the just war doctrine, but to focus on the imperative need to abolish war.[10]

To achieve this end John insisted on the inescapable necessity of establishing a world federal government. He praised the United Nations' Declaration of Human Rights, and called for the mutual trust and initiatives necessary to make of that world body a real government. Much of the encyclical is given to a presentation of the divine order of human rights, obligations, and relationships which must be respected in order to achieve a just and peaceful society. John reaffirmed the traditional emphasis of Catholic social teaching that the dignity of the individual human person is the basis and goal of society. To achieve this end, world development must respect all peoples of the world and their cultures. All forms of racism and colonialism must be abolished.[11]

Such internationalist idealism was warmly applauded by American nuclear pacifists like Justus George Lawler, who interpreted the global perspective espoused by Pope John as essential to finding resolutions to the nuclear stalemate ensnaring international relations. Yet that very internationalist thrust of John's teaching caused significant concern for realist thinkers, both Catholic and Protestant. Perhaps the most thorough critique was developed by Paul Ramsey, who voiced the realists' contention that John's internationalist idealism did not address the problem of how to concretely move to establish

the world order he called for. Catholic realists such as John
Courtney Murray and William O'Brien cited the danger of what
they saw as the naive failure of the Pope to test his idealism
against the reality of the world's ideological divisions.[12] For
realists in general, *Pacem in Terris*, as the internationalist
tenor of most subsequent Church teaching, demonstrated little
comprehension of the difficulty of transposing into international legal and institutional arrangements the principles of a
just world order which they espoused.

Thus, John XXIII's encyclical placed at the heart of recent
Church social teaching the internationalist perspective which
was to serve as the crux of much of the American Catholic
debate on war and peace. Without rejecting the just war tradition, John sought to shift Catholic thought to a reconsideration of war with the "entirely new attitude" which the Second
Vatican Council would call for. In this perspective war is clearly
branded as no longer a rational instrument of justice, and the
issue of war is intimately linked with the task of establishing
an order of justice within and between nations. Essential to
such a task is the willingness to view the issues affecting the
world's peace, not from the perspective of national interests,
but from the perspective of the requirements of the common
good of the human race. Proponents of this internationalist
perspective would herald it as a creative and essential challenge to rethink the basic terms with which we have defined
national interest and international relations. Realist opponents would continue to raise the hard question of implementation. Yet the internationalist idealism articulated by John
XXIII would continue to be a significant element in official
Church teaching.

Three other elements characterizing recent universal Church
teaching on war and peace appeared in the teaching of Vatican
II. In its document *Gaudium et Spes* (G.S.) under the section
"The Fostering of Peace and the Promotion of a Community of
Nations," the Council set the moral context for the Catholic
debate on war for the following two decades. The Council's
teaching also reflects elements of ambiguity and conflict which
would characterize American Catholic efforts to grapple with
the dilemma of war during these years. The three themes of

the Council's teaching which are of concern here are: 1) the recognition of both pacifism and the just war tradition; 2) the condemnation of "total war"; and 3) ambiguity toward nuclear deterrence.

The Council made a significant step beyond previous papal teaching in both affirming the right of self-defense in the absence of a world authority, and also recognizing those who have dedicated themselves to non-violent means of defense, "provided that this can be done without injury to the rights and duties of others or of the community itself."[13] While not a ringing endorsement, it was the first official recognition in modern Church teaching of pacifism as a legitimate option for Catholics.

Similarly, while commending those in military service to be agents of peace and freedom, the Council also called for legal acceptance of conscientious objectors. This, together with the acceptance of pacifism, signalled a significant change in Catholic teaching on war, which was seen by many as traditionally allowing only for the just war theory. With this change the Council was now seen as endorsing a pluralism of conscientious positions which Catholics could take.[14]

Obviously, American Catholic pacifists would find this official recognition of conscientious objection encouraging. Yet, while recognizing conscientious objection as a valid option for individuals, the council did not treat pacifism as an option for governments. Neither did it lessen the status of the just war theory as the dominant method of morally evaluating questions of war and peace for the Catholic community. The council's own approach to these issues was that of the just war methodology. Yet with the escalation of the Vietnam war, Catholic conscientious objectors could find in the council's recognition support for their position in the face of local draft boards, who often denied that Catholics could take such a stance within their own moral tradition.

The Council's recognition of conscientious objection, however, was one of endorsing a general principle. The Council made no attempt to address how the legal recognition of conscientious objection should be implemented. In particular, the Council did not address the question of selective conscientious objection to particular wars deemed to be unjust. The Council's action, however, would serve as a spur for the American bishops to later take up the question of total and selective conscientious objection to participation in war.

In addressing the question of the use of force in war the Council reaffirmed the condemnation of "total war" which was a traditional part of Church teaching and which had been strongly asserted by Pius XII and John XXIII. It also specifically spoke to the use of modern scientific weapons in stating that "any act of war aimed indiscriminately at the destruction of entire cities or of extensive areas along with their populations is a crime against God and man himself.... The unique hazard of modern warfare consists in this: it provides those who possess modern scientific weapons with a kind of occasion for perpetrating just such abominations."[15] This clearly constituted a rejection of nuclear "counter-city" warfare, as well as conventional "obliteration bombing" as practiced in World War II.

Yet the Council made no attempt to directly address the fact that the nuclear arsenals of the major powers were constructed around weapons designed for such attacks upon cities or large population areas. Neither did the Council address the question of "tactical" nuclear weapons. That is, can there be a moral use of some nuclear weapons which would be within the limits of discrimination and proportionality? If so, what would those limits be? Thus, the Council's statement was both strong and ambiguous enough to fuel the debate among American Catholics. Pacifists like James Douglass could interpret the condemnation of total war as effectively outlawing almost all actual uses of nuclear weapons, and expressing what he saw as the "pacifist intent" of the Council. Yet realists like William O'Brien could argue that the Council did not rule out all uses of nuclear weapons. In fact, realists would contend that such condemnations without an attempt to address the just war possibilities of a legitimate nuclear defense was a failure on the part of Church leadership. Beneath such conflicting interpretations of the meaning of the Council's statement were also differing judgments as to whether or not nuclear weapons were inherently indiscriminate. This question the Council did not address. Thus, in light of the differing perspectives discussed in the previous chapters it is possible to see how the Council's statements could be criticized as inadequate by both pacifists and realists, and yet also used by both as ammunition to defend their differing positions. This character of Vatican II's statements on war and peace is even more apparent in the matter of nuclear deterrence.

On the issue of nuclear deterrence the Council reflected an ambiguity which has marked official Church statements since then. The Council recognized that the stockpiling of massive nuclear weapons was being done with the intention of deterring war, and that many see this as the best available means of preserving a peace of sorts. It did not directly judge this deterrent possession of nuclear weapons, despite the fact that the present deterrence system rests upon the threat to do what the Council had just condemned as morally unthinkable. Instead, the Council passed over the question of deterrence with the conclusion, "Whatever be the case with this method of deterrence, men should be convinced that the arms race in which so many countries are engaged is not a safe way to preserve a steady peace. Nor is the so-called balance resulting from this race a sure and authentic peace. Rather than being eliminated thereby, the causes of war threaten to grow gradually stronger." This arms race was further condemned as a treacherous trap for mankind, which injures the poor to an intolerable degree by diverting resources away from human needs.[16]

Thus, in its stated desire to look at war with an entirely new attitude,[17] the Council endorsed John XXIII's rejection of war as a rational instrument for justice in the nuclear age, and reinforced his call for changes in the international system to effect its elimination. Yet in its specific moral precepts the Council could not get past the tension and ambiguity of effectively outlawing the actual use of most nuclear weapons which were designed for mass destruction, while tolerating a system of deterrence based on the threat of such usage. It is clear, however, that the Council held that the present state of deterrence cannot be accepted as a permanent state of affairs, and must be eliminated by a negotiated movement toward disarmament.

Following the Council Paul VI devoted much of his ministry

to the cause of peace, the theme of which he summed up in his
address to the United Nations on October 4, 1965. Here Paul
reaffirmed the right of self-defense as justified by Pius XII, but
he also chose to focus on the emphasis of John XXIII that the
modern world can no longer afford war as a means of justice
and political policy: "It suffices to remember that the blood of
millions of men, that numberless and unheard sufferings, use-
less slaughter and frightful ruin, are the sanction of the past
which unites you with an oath which must change the future
history of the world: No more war, war never again!"[18]

Most significantly, Paul developed two themes which also
had their roots in the teaching of his predecessors and Vatican
II: 1) the linkage of the issue of war with that of world economic
reform and development; and 2) the development of a new appreciation of politics. In *Populorum Progressio* Paul stressed
the need for reform of the world economic order, for the social
question of the nineteenth century had become a global question of survival and justice in the twentieth. He stressed that
all people had the right to development and that in the present
era *development* is actually the new word for peace.[19]

By development, however, Paul meant not purely economic
development, but rather an integral development which addressed the spiritual and cultural needs of people as well as
material well-being. He also adamantly stressed that development did not mean absorption of the poor nations into the
Western industrial-cultural system. True human development
required respect for the higher cultural values and expressions
of the world's peoples and these should not be traded off for
material prosperity from the richer nations.[20] In this Paul VI
clearly tried to distinguish his definition of "development" from
the way that word was normally used in Western industrial
nations, equating development with economics and therefore
implying the cultural superiority of the West over the so-called
"under-developed" countries.

In this presentation of the necessity of world development
Paul took the focus of Church teaching on peace and justice off
of the ideological East-West conflict and placed it on what was
called the North-South conflict between the industrialized and
the non-industrialized nations (the so-called Third World). In

so doing Paul wished to place the Church on the side of the "South" in calling for greater justice in the world economic system.[21] In his address to the 1974 World Food Conference in Rome, Paul VI expanded on the linkage of the development question and war by referring to the perverted "aid" programs of the industrial nations as a new way of making war on the world's poor. These were seen as substituting birth control for economic justice and even using food as a weapon, designed to limit the population of the poor so as to keep them from their fair share of the world's goods.[22]

This shift of focus to the problem of development and the North-South conflict also entailed an effort on the part of Paul VI to move the Church away from its historical identification with the West. Paul took care to criticize Western liberalism and materialism along with Marxist atheistic socialism. In *Populorum Progressio* he charged Western liberalism, with its exaggerated individualism, with the responsibility for perverting industrialization into a profit-seeking system based on what Pius XI had condemned as the "imperialism of money."[23]

In 1971 Paul sought to add his own contribution to the teachings of *Quadragesimo Anno* and *Mater et Magistra* with his encyclical *Octogesima Adveniens*. In this letter Paul attacked the dehumanizing character of ideological conflict in the modern world, and charged that both Marxism and Western liberalism falsified life by imposing their incomplete visions upon it.[24] Clearly, the duty of the Christian for Paul was to view issues of war and world development not from the perspective of either ideological camp, but rather from the perspective of the concrete common good of humanity. To this end Paul saw the Church as giving the ideologically divided world its most precious gift, a universal vision of the nature of the human person and the destiny of the human race.[25]

Thus Paul VI wedded the internationalism of modern papal teaching and the call for reform of the world's economic structures into the theme of global development, and held that global development to be an intrinsic part of the preservation of world peace. As this theme emerged as such a strong part of papal teaching and would consequently be incorporated into episcopal statements, it would naturally serve as a key focus of contro-

versy in the American Catholic debate over the definition of
the problem of war in the modern world. This internationalist
stress on world economic reform would be an obvious challenge
and exasperation for realists, who insisted that the problem of
security could and must be treated separately from the question
of economic development. Their consistent contention had been
that the major threat to world peace was not unfair development of the world's resources, but rather Soviet military might
and expansionism. This military threat, they argued, could not
be countered by economic reform. Most realists, like William
O'Brien, thus contended that the issue of economic reform and
development was really a red herring, which pacifists and idealists used to avoid dealing with the problem of military security. O'Brien argued that, even if defense budgets were cut,
it was not likely that the money would be redirected to economic aid. Perhaps the most telling argument realists could
raise was that greater reliance on nuclear weapons was much
cheaper than maintaining larger conventional forces. Consequently, significant reductions in defense budgets for the sake
of economic development could force the major powers into a
less flexible position on the use of nuclear weapons to respond
to aggression.

Papal teaching did not directly address this form of argumentation from the realists, but it was clearly opposed to their
attempt to separate the issue of war from the issue of world
economic development. In this, many idealist and radical Catholics could find support for their contention that the East-West
conflict was often used as a smoke-screen to hide the unjust and
destructive economic domination of Third World countries by
the industrialized nations, which had nothing to do with providing for the security of the West. Pope Paul's statements on
the dehumanizing character of modern ideological conflict also
seemed to echo earlier statements by American Catholic pacifists such as Thomas Merton and Gordon Zahn. While more
polemical, Merton's attack on the false ideological consciousness supporting the American-Soviet rivalry does not seem too
dissimilar from Paul's attempt to get Christians to reject the
incomplete visions of the human person in both Marxism and
Western liberalism. Obviously, Paul's attempt to get past ide-

ological conflict to a consideration of the common good of humanity would receive from realist thinkers the same judgment of naiveté that Paul Ramsey and John Courtney Murray had placed upon *Pacem in Terris.*

A final theme of papal teaching, which also echoed what had been a constant theme of radical and pacifist Catholics during these years, was the call of Paul VI for renewed appreciation of politics and political power. For Paul it was essential to break the control of society by economics, and to destroy the psychological atmosphere of fatalism that stemmed from viewing the world as controlled by impersonal "forces" (for example, the laws of the market). This fatalism and the economic imperalism which fed upon it had to be countered by a renewed personal and collective sense of the responsibility and competency of the individual conscience, and the belief that people can change the world which people created. This meant a renewed sense of politics as the public realm in which the human will directed the social enterprise. As Paul defined it:

To take politics seriously at its different levels—local, regional, national and worldwide—is to affirm the duty of man, of every man, to recognize the concrete reality and the value of the freedom of choice that is offered to him to seek and bring about both the good of the city and of the nation and of mankind. Politics are a demanding manner—but not the only one—of living the Christian commitment to the service of others.[26]

The particular style and content of this political engagement of Christians was left by Paul to each local church to discern.[27] Yet the need for a revival of personal responsibility in the political realm was, for Paul, an essential element in the modern papal call for reform of the international order. The Roman Synod of 1971 reaffirmed this theme in its statement that working for justice was a constitutive element of preaching the Gospel to the world. In the Synod's view, embracing the world's struggle for justice and infusing politics with a sense of responsibility for the common good are a vital service of Christians to a world caught in the paradox of a simultaneous emergence of a planetary society and the increase of forces of division and antagonism.[28]

American Catholic pacifists could find in Paul's statements
support for their efforts to heighten the sense of the individual's
moral responsibility and competency in the face of the immense
power of the modern state. Yet perhaps more significant is the
fact that the insistence of Paul VI and the Synod on the importance of political involvement for the Christian vocation
could serve as a spur to national episcopal conferences to address the issues of war and world development.

AMERICAN EPISCOPAL TEACHING

These major themes of papal and conciliar teaching over the
past twenty years greatly influenced and helped shape the American Catholic debate on war and peace. The conflicting responses
of the different schools of American Catholic thought to this
teaching reflected the varied ways in which it was received and
interpreted within the American Catholic community. The
global vision expressed in papal teaching posed special challenges to the American hierarchy as they faced the task of
applying that vision to their own national situation and addressing the issues to which American defense and foreign
policy gave rise.

This presentation will focus on the teaching of the American
bishops as they addressed issues of war and peace in four major
areas: the Vietnam War, conscientious objection, the linkage
of war with international reform and development, and nuclear
weapons.[29] It was in addressing these issues that the bishops
developed many of the positions which found expression in their
1983 pastoral. In particular, attention will be given to the tensions within the bishops' teaching as they addressed these issues, and the tension between the positions taken by the bishops
and the policies of the United States government.

Vietnam

A series of episcopal statements from 1966 to 1971 were
progressively skeptical of the morality of the American intervention in Vietnam. In these statements the bishops reflected a
desire both to uphold the general principles expounded by Vat-

ican II and to grant a presumption of justice to American policies. Their first joint statement on the war in November, 1966,
was in fact a juxtaposition of these two factors. The bishops
listed the principles found in the teaching of Vatican II which
they held must be used to evaluate the morality of the war.
These were: the distinction between true and false patriotism;
the right to legitimate self-defense; the necessity to keep the
waging of war within moral limits; the arms race is not a safe
way to preserve peace; people in the armed forces must act as
agents of security; provisions must be made for conscientious
objection.[30]

They followed the listing of these principles with an assertion
of confidence in the intentions of American leaders and supported the justice of the government's decision. The bishops,
however, gave no argument on how this conclusion was reached.
They further insisted that the government had an obligation
to keep the people adequately informed on the war, and that
citizens had a duty to protest when the war threatened to ex-
ceed moral limits. Support for the war, the bishops argued,
must be accompanied by support for disarmament negotiations.
The bishops' chief fear was that the war would lessen the American people's sensitivity to the moral evils of war.[31] A year later
the bishops reaffirmed their 1966 statement, and encouraged
the government to continue to pursue negotiations "despite the
rebuffs to these efforts."[32]

In 1968 the bishops issued a major pastoral statement, *Human Life in Our Day*. Without altering their previous judgment
on the war, the bishops raised the question of whether or not
the war had exceeded the bounds of proportionality in the destruction it was causing, assuming the justice of the American
cause and intentions. The bishops recalled the teaching of Pius
XII in 1953, stating that even a legitimate war of defense can
cross the point of proportion where the destruction wrought is
disproportionate to the injustice to otherwise be tolerated. This
question the bishops left unanswered.[33]

The doubts which the bishops exhibited in 1968 on the continuing justification of American involvement in Vietnam grew
until finally in 1971 they stated that "at this point in history
it seems clear to us that whatever good we hope to achieve

through continued involvement in this war is now outweighed by the destruction of human life and moral values which it inflicts." The bishops therefore called for an end to the conflict without further delay, but did not demand immediate withdrawal. They did, however, go on to stress that the United States had an obligation to help rebuild Southeast Asia as it had for Europe after World War II. They also called for higher G.I. benefits for veterans and pardon for draft resisters.[34]

The 1971 resolution declaring the Vietnam War no longer to be just was a most significant experience for the bishops. It was the first time that, as a body, they had publicly opposed their government on a major foreign policy issue. Despite its unprecedented nature, this resolution did not receive anything like the attention or reaction that was to greet the 1983 pastoral on war and peace. By 1971 the bishops' resolution, which did not demand immediate withdrawal, could be expected to appear rather tame and belated to the chief proponents of Catholic anti-war activity. As previously stated, numerous liberal and moderate Catholic journals and papers had preceded the bishops in condemning the war. Rather than charting a course of leadership, the bishops' resolution seemed to reflect a growing national trend of mainstream disillusionment with the war in Southeast Asia. Yet the 1971 resolution was significant for the development of the bishops' approach to teaching on issues of war and peace. It helped to move them in the direction of a greater willingness to address negative judgments against major government policies, which would find more controversial expression in the 1983 pastoral, *The Challenge of Peace.*

It is also significant for understanding the bishops' perspective that their final rejection of the war was based on the principle of proportionality and did not involve any attempt to judge the justice of America's involvement in Indochina. The rejection of the morality of the war was somewhat expanded in the 1973 statement of the United States Catholic Conference (USCC) committee on Social Development and World Peace, which responded to the expansion of the war into bombing raids on Cambodia. The statement lamented the general climate of uncertainty about moral issues in the United States which created a vacuum in which political and military decisions became the moral judgments of the moment. The committee rejected the bombing as immoral on three counts. First, it rested on dubious legal authority given the repeal of the Gulf of Tonkin resolution and various congressional resolutions against it. Second was the dubious utility of using force to uphold a shaky government in Cambodia. Third, the tactic of "carpet-bombing" entire areas was condemned as the indiscriminate warfare rejected by recent popes and Vatican II.[35] This statement was one of the most specific criticisms of United States military policy in Southeast Asia issued by the USCC during the war. Yet even in light of the National Conference of Catholic Bishops' (NCCB) rejection of the morality of continuing the war, this criticism was never expanded into a consideration of the wider dimensions of the purposes and goals of American policy in the continuance of the war.

Conscientious and Selective Conscientious Objection

In the sixties the draft became a major target of much antiwar activity. As the Catholic resistance movement made draft boards the focus of their campaign of disruptive civil disobedience, conscientious objection to military service became a chosen option for unprecedented numbers of draft-eligible Catholic men. Because of the strong identification of the Catholic moral tradition with the just war tradition, gaining acceptance of CO status from local draft boards often proved to be difficult for Catholic objectors. Vatican II recognized the right of Catholics to be conscientious objectors, but many American Catholic pacifists, like Gordon Zahn, argued that the just war tradition of the Church also logically called for recognition of selective objection to particular wars. United States law provided for CO status but did not recognize the right to selective objection. For many Catholic pacifists and radicals the issue of selective or total conscientious objection was but a part of pressing their more radical critique of American society and even anarchistic attitudes towards the state. Consequently, the arguments between Catholic pacifists and realists over conscientious objection became a focal point for debate over the relative status of pacifism and the just war tradition within the Catholic community. This in turn was but an instance of the wider Catholic debate over American policies and goals and the place of the Church in modern society. Because of the importance of the bishops' statements for the Catholic debate over conscientious objection, it seems best to briefly treat the significance and difficulties of this issue here.

In their 1968 pastoral, *Human Life in Our Day*, the bishops went beyond Vatican II, and were probably in advance of much of their own flocks in calling for legal recognition of both conscientious objection and selective conscientious objection to particular wars, as well as an end to the peacetime draft. In rejecting the peacetime draft, the bishops cited the position of Pope Benedict XV, who criticized this practice as contributing to the breeding of actual wars. They therefore joined their voices with those who called for a review of the draft system and the establishment of a volunteer army adequate for the purposes of defense.[36]

The bishops argued that the present and future generations of young men who bear the burden of fighting wars will be less willing to leave the decisions regarding issues like Vietnam entirely to political and bureaucratic processes. They further asserted that if war is ever to be outlawed and international institutions established on a belief in the universal common good, it will be because of these citizens who reject exaggerated nationalism and insist on principles of non-violent political and civic action in both domestic and international affairs. The bishops joined with Vatican II in praising those who renounced the use of violence and took up methods of non-violent defense. In this spirit the bishops called for a modification of Selective Service laws to allow recognition for those selective conscientious objectors refusing to serve in particular wars they believe to be unjust, as well as those who reject participation in all war.[37]

This position was reiterated in a 1971 declaration of the USCC which stressed the Church's traditional teaching on the central importance of conscience. It argued that while the Church's insistence on serving the common good included participation in a just defense, it was also in conformity with Catholic moral teaching to refuse participation in military efforts either totally or in reference to a particular war judged to be unjust. The declaration recognized the administrative difficulties in allowing selective conscientious objection, but urged the government to accept the task of working to reconcile the demands of the civic and the moral order on this issue.[38]

The major division in Catholic thinking on the issue of conscientious objection was clearly drawn in a debate which was itself sponsored by the USCC in 1973, and which focused on the position taken by the bishops. The debate was between two committees, one having Major General Thomas A. Lane (U.S. Army Ret.) as its chairman, and the other under Auxiliary Bishop John J. Dougherty of Newark. The debate between these two groups reflected the discussion within the wider Catholic community, and also served to bring to the surface an unaddressed tension within the bishops' own position.[39]

The Lane committee objected to the 1971 statement as erroneously placing pacifism and the just war theory on an equal footing in Catholic moral teaching. They argued that pacifism was a dissent from the Church's traditional teaching on the obligation of individuals to share in the just defense of the common good. They further contended that since it is the state's right to judge the conscientious objection of individuals, the granting of recognition to selective conscientious objection would create an unmanageable problem and subject the state's decision to the veto of individuals.[40]

The Dougherty committee argued that even within the just war tradition it is still a debatable question as to what are the limits in granting to the state's decisions a presumption of justice. In any event, the committee stressed that what is not debatable is the rights of individual conscience defended in Vatican II's recognition of conscientious objection and pacifism. The Dougherty committee claimed that the recognition of conscientious objection by the Council and the American bishops encompassed the three forms that such dissent could take: complete pacifism based on Scripture and the example of the early Church; pacifism based on the conviction that no modern war could meet the terms of the just war theory; and objection to a particular war as failing the test of the just war theory.[41]

Thus, in equating total and selective conscientious objection as having the same rights before the state, the bishops raised, without ever addressing, the question of the individual's relationship to the state and the manner in which that relationship is mediated by the Church. The problem posed by selective conscientious objection is more complex than the bishops' statements acknowledged.[42] Total conscientious objection does not pose a direct challenge to the competency or justice of the state's exercise of its prerogative to make decisions regarding the public defense. From the state's perspective the pacifist has absented himself from the realm of political decision making in which the state claims sovereignty. Selective conscientious objection, however, challenges the state precisely in the area where the state claims sovereignty by challenging the morality or legality of a particular decision of the state on the use of armed force. To grant the right of selective conscientous objection thus extends by implication beyond the waging of war to all other exercise of political power by the state. In effect, the demands of selective conscientious objection would have the state grant the individual in advance the right to disobey the law, which the state, *qua* state, cannot do.

Selective objection follows directly from the just war tradition of the Church, and the bishops logically defended it. The Christian must dissent from unjust war as he must refuse to obey unjust laws. It is also true, however, that the state, *per se*, cannot be expected to grant the right of disobedience. Thus, the problem of how to recognize selective conscientious objection and still reconcile the individual's obligation to the state remains unaddressed in the bishops' teaching. It is easy to understand how pacifists would welcome the recognition of selective objection as bolstering the rights of individual conscience against the state. Catholic realists, however, would naturally view this position as a threat to the stability of the political order. The fact that the bishops did not address the practical problems entailed in this recognition of selective conscientious objection could only serve to reinforce realist fears that Church teaching was unreflectively moving in a direction that threatened the relationship of the Church to American society.[43]

Part of the problem entailed in the bishops' position on conscientious objection was a dilemma long associated with the just war tradition, namely, how to apply a negative moral judgment on a war against the state. The implication of selective conscientious objection is the possibility of a clash between the state and individual Christians or even large segments of the Christian community, if not the official Church structure itself. Implicit in the efforts of the bishops to gain recognition for selective as well as total conscientious objection was an effort to diffuse the potentialities of such a clash by providing legal protection for all conscientious dissent from the government's defense policies. This effort, however, presupposed the protection of all positions of the individual conscience without addressing the inherent conflict between these positions or the state's ability to accommodate them. Most significantly, it also took the focus off consideration of the bishops' own role in pressing moral judgments against the state by placing the bishops in the role of guardians of the individual conscience, whose primary task was to provide a place for each conscience rather than to prophetically pursue their own moral judgments on public policy.

The desire of the bishops to recognize total and selective objection to war was part of their desire to follow Vatican II's recognition of both the just war and pacifist positions within the Church.[44] The unaddressed conflicts in the bishops' stance on conscientious objection reflected the tension involved in their attempting to mediate these divergent positions within the ecclesial community, as well as to balance their own role of moral leadership with the desire to avoid the possibility of a radical confrontation with the government.

The Linkage of War with World Development

Another major theme of the bishops' statements on war and peace was their affirmation of the internationalist ideals that were such a clear part of modern papal teaching. In *Human Life in Our Day* (1968) and *Human Solidarity* (1970) the bishops urged support for the United Nations and other international agencies, and followed the papal lead in strongly linking the solution to the problem of war to reform of the world economy. The bishops specifically laid responsibility on the United States, because of its immense power, to work with the United Nations to eliminate the unilateral use of force. In 1974 the bishops issued several statements stressing the theme of world development and America's role in it. The thrust of these statements reflected again internal tensions in the bishops' attempt to evaluate American policies and goals while not denying their intrinsic justice. In October, 1974, the USCC Executive Committee issued a statement on the global food crisis. The committee asserted that the United States must treat its food resources as a sacred trust and not as a weapon or as merely a matter of markets and money. It insisted that "the law of the market" is a human invention which must recognize moral limits. If it denies food to the starving, it must be changed. The committee further urged the government to approach the upcoming World Food Conference with an open policy supporting an international food reserve for global emergencies, an increase in short-term emergency relief to threatened areas, and an offer of technical assistance to nations in need of increasing their food supply.[45]

The food crisis and its relation to world development, the bishops asserted, posed serious implications for the United States both at home and abroad.[46] These implications were in part articulated in a statement of the USCC Department of Social Development and World Peace in August, 1974, entitled *Development-Dependency: The Role of Multinational Corporations.*

The statement referred to the encyclical *Populorum Progressio* and its recognition of the historical emergence of industrialization as providing the potential for both true human development and for what Pius XI called the tyranny of the "international imperialism of money." The statement also cited the fact that recent efforts of Latin American bishops to address the problems of their countries usually focused much of their criticism on the effects of Western capitalism. The committee lamented that in hearing the words of the Pope and Christians from other countries, Americans could not perceive the full truth being expressed because their perceptions were filtered through the culture of capitalism.[47]

The committee felt that the crisis of the present moment was clearly reflected in the 1974 United Nations session called to hear the complaints of the nations of the Third World about the international economic system. This session served to dramatize the increasing concentration of power and wealth in relatively few multinational corporations and banks. This fact, the committee argued, served to deter real international development and justice.[48]

The committee insisted that it was necessary for Americans to admit that a real dilemma exists. On one hand, Christians must be committed to the ideal that all nations have a right to self-determination and economic development. On the other, the United States is committed to protect its national interests narrowly defined in economic and political terms. The identification of free enterprise and our political system, the committee argued, set national policy to providing a favorable world climate for American business. The result of this policy was to reduce most of the poor nations to a position of dependency and therefore control by the multinational corporations which dominated Western capital and technology.[49]

The committee argued that Americans must realize that the multinational corporations which dominate the international economy also control their domestic economy. Many domestic economic problems resulted from the service the political and economic system renders to the needs of the multinationals, to the detriment of Americans just as to the detriment of foreign populations. The committee was glad that many Catholics in the world were becoming increasingly aware of the interlocking of American domestic and foreign policies to serve the interests of transnational business enterprises.[50]

Most emphatically, the committee argued that the time had now come to question the motivation as well as the possession of such power by these institutions. "For the motivation continually to increase profit emerges from values which promote excessive individualism, unnecessary consumption, and disregard for the quality of human life, all of which are contrary to the deepest values of the Judeo-Christian tradition." Consequently, the committee maintained that the American Church must come to see itself as a prophetic voice apart from the forces controlling society, and that it could learn much of how to function in this way from the experience of the Church in the Third World.[51]

The questions raised in this statement about American foreign, military, and economic policies and goals were extremely pointed and carried a strongly negative implication for the moral and human value of America's role in the world. Here again, however, this questioning of America's influence on world development was not pursued into more specific judgments on American policies which could have created the possibility of a direct confrontation between the Church and the government. Yet this statement remains one of the sharpest indications among the documents issued under episcopal auspices that the government's policies were in direct contradiction to the values which the bishops upheld as fundamental to global human welfare. Two years later in a pastoral letter of the NCCB, *To Live in Christ Jesus*, the section on world development did not continue this more pointed line of criticism. Rather, it reasserted the more general principles of world development, and the criticisms of the present international system, which the bishops had previously made.[52]

Thus, the American bishops embraced the internationalism of modern papal teaching and especially the theme of world development that was a central part of the teaching of Paul VI. As such the bishops' teaching would invite the same conflicting responses of Catholic idealists and realists that greeted papal teaching. Yet episcopal statements did not receive the same prominence as the papal encyclicals and consequently were not the focus of the same degree of pointed commentary as were *Pacem in Terris* and *Populorum Progressio*. The most critical USCC statement on American economic practices, *Development-Dependency*, did not receive the reaction one would anticipate. Almost ten years later, as the bishops considered their 1983 pastoral, this earlier statement did not seem to be well remembered, and was not cited in the 1983 pastoral as other previous USCC statements were. In their statements the bishops did not substantively go beyond Papal teaching, but they did move toward accepting the need to apply that teaching to an evaluation of American responsibilities and practices. The principles which the bishops upheld for international development and justice called for negative judgments on many American economic policies and goals, yet the bishops' criticisms were only a bit stronger than their commentary on Vietnam. The fact that episcopal teaching on this issue moved away from its strongest indictment of American economic practices to a more general statement of principles and exhortations would seem to reflect a desire not to push judgments on the justice of American policies to the point of direct confrontation with the government or the further polarization of the Catholic community.

Nuclear Weapons

It was on the issue of nuclear weapons that the bishops made their sharpest presentation of the conflict between Christian moral principles and American practices. In 1968 (*Human Life in Our Day*) the bishops reiterated Vatican II's condemnation of the arms race and questioned the rationality of seeking security through the threat of mutual societal destruction. The bishops recalled that Vatican II, while not condemning nuclear deterrence in itself, had gone on to condemn the arms race and the balance of terror as a means of preserving peace. In that spirit, the bishops did not address the issue of deterrence, but expressed hope that the Partial Test Ban Treaty would help lead to a cessation of arms development, and they urged the Senate to ratify the Nuclear Non-Proliferative Treaty between the United States and the Soviet Union, which committed the signatories to balanced reductions of nuclear weapons and the peaceful use of nuclear energy. They further urged the United States to take initiatives in reducing tension and building a climate of trust by inviting the United Nations' Atomic Energy Commission and other world agencies to inspect our nuclear facilities.[53]

The bishops seriously questioned the basic policy of seeking superiority in the capacity for mutually assured destruction

(MAD) as a means of security. They argued that, although for some years there had been an effective parity in MAD capability between the superpowers, the result had been less security, not more. They also specifically addressed the American decision to deploy a "thin" anti-ballistic missile (ABM) system. They deplored this decision as the latest act in the arms race and a prelude to an even bigger ("thick") ABM system. Though the ABM was deemed a purely defensive weapon, the bishops labeled it as dangerously destabilizing to the "balance of terror," likely to cause the other side to increase its offensive capability.[54]

In this, the bishops did not go beyond what Vatican II had stated on the question of nuclear arms. When the bishops did eventually move to address more specifically the issue of nuclear deterrence and the use of nuclear weapons, their statements must be understood in the context of a new phase in the "nuclear debate" which arose in the mid-seventies.

The structure of the renewed debate on nuclear weapons strategy actually emerged in the mid-sixties but was obscured by the furor over Vietnam. A chief factor in its emergence was the desire of the superpowers to stabilize their relations so as to lessen the danger of all-out nuclear war. Another factor was the development of weaponry which made arms control more difficult, notably ABM defense systems and MIRV warheads (multiple independently targeted re-entry vehicles—more than one warhead in a missile, each capable of being released and directed at a separate target).[55]

The introduction of Multiple Independently Targeted Reentry Vehicles (MIRV's) allowed the superpowers to increase their striking capability geometrically, which threatened to destabilize the balance of terror by creating in the adversary's mind the fear of an imponderable striking power in his opponent. ABM systems, as a defense for cities against enemy missiles, threatened to destabilize the nuclear deterrence system by promising to limit the threat of MAD. The Strategic Arms Limitation Talks (SALT I) agreements of 1972 limited the deployment of ABM systems but solidified the superpowers' deterrence posture on the use of offensive weapons employing MIRV's.[56]

The debate over the ABM system and SALT I also served to raise renewed questioning of the morality of attacking cities and the MAD doctrine which was the basis of nuclear deterrence. In this context Secretary of Defense James R. Schlesinger revived earlier proposals of Secretary McNamara's to move the United States to a "counterforce" nuclear strategy, that is, a more flexible nuclear capability with which the United States could engage in a limited nuclear war with the Soviet Union. The reasons given as motivating the shift of policy were: the immorality of indiscriminately striking cities, a dissatisfaction with not being able to limit and control a nuclear exchange, and the desirability of matching the Soviet capacity for selective attacks on a variety of targets. To keep this counterforce strategy in perspective it must be understood that counterforce strategy would not eliminate MAD. Rather, it would presuppose a MAD capability as the ultimate threat designed to keep any limited nuclear exchange limited. Therefore, the role of city hostages remained at the heart of nuclear policy.[57] It was in the context of this technological escalation and a conceptual shift of strategic policies to fighting a limited nuclear war that the American bishops had to address the problem of nuclear deterrence in the late seventies and early eighties.

Episcopal statements on nuclear deterrence during these years reflected the influence of a position developed for the bishops by Father Bryan Hehir. Hehir was director of the USCC Office of International Justice and Peace, in which capacity he had considerable influence on the content and composition of official statements. Hehir would later be one of the principal staff persons for the Bernardin committee during the formulation of the 1983 pastoral letter, *The Challenge of Peace*. Consequently, his influence was most important to the development of episcopal statements on war and peace from the mid-seventies to the present.

Hehir's position was a nuclear pacifist stance focusing on three operating principles: first, the distinction between possession and use of nuclear weapons, allowing their interim possession for deterrence purposes while prohibiting any use; second, a rejection of any weapons development which de-

stabilizes the balance of terror or promises a "limited" use of
nuclear weapons; and third, the necessity to be seriously committed to negotiations for arms reduction and elimination of
nuclear weapons.

In effect Hehir sought to sever the linkage by which one's
response to the matter of deterrence is governed by one's prior
judgment on the use of nuclear weapons. Hehir stressed that
consideration must be given not only to the physical but also
to the psychological impact of nuclear weapons. He argued that
even if tactical nuclear weapons could be controlled within the
limits of proportionality and discrimination, the psychological
impact of moving from conventional to nuclear weapons was
immense. Such a shift introduced a new order of combat with
continuing potentialities for levels of escalation far exceeding
all proportion and discrimination, and therefore constituted a
qualitative breech in the use of force which should be trans-
posed into an ethical limit: no use of nuclear weapons.[58] Yet
Hehir accepted the position that today nuclear deterrence functions as a legitimate instrument of policy and in the present
international system serves to prevent the outbreak of a major
world war. In such a system, to reject deterrence immediately
would practically be tantamount to unilateral disarmament.
As Vatican II asserted, however, deterrence as a long-term goal
constitutes a high risk of nuclear war. Therefore, Hehir concluded that nuclear deterrence is acceptable as an *interim* instrument of policy, not as a permanent state of affairs. The
implication here is the necessity of seriously pursuing negotiations for arms reduction and elimination of nuclear weapons.
It also followed from Hehir's position that the only legitimate
use of nuclear weapons was to deter. If deterrence failed, another policy of response not employing nuclear weapons would
be morally required.[59]

Realist advocates of a counterforce strategy would criticize
Hehir's position as unrealistic because it ignored the fact that
any real deterrent must involve the intent to carry out the
threat, and that therefore we must develop a usable nuclear
system in the event that deterrence should fail. Hehir's response was that his position was no less realistic than that of
his realist opponents. Both were based on a bet. Hehir bet that

deterrence would not fail; they bet that nuclear war could be limited. Given his belief that nuclear weapons had snapped the classical linkage of military power and political purpose, Hehir felt his position was the only realistic approach to the present moral dilemma of nuclear deterrence.[60]

Following from these premises, Hehir argued that strategic policy must be geared to maintain the "firebreak" between conventional and nuclear weapons. He therefore insisted that the move to a counterforce strategy only made nuclear war or a first strike more likely by creating the illusion of a limited nuclear war and encouraging the development of more sophisticated and destabilizing weaponry. Hehir therefore argued for maintaining the MAD deterrence, because even though it was morally unusable, its complete nature made it less likely that it would be used. Thus, in the existing situation of bad choices, Hehir opted to reinforce the existing nuclear "bluff" as the least objectionable.[61] Hehir saw his position as providing a middle ground between the pacifist and realist positions, which would allow Catholics to tolerate the present possession of nuclear weapons while working for their elimination. Yet Hehir's position would naturally produce continued opposition from both the pacifist and realist camps because it violated the basic premise of each: the pacifist contention that nuclear weapons were inherently evil and could not be morally possessed, and the realist contention that a moral, limited use of nuclear weapons was essential to a realistic deterrent and defense. The controversy over the adequacy of this approach to deterrence would obviously increase as Hehir's thinking would shape later episcopal statements and eventually find expression in the bishops' 1983 pastoral.[62]

In November, 1976, the NCCB issued a pastoral letter, *To Live in Christ Jesus*, in which the bishops made a statement of major significance about nuclear deterrence. The pastoral declared that "as possessors of a vast nuclear arsenal, we must also be aware that not only is it wrong to attack civilian populations, but it is also wrong to threaten to attack them as part of a strategy of deterrence."[63] This condemnation struck at the heart of the deterrence strategy of both the United States and the Soviet Union, which are based on the ultimate threat to attack cities. This statement was regarded by many as the most dramatic development in Church teaching since Vatican II. For up to this time that teaching condemned the act of directly attacking civilians, but had made no direct moral judgment on the threat to do so in the present system of nuclear deterrence. The irony of the statement was that it was passed with little debate or controversy and did not become the storm center of reaction as one might have expected. In large measure this was probably due to the fact that the pastoral, while dealing with numerous issues, was seen as primarily focused on sexual morality, and the section on nuclear weapons did not receive primary attention. Yet given the significance of the statement on the morality of the deterrent threat and the later debate surrounding the 1983 pastoral, it is hard to avoid the conclusion that in 1976 many bishops were not fully aware of the implications of their statement. They apparently simply followed traditional Catholic morality, which holds that it is immoral to threaten to do what it is immoral to do. The logical question of what stance must then be taken toward actual American nuclear defense policy was neither raised nor addressed. If it is evil to threaten direct attack on civilians, and American and Soviet nuclear deterrent policy is based on this threat, must that defense system be outrightly rejected as immoral? Is it even moral then to possess nuclear weapons? Would Catholics then be morally obliged to remove themselves from the military or at least the nuclear defense system?

The position by which the bishops would attempt to respond to such questions found official expression in the 1979 testimony of Cardinal John Krol of Philadelphia before the Senate Foreign Relations Committee. Krol testified on behalf of the USCC as part of the Senate's hearings on the SALT II Treaty. Krol's testimony is the most developed episcopal statement on nuclear weapons prior to the 1983 pastoral, and clearly reflects the adoption of the position developed by Bryan Hehir, who himself helped to write Krol's testimony.

Krol stated that the American bishops believed that we have too long been preoccupied with preparations for war, guided by false criteria of equivalence or superiority in armaments. It was time, he insisted, to take the first steps toward peace and negotiated bilateral disarmament.[64] He further stated that while he allowed legitimate just war defense, this could not include nuclear war. The primary imperative of the nuclear age, he argued, was to prevent the use of strategic nuclear weapons. Thus, in nuclear deterrence is found the paradox of war prevented by the threat of doing what the Christian conscience could not tolerate. Krol clearly stated that the bishops accepted nuclear deterrence only as a lesser evil, and only as long as the hope of a reduction in weapons is possible. He made clear the implication of this qualified acceptance in stating that if negotiations for disarmament do not seriously proceed, then the Catholic Church would have to move officially to condemn the possession as well as the use of nuclear weapons.[65]

The SALT I treaty had given the hope of leading to actual reductions in nuclear arms, Krol observed, but that hope had not materialized in SALT II, which was only a deceleration, not a reversal of the arms race. It was for this reason that some bishops would not support SALT II, seeing it as substituting the illusion of arms control for a serious effort at disarmament.[66] Krol rejected the view of those who felt that SALT II would weaken the United States and allow the Soviets a first-strike ability. He further specified that if the United States used SALT II to expand strategic and conventional forces, it would eliminate any reason for the bishops to continue their qualified acceptance of deterrence. Krol claimed that "strategic equivalence" was only the new name for the arms race, and that it would distort the bishops' support of SALT II to link this with new military expenditures within the terms of the treaty. He also urged the United States to consider the new MX missile and Trident submarine programs as negotiable in return for Russian concessions, and to work to eliminate MIRV's, which SALT I had failed to do.[67]

Thus Krol's testimony shows that the bishops' position on nuclear weapons had been brought by 1979 to the near breaking point of confrontation that they had avoided on other issues of war and peace. The clearly conditional acceptance of deterrence recognized the incompatibility of present American policy and Christian moral principles. It also clearly served notice to the government that if changes were not made the Church would have to dissociate itself officially from American nuclear defense policies. Since such a stance of condemnation would be seen by realists and pacifists alike as banishing Catholics from participation in the present American strategic defense system, the implications of Krol's warning were far-reaching.

NOTES

1. Joseph Gremillion, ed., *The Gospel of Peace and Justice: Catholic Social Teaching since Pope John* (Maryknoll, New York: Orbis Books, 1976), p. 47; Pope Pius XII, "Christmas Message," in Robert Heyer, *Nuclear Disarmament: Key Statements of Popes, Bishops, Councils and Churches* (New York: Paulist Press, 1982), p. 13.

2. J. Bryan Hehir, "Foreword: Reflection on Recent Teaching," in Heyer, *Nuclear Disarmament*, pp. 3–4. Hehir is associate secretary of the Department of Social Development and World Peace of the United States Catholic Conference.

3. Pope Pius XII, "Christmas Message," 1956, cited in James R. Jennings, ed., *Just War and Pacifism: A Catholic Dialogue* (Washington, D.C.: United States Catholic Conference, 1973), p. 8.

4. *Mater et Magistra*, par. 157–159. Since the major papal encyclicals and other documents cited are printed in numerous collections and journals, citations here will refer to the paragraph numeration of the documents. All of the documents cited here can be found in Gremillion, *The Gospel of Peace and Justice*. Also another collection of some of these documents can be found in David J. O'Brien and Thomas A. Shannon, eds., *Renewing the Earth: Catholic Documents on Peace, Justice and Liberation* (Garden City, New York: Image Books, 1977). In *Mater et Magistra* John sought to update Catholic teaching on social justice previously addressed by the seminal encyclicals of his predecessors Leo XIII, *Rerum Novarum* (1891), and Pius XI, *Quadragesimo Anno* (1931).

5. Ibid., par. 27–40.

6. Ibid., par. 41–45.

7. Ibid., par. 61–67.

8. Gremillion, *The Gospel of Peace and Justice*, pp. 69, 71.

9. *Pacem in Terris*, par. 127.

10. Hehir, in Heyer, *Nuclear Disarmament*, p. 4.

11. *Pacem in Terris*, par. 132–134, 142–145, 121–125, 80–88. A listing of human rights in modern society by John XXIII is given in par. 1–74.

12. Paul Ramsey's analysis and critique of *Pacem in Terris* is found

in chapter 4 of his *The Just War: Force and Political Responsibility* (New York: Charles Scribner's Sons, 1968), pp. 70–79. The reaction of realists John Courtney Murray and Reinhold Niebuhr to the encyclical has been previously cited: Murray, "Things Old and New in Pacem in Terris," *America* 108 (April 17, 1963): 612–614, Niebuhr, "Pacem in Terris: Two Views," *Christianity in Crisis* 23 (May 13, 1963): 81–83. Murray had previously made similar criticism of the internationalism of Pius XII. In referring to Pius' rejection of aggressive war Murray said, "Pius XII did not enter the formidable technical problem, how this legal transcription of a moral principle is to be effected.... This problem has hitherto been insoluble." "Remarks on the Moral Problem of War," *Theological Studies* 20 (March 1959):47.

13. *Gaudium et Spes*, par. 78.

14. Ibid., par 79.

15. Ibid., par 80.

16. Ibid., par. 81. John XXIII also treated the issue of deterrence in a similar manner, by acknowledging that the intentions of statesmen were to deter war, but that the result of the stockpiling of modern weapons was only a climate of fear and insecurity. *Pacem in Terris*, par. 109–119.

17. Ibid., par. 80.

18. Pope Paul VI, Address to the General Assembly of the United Nations, October 4, 1965, par. 19.

19. *Populorum Progressio*, par. 76.

20. Ibid., par. 14, 40–41.

21. This theme was further reinforced by the address of Cardinal Maurice Roy, President of the Pontifical Commission on Peace and Justice, in his address to the U.N. on the occasion of the launching of the Second Development Decade in 1970. Roy rejected the method of Western industrialization as the "model" for the "development" of the rest of the world. He charged that the "free competition" of the world market only served to benefit the wealthy nations and their favored elite in nonindustrial nations. The result of the present world order was a planetary society controlled by "the few" who managed the world's resources. He urged the reform of the international political and economic structure to correct this. Maurice Cardinal Roy, "Message on the Occasion of the Launching of the Second Development Decade," November 19, 1970, par. 4–8, 10, 13–17.

22. Pope Paul VI, Address to the Participants of the World Food Conference, Rome, November 9, 1974, par. 6.

23. *Populorum Progressio*, par. 26.

24. *Octogesima Adveniens*, par. 32–35.

25. *Populorum Progressio*, par. 13.

26. *Octogesima Adveniens*, par. 46.

27. Ibid., par. 4.

28. Synod of Bishops, Second General Assembly, "Justice in the World," November 30, 1971, par. 6–9.

29. The Catholic bishops of the United States are presently organized nationally as the United States Catholic Conference (USCC) and the National Conference of Catholic Bishops (NCCB). Both groups were established in 1966, replacing the National Catholic Welfare Conference (NCWC). The NCCB is a canonical body established by Church law like other national bishops' conferences. The USCC is a civil entity whose members are the bishops, but whose policy-making structures include others as well. The statements treated in this section are primarily those issued by the USCC or the NCCB as position statements on the issues of war and peace published under American episcopal auspices. Representative statements of American bishops on the question of nuclear weapons can be found in Heyer, *Nuclear Disarmament*. A more complete collection of NCCB and USCC statements on social justice can be found in J. Brian Benestead and Francis J. Butler, eds., *Quest for Justice: A Compendium of Statements of the United States Catholic Bishops on the Political and Social Order 1966–1980* (Washington, D.C.: United States Catholic Conference, 1981). The documents cited here will also be cited according to paragraph number. Those documents not published in this form will be cited according to the page number of the collection in which they are found.

30. *Peace and Vietnam*, NCCB, November 18, 1966, par. 5–9.

31. Ibid., par. 11–16.

32. *On Peace*, NCCB, November 16, 1967, par. 2–3.

33. *Human Life in Our Day*, par. 137–138.

34. *Resolution on Southeast Asia*, NCCB, November 1971, in Benestead, *Quest for Justice*, p. 78. The call for negotiations was repeated on November 16, 1972, in the NCCB *Resolution on Imperatives for Peace*, in Benestead, pp. 80–81.

35. *Statements on U.S. Bombing Operations in Cambodia*, USCC Committee on Social Development and World Peace, July 15, 1973, in Benestead, *Quest for Justice*, p. 82.

36. *Human Life in Our Day*, par. 123.

37. Ibid., par. 143, 148–149, 151–152.

38. *Declaration on Conscientious Objection and Selective Conscientious Objection*, USCC, October 21, 1971, in Benestead, *Quest for Justice*, pp. 74–77.

39. Jennings, *Just War and Pacifism*. This booklet is the reports of these two committees.

40. Ibid., pp. 4, 10–13.

41. Ibid., pp. 20–24, 36.

42. A thorough treatment of the problem of selective conscientious objection and Catholic teaching can be found in John A. Rohr, *Prophets Without Honor: Public Policy and the Selective Conscientious Objector* (Nashville: Abingdon Press, 1971).

43. John Courtney Murray was an exception to the realist rejection of selective objection. He stated his views in a minority position as a member of a presidential committee which recommended against recognition of selective objection. Yet Murray also believed that such recognition would require a degree of moral and political discernment in judging claims to selective objection which the present cultural climate of the U.S. did not exhibit. See John Courtney Murray, "War and Conscience," in James Finn, ed., *A Conflict of Loyalties* (New York: Pegasus, 1968), pp. 19–30.

44. *The Gospel of Peace and the Danger of War*, USCC Administrative Board, Feb. 15, 1978, in Benestead, *Quest for Justice*, pp. 84–85. The bishops stated here that in their statements on war and peace, they would draw from both the just war and pacifist positions.

45. *Statement of Global Food Crisis*, USCC Executive Committee, October, 1974, in Benestead, *Quest for Justice*, p. 101. The bishops also stressed that the burden of economic change here should not fall on the independent farmer.

46. *Statement of the World Food Crisis: A Pastoral Plan of Action*, NCCB, November 21, 1974, in Benestead, *Quest for Justice*, pp. 102–105. The bishops also reiterated their call with specific proposals in 1975, *Food Policy and the Church: Specific Proposals*, USCC Administrative Board, September 11, 1975, in Benestead, pp. 113–116.

47. *Development-Dependency: The Role of Multinational Corporations*, USCC Department of Social Development and World Peace, August, 1974, in Benestead, *Quest for Justice*, pp. 105–106.

48. Ibid., pp. 107–108.

49. Ibid., pp. 109–110.

50. Ibid., pp. 110–112.

51. Ibid., p. 112.

52. *To Live in Christ Jesus: A Pastoral Reflection on the Moral Life*, NCCB, November 11, 1976, in Benestead, *Quest for Justice*, pp. 41–43.

53. *Human Life in Our Day*, par. 105–109.

54. Ibid., par. 110–112. The bishops also singled out the proposed

neutron bomb, which was designed to kill people and leave cities intact. They termed this weapon symbolic of our civilization and the technological advance of warfare against life itself. Par. 103–105.
    55. Robert A. Gessert and J. Bryan Hehir, *The New Nuclear Debate* (New York: Council on Religion and International Affairs, 1976), pp. 53–55.
    56. Ibid., pp. 55–56.
    57. Ibid., pp. 56–58.
    58. Ibid., pp. 35–46.
    59. Ibid., pp. 50–51.
    60. Ibid., pp. 51–52, 91–93.
    61. Ibid., pp. 60–64, 91.
    62. In contrasting the realist and pacifist positions Hehir used Paul Ramsey as representative of a traditional just war approach to the use of nuclear weapons, and the English pacifist Walter Stein as his counterpoint (*New Nuclear Debate*, pp. 35–46). Hehir also acknowledges the importance of the work of Paul Ramsey in the development of modern just war theory, even though he arrives at different conclusions. Episcopal statements of these years reflecting Hehir's influence can be seen in: Archbishop Peter Gerety of Newark, "Testimony before the U.S. Foreign Relations Committee," Jan. 21, 1976, in Heyer, *Nuclear Disarmament*, pp. 87–88. Gerety argued for the maintenance of a firebreak against any use of nuclear weapons; Archbishop John Quinn of San Francisco, "Remarks as President of the NCCB on President Carter's decision to defer production of neutron warheads," April 14, 1978, in Heyer, *Nuclear Disarmament*, pp. 95–96. Quinn rejected the neutron weapons as destabilizing of the balance of power and escalating the arms race.
    63. *To Live in Christ Jesus: A Pastoral Reflection on the Moral Life*, NCCB, November 11, 1976, in Benestead, *Quest for Justice*, p. 44.
    64. John Cardinal Krol, "Testimony on behalf of the USCC before the Senate Foreign Relations Committee," Sept. 6, 1979, in Heyer, *Nuclear Disarmament*, p. 101.
    65. Ibid., pp. 103–104.
    66. Typical of this reaction among the American bishops were Auxiliary Bishop Thomas Gumbleton of Detroit and Bishop Carroll Dozier of Memphis. Both are members of the pacifist organization Pax Christi. Cited in Jim Castelli, *The Bishops and the Bomb: Waging Peace in a Nuclear Age* (Garden City, New York: Doubleday and Co., 1983), p. 23.
    67. Krol, in Heyer, *Nuclear Disarmament*, pp. 105–110.

7

The State of the Question

THE CHALLENGE OF PEACE

The previous chapters presented the major analytical perspectives that emerged among American Catholics as they grappled with the issues of war and peace from 1960 to the latter years of the seventies, as well as the chief themes of official Church teaching in response to these issues. This chapter will seek to pull together the strands of these perspectives as they constitute the American Catholic debate emergent at the beginning of the decade of the eighties. In this debate can be found the present state of the question on war and peace among American Catholics as their differing outlooks continue to battle for dominance and consensus. In this debate can also be found the same questions and points of division which in the past twenty years have led the American Catholic community from an apparently monolithic, nationalistic stance toward issues of war and peace, to a debate of growing intensity and confusion on what has become recognized as one of the paramount issues of our times.

By the late seventies the American bishops had shown an unprecedented willingness to address issues of war and peace and to take a more critical approach to United States defense policies. Their willingness to continue to pursue these issues in the first few years of the eighties can in fact be seen as the chief stimulus provoking renewed Catholic debate on the subject as well as providing a focal point for that debate.

The major concern of episcopal teaching continued to be nuclear arms and nuclear deterrence, which had emerged after

the Vietnam War as the focal issues of American debates on
war and peace. The central position of the nuclear question as
the decade of the eighties opened was given greater urgency
by the convergence of a number of factors. First was the continuing and dangerous tension between the United States and
the Soviet Union. Second was an emergent debate within the
NATO alliance over the first use of nuclear weapons. Third
was the developing technological capacity for "first-strike"
weapons, such as the MX and Trident II missiles, and the cruise
missile, which, while sub-sonic, is extremely difficult to detect.
Fourth was the growing public awareness and fear of the possibilities of nuclear war, which were manifested in a renewed
European peace movement and a strong antinuclear movement
in the United States.[1]

The year 1981 saw the emergence of a very visible and vocal
segment of the hierarchy in opposition to the arms race and
American nuclear policy. These bishops urged a renunciation
of the use of nuclear weapons by the United States, and some
of them declared their own arrival at absolute pacifist convictions.[2] For example, Bishop Leroy Matthieson of Amarillo,
Texas, in whose diocese the Pantex Corporation runs an assembly point for American nuclear weapons, urged Catholics
working there to seek other employment which did not contribute to the arms race. Archbishop Raymond Hunthausen of
Seattle, in whose jurisdiction the new Trident submarines are
based, took a similar stance against American nuclear policies.
He also became the first American Catholic bishop to engage
in and publicly advocate tax resistance, by refusing to pay the
percentage of his federal taxes which were used for military
purposes. In October 1981, twenty-nine bishops signed a statement that possession of nuclear arms is immoral.[3]

This rising concern over the nuclear question had been given
added stimulus in the minds of many bishops by the 1980 election of Ronald Reagan as president. Many of the governmental
arms policies and strategic doctrines with which the bishops
would be concerned in the early eighties obviously had their
origins in previous administrations. The emphasis on military
strength and more strident rhetoric which Reagan brought to
the White House, however, served as an immediate influence

motivating many bishops to examine more seriously the issue of nuclear arms development.[4]

Catholic episcopal concern with the escalating arms race was itself part of a rising national wave of alarm over this issue. The idea of a bilateral agreement freezing the development and deployment of nuclear weapons gained increasing support in the late seventies and early eighties and was a debated part of the 1980 elections. The idea gained in prominence when a series of town meetings in Vermont voted to support a "nuclear freeze," and provided concrete evidence that the concept had grass-roots support. The concept of a freeze gained wide-based political support from politicians and numerous religious and peace groups which organized to promote it. The "nuclear freeze movement" became a formidable presence in the American political scene. The national mood which this movement reflected would naturally serve to give increased political significance to any action on the nuclear issue by the Catholic bishops.[5]

The rising concern among many of the bishops with the nuclear question was reflected in the annual meeting of the NCCB in November of 1980. At this meeting Auxiliary Bishop P. Francis Murphy of Baltimore, supported by fellow episcopal members of the peace organization Pax Christi, called for the conference to address the issues of war and peace in a pastoral letter. In the lengthy discussion that followed, Murphy's proposal received support, not only from like-minded bishops such as Detroit Auxiliary Bishop Thomas Gumbleton and Bishop Walter Sullivan of Richmond, but also from noted conservatives like Bishop Edward O'Rourke of Peoria and Archbishop John Whelan of Hartford. O'Rourke had disagreed with the bishops' earlier rejection of the neutron bomb, and Whelan had felt that their 1968 position on conscientious objection was too vague. Thus, even the conservative opposition to recent trends in episcopal teaching served to bolster a general consensus on the need to review the Church's teaching on war and peace and to clarify the conferences' consensus on the issue.[6]

In response to this sentiment among the bishops, the president of the NCCB, Archbishop John Roach, appointed an *ad hoc* committee headed by Archbishop Joseph Bernardin of Chicago. The committee was to prepare a draft of a pastoral on war and peace to be submitted to the conference for debate and approval. The committee began extensive hearings in July, 1981, and a year later presented a first draft to the bishops for comments. By November, 1982, the committee had produced a second draft which was discussed at the annual NCCB meeting and, with suggested amendments, was to be brought before a special NCCB meeting in May, 1983, for final debate and decision.[7]

The process of the Bernardin committee's formulation of the pastoral letter served not only to bring national attention and controversy to the bishops, but also to bring the various schools of thought on the subject to array themselves in the latest round of American Catholic debate on war and peace. Consequently, the development of the second draft to the final version of the pastoral letter, *The Challenge of Peace*, can serve as a prism for viewing the present "state of the question" in this debate. For the purposes of presentation it seems best to first present the positions set forth in the second draft and then to treat representative statements of the major reactions to the document in the debate surrounding its transition to a third and final draft. The examination conducted here is not meant to be an exhaustive exegesis of the entire document or the process of its development, but a presentation of the major positions of the bishops and the reactions they incurred that are relevant to the concerns of this study. Specifically, focus will be given to the development of the pastoral's positions on the use of nuclear weapons, nuclear deterrence, and the internationalist themes which had been a consistent part of papal and American episcopal teaching on war and peace.[8]

The second draft opened with the urgent tone which marked the atmosphere in which the bishops felt they undertook their considerations of the issues of modern war. It began with an affirmation of Vatican II's reading of the signs of the times indicating that the human race is at a moment of supreme crisis. It cited Pope John Paul II's speech at Hiroshima: "From now on it is only through a conscious choice and through a deliberate policy that humanity can survive."[9] The draft recognized that as citizens of the first country to develop nuclear weapons, and the only one to use them, Americans had a particular responsibility to see that such a "conscious choice" is made to save humanity. Three signs of the times were cited as revealing the need for this further attempt of the bishops to address the contemporary threat of war. First was the increased expression by the peoples of the world for peace and their fear of nuclear war. Second was the condemnation by Vatican II of the arms race. Third was the fact that the unique dangers and dynamics of the nuclear arms race presented a qualitatively new problem for traditional moral principles.[10]

The draft also recognized the differences in the audiences which the bishops must address and the differing methodologies which they must employ. The document must speak to both the faithful and the civil community, and seek both to form the conscience of the believer and to contribute to the wider public policy debate. The bishops would therefore have to employ distinct but complementary styles of address which combine both prophetic and philosophical modes of discourse.

The draft also acknowledged that within the Catholic community itself there was significant divergence on how these issues should be approached. It asserted that since Vatican II it was clear that Catholics could morally follow both the just war and the pacifist traditions. The attitude set forth in the draft was to accept and endorse the ethical pluralism of just war and pacifist options and to seek to articulate the common ground that all Catholics could and must accept. It asserted the common presumption of both traditions against the use of armed force. The draft upheld the traditional just war principles of discrimination and proportionality in discerning the moral limits of violence, but it also acknowledged that historically Catholic theology on war had been too narrowly focused in only seeking to define these limits. It was necessary now to follow the Council's call for a fresh reappraisal of war itself.[11]

Part of this reappraisal envisioned by the draft was the necessity of seeing that the classical moral positions on war were faced with a unique challenge in the nuclear age. The starting point, therefore, of any moral discussion on war must be the recognition that nuclear war, as planned today, constitutes a new moral issue. It is consequently inadequate simply to repeat the moral formulations of previous eras.[12]

In an effort to undertake such a re-evaluation the second draft employed the just war criteria to the use of nuclear weapons to arrive at a position of virtual nuclear pacifism, on which it was believed both the just war and pacifist traditions could converge. Counter-population warfare was, of course, rejected as clearly contrary to the condemnation voiced by Vatican II and modern popes against indiscriminate acts of destruction. The draft acknowledged that Vatican II's condemnation referred to direct attacks on civilians which clearly violated the principle of non-combatant immunity. The Council did not address situations in which some just war moralists would use the traditional "double effect" reasoning to justify counterforce nuclear strikes, in which civilian casualties were accepted as the unintended and indirect result of attacks on military installations. Here the draft made a significant move in rejecting such use of the double effect principle:

Aware of the controverted nature of the issue, we nonetheless feel obliged as a matter of practical moral guidance to register our opposition to a policy of attacking targets which lie so close to concentrations of population that destruction of the target would devastate the nearby population centers. The relevant moral principle in this case is the disproportionate damage which would be done to human life. We are moved to specify this practical moral conclusion because recent policy proposals seek to justify attacks on militarily related industries situated in populated areas.[13]

Thus, while not rejecting all use of "double effect" reasoning, even in cases of armed violence, the draft clearly used the principle of proportionality to reject it as applicable to the case of nuclear warfare. In so doing, the draft made the significant move of seeking to link the traditional condemnation of attacks upon civilians with a rejection of the current development of strategies for fighting "limited" or counterforce nuclear war.

In regard to the first use of nuclear weapons the draft stated: "We do not perceive any situation in which the deliberate initiation of nuclear war, on however restricted a scale, can be morally justified. Non-nuclear attacks by another state must be resisted by other than nuclear means."[14] This constituted a rejection of the stated defense policy of the United States and

NATO that smaller "tactical" nuclear weapons would be used on a "limited scale" to repel an overwhelming conventional attack in Europe. In its rejection of the first use of nuclear weapons, the draft had adopted the conception of the absolute need to maintain the strongest barriers against any move toward nuclear war, as had been expressed in the 1979 testimony of Cardinal Krol written by Father Bryan Hehir. The draft argued that discussion should not be limited to the size and numbers of weapons to be employed in any nuclear exchange, but must also deal with the psychological significance of moving to the nuclear level of warfare. Such a move would place us in a world of which we have neither experience nor any clear conception of how to continue any control of events.[15]

This position expressed the conviction of the drafting committee that any use of nuclear weapons posed an unjustifiable risk of escalation into all-out nuclear war. On the basis of the teaching of Vatican II and modern popes, however, the committee could not state that Catholic moral teaching absolutely forbade any use of nuclear weapons under any circumstances. Yet they wished to reject the thinking of those moralists who argued for the theoretical possibility of a limited use of nuclear weapons within the bounds of discrimination and proportionality as part of a "counterforce" war strategy. They thus opted for stressing the creation of "barriers" to the use of nuclear weapons by stating their studied conclusion that there is no rational moral justification for such a move. This conviction was clearly set forth in the second draft's evaluation of the concept of "limited nuclear war."[16]

The document asserted that the only question to be addressed was the *real* possibility of a truly limited nuclear exchange and not the *theoretical* possibility of such an occurrence. The pastoral questioned the validity of using the word "limited" to describe any real situation that would exist in the event of nuclear war. It was maintained that the technical literature on the subject and the testimony of public officials did not refute the charges of the critics of counterforce strategy that any nuclear exchange could not be kept limited. The draft cited a study conducted by a commission of the Pontifical Academy of Sciences which had concluded that the medical aspects of any

significant nuclear exchange made absurd any talk of winning
or surviving a nuclear war. The pontifical commission had also
argued that any counterforce war which only directly attacked
military targets would still require the use of so many nuclear
weapons that radiation and other effects would still devastate
the majority of a nation's population. This led John Paul II to
conclude that the only course left to humanity was the reduction and eventual elimination of such weapons. The draft joined
in this conclusion that the moral imperative of the present was
the rejection of nuclear war as in any way morally tolerable.
The second draft of the pastoral sought to translate this conclusion into an ethical norm and state a definite *no* to nuclear
war.[17]

Having rejected the use of nuclear weapons, the draft moved
to consider the question of deterrence, where it acknowledged
most of the present debate is centered. The draft in effect adopted
the basic stance toward nuclear deterrence which was set forth
in the 1979 testimony of Cardinal Krol. The document recalled
that in Krol's Senate testimony and in the 1976 statement of
the NCCB, the bishops had gone on record as affirming that it
was immoral to threaten what one cannot morally do, and that
the declared intent of United States and Soviet deterrence policy was to engage in nuclear warfare, including massive counter-
city warfare, and that this was totally immoral. Therefore, the
draft was clear in stating that its rejection of the use and actual
intent to use nuclear weapons was in direct contradiction with
essential features of the defense policies of the superpowers.[18]

Yet the draft also affirmed the distinction made in the Krol
testimony between possession of nuclear weapons and the intent to use them. It cited the message of John Paul II to the
United Nations Special Session on Disarmament in which the
Pope termed nuclear deterrence morally acceptable within the
context of serious attempts to diffuse the present state of international tension and to move toward disarmament.[19] Many
had interpreted the Pope's statement as an acceptance of present deterrence policies. The draft, however, stressed that such
an interpretation was erroneous. The document maintained
that the Pope had made it clear that the present structure of
nuclear deterrence was not a safe way to preserve peace, and

that the development of nuclear weapons and even their possession must be eliminated if the world is to escape a suicidal holocaust. In the same manner, the draft presented the bishops as tolerating nuclear deterrence as a concession to the present international *status quo* and the stated intentions of government officials to be interested in arms reduction. Yet the bishops' toleration of the continued *possession* of nuclear weapons was premised upon the rejection of any intent to use them or threaten their use, and even the possession of these weapons was to be tolerated only as an *interim* measure to refrain from destabilizing international relations while negotiations were in progress for their elimination.[20]

Thus, the draft's conditional toleration of continued possession of nuclear weapons served to create a mandate and a basis for examining the direction of United States policy in this area. For many bishops, as well as other Catholic leaders in the debates on war and peace, the evaluation of the moral acceptability of the continued possession of nuclear weapons was directly linked to their assessment of the goals of American foreign policy and the sincerity of the government in seeking to eliminate these weapons. Differences over this evaluation would continue to be at the heart of debates over nuclear deterrence both within and without the episcopal conference.[21] The second draft continued the implied threat of the 1979 Krol testimony that if the bishops decided that the government was not seriously pursuing disarmament negotiations, they would have to reject the morality of even possessing nuclear weapons. This threat was strengthened in the concluding section of the draft which addressed pastoral admonitions to different groups of people. In the section addressed to Catholics working in industries producing nuclear weapons, the draft stated that because the bishops have conditionally allowed possession of nuclear weapons, they cannot *at this time* require the resignation of Catholics from such employment. The document warned, however, that if the bishops changed their position on the possession of nuclear weapons, they would also have to condemn any involvement in their production.[22]

The draft specifically warned that toleration of the present nuclear arsenal was not to be construed as toleration for continued development of new weapons, especially those designed for a "first strike" capability.[23] Also the document rejected any defense strategies aimed at developing nuclear war-fighting capabilities, or any policies which would make the transition from conventional to nuclear weapons more likely. Rather, the draft's toleration was envisioned as a call to use the present time to pursue the goals of: bilateral agreements halting the testing and development of new weapons; reduction in the present arsenals; a comprehensive test ban treaty; strengthening controls to avoid inadvertent or unauthorized use of nuclear weapons; eventual elimination of nuclear weapons; and reductions in conventional forces. This last object was also stressed, so as not to have the document's concentration on the nuclear question to be used as a tool in "making the world safe for conventional war."[24]

Two other areas treated by the second draft of the pastoral which are of particular relevance to the issues and arguments being treated here were the superpower rivalry and the linkage of the issues of war and world development.

The draft specifically called upon the government of the United States to take unilateral initiatives in seeking to reduce political tensions with the Soviet Union and to initiate serious arms reductions. It was stressed that the bishops did not wish to be associated with calls for unilateral disarmament. Rather, unilateral initiatives were defined as carefully chosen policy steps designed to induce the Soviet Union to make a reciprocal response. If the Soviets did not respond, the United States would not be bound by the steps it had taken.[25]

In this regard, an important aspect of the draft was its attempt to view American-Soviet relations within the context of world conditions and the need of the world to develop international co-operation and structures commensurate with its spiritual unity and practical interdependence. The document stated that the bishops did not deny that the Soviet Union constituted a threat to the United States. It did, however, charge that a great danger was posed by those who argued that the only way to meet that threat was militarily and who were excessively preoccupied with the imputed irrationality of Soviet policy, seeing it as insanely striving for world conquest.

The attitude expressed in the draft was neither to deny the Soviet threat nor to engage in a distorted anti-Sovietism. Rather, a third view was preferred which concentrated on the mutual interests of both sides on which agreements could be made that would free the world from the threat of nuclear destruction. This required a willingness to see the other as potentially more than an adversary, and the draft stressed the need for the United States to seek maximum political engagement where mutual interests could be constructively dealt with.[26]

The internationalist ideals which the bishops continued to hold to were also given expression in the second draft's linkage of the issue of war with the issue of world development. The document cited John Paul II, who in referring to the chasm of living standards between the industrialized nations of both the East and West and those of the so-called "developing" countries, had stated that the problem was so widespread that it called into question the basic financial, monetary, production, commercial, and political structures which support the world economy. The draft contended, along with the Pope, that the present structure of the world economy was proving incapable of remedying the injustices of the past or meeting the challanges and ethical demands of the present. The document lamented that the East-West rivalry ignored this moral question, which rivaled the nuclear one in human significance. Both superpowers were charged with failing seriously to address this question which directly determined the fate of most of the world's population.[27]

In regard to this issue of world development, the draft also directed specific criticism at the United States. It contended that the ability of the United States to act in multilateral cooperation for reform of the world economy should not be subordinated to strategies of countering Soviet policy. Yet the present American posture toward the concerns of the so-called "Third World" was judged to be at least minimalist and even obstructionist. The second draft did not develop this criticism, nor did it attempt an analysis or judgment of the reasons behind American failure to work for world economic and political justice.

This criticism of the United States was expressive of the document's general tone of not wanting to place the bishops in a position of simply taking sides within the ideological conflict of East and West. The draft took the course of criticizing both superpowers for the threat their conflict posed to the world and their neglect of the pressing problems of world development. The specific criticism of the United States seemed in line with previous statements of the bishops in aiming their concerns most specifically at the responsibility of their own government. The criticism of the nation's failure to foster the creation of international co-operation and strengthening the role of international institutions was also an expression of adherence to the strong stress on international institutions in papal teaching. To this end the document stressed that the United States must aid the expansion and strengthening of the role of the United Nations. The document also recognized the controversy over the precise relationship between the arms race and world development, but stressed the bishops' continued insistence that the continuance of the arms race would only increase the toll taken by world poverty.[28]

Thus, the second draft of the proposed pastoral consolidated and strengthened positions the bishops had articulated in the late seventies. Perhaps the most significant feature of this document's development of episcopal teaching was that it used just war criteria to commit the bishops to a position of virtual nuclear pacifism, while affirming an ethical pluralism of both just war and pacifist traditions as valid positions of conscience for Catholics. Yet this document also continued and even heightened tensions present in the previous position statements of the NCCB.

The draft's position on the question of deterrence was in substance a reaffirmation of the 1979 Krol testimony before the Senate. Because of the casuistic distinction between the possession of nuclear weapons and the intent to use them, an immediate and total break between the bishops and their government over defense policies was avoided. The document's commitment to nuclear pacifism and its rejection of the deterrent threat of counter-population warfare, however, already put the bishops against essential elements of American defense doctrine. The conditional acceptance of possession of nuclear weapons also committed the bishops to monitor and evaluate American policy to judge whether or not the intentions and goals of the government were in fact moving to a position compatible with the moral principles expounded by the bishops.

Similarly, the censure of the American failure to promote reform of the world economy and of international institutions recalled earlier criticisms by USCC statements. Here too the implication was that the United States was not committed to those goals and ideals of a new international order which the bishops, in conformity with papal teaching, upheld as essential to world peace and development. These implications were not developed in the second draft, but would seem to be an essential part of the future evaluation of American policy to which the bishops' stated positions had in fact committed them. The warning given to Catholics working in the production of nuclear weapons, that they may be called upon to resign their positions, clearly implied that the bishops were open to a more critical and confrontational development of their stance toward government policies.

These implications were not lost on either the government or the leaders of the conflicting schools of American Catholic thought on war and peace. The Reagan administration had strong objections to the draft's stand on the use of nuclear weapons, especially its rejection of first use, as well as the strong language favoring a freeze in the development and deployment of nuclear weapons. Given that there was already a strong national movement for a nuclear freeze, the administration saw the bishops' pastoral heading in the direction of providing strong support to its political opponents. Without directly attacking the bishops, President Reagan himself led his administration in attacking the positions that the bishops seemed to be moving toward embracing.[29] The attention which the administration gave to the draft served to heighten the significance of the document in the public mind, which in turn only fostered the already growing Catholic debate over the pastoral. This debate drew into itself all of the schools of thought which had made up the Catholic debate on war and peace in the past twenty years.

THE DEBATE

Catholic realists could obviously be expected to be opposed to much of the development in episcopal teaching on nuclear weapons and deterrence. The second draft of the pastoral served to feed the growth of conservative groups organized to fight what they saw as an anti-capitalist, anti-American trend in the bishops' social teaching. Michael Novak, who in the sixties had appeared as more of a critic of American policies, re-emerged in the latter seventies as a major spokesman for American defense programs. He became one of the most vocal and prominent Catholic realists organizing opposition to the bishops through such groups as the American Catholic Committee, and the American Enterprise Institute, a Washington-based "think-tank" for which he is a staff member.[30] Other organizations prominent in opposing the bishops have been the Ethics and Public Policy Center, another Washington-based "think-tank" headed by Ernest Lefever, and the Catholic Center for Renewal, an offshoot of the Heritage Foundation.[31]

The most systematic and developed realist response to the second draft came from a man who had been one of the most prominent representatives of that school of thought within the Catholic community for the past twenty years, Dr. William V. O'Brien of Georgetown University. O'Brien testified before the Bernardin Committee in the drafting process prior to the November, 1982, discussion of the second draft. In the Spring issue of the *Washington Quarterly* (1982), and in an address before a Bishops and Scholars Colloquium held in Washington, D.C., the following September, O'Brien set forth his objections to the direction in which the bishops were apparently heading.

O'Brien's criticisms could generally be grouped around the major division of the just war criteria for evaluating the use of armed force: the *jus ad bellum*, or the just cause for resorting to war, and the *jus in bello*, or the limits of the use of force in war. O'Brien felt that the most serious lacuna in the bishops' position was a lack of attention to the *jus ad bellum*, that is, to the question of just cause. By this O'Brien meant that no discussion of the morality of American defense and deterrence policies could be adequate if it did not examine the actual threats faced by the United States and the justice of the American cause in the face of these threats. He argued that the bishops had never really addressed the question of whether there is a real threat of aggression against the United States and what it would mean if that threat were to be successfully realized. Consequently, O'Brien contended, there is no real just cause in the bishops' teaching to which their discussion of nuclear deterrence could be related. Eschewing recognition of an actual aggressor and the relative merits of conflicting "causes," the bishops had developed no real calculus of proportion in their evaluation and application of the just war criteria. O'Brien argued that in order to regain such a means of moral measurement it was essential for the bishops to begin with a more specific and in-depth analysis of the United States and the Soviet Union as societies and of their roles in fostering world peace. This evaluation was most crucial for O'Brien because he saw the bishops' nuclear pacifism as challenging the defense structure of the West, without ever seriously addressing the consequences.[32]

O'Brien did not specifically address the question of world economic development and the American role in it except in so far as he argued against those who would claim that the only threats faced by the United States were rooted in the problems of the world economy. He contended that the greatest threats faced by America and its allies and the greatest threat to the peace of the world came from the real intent of communist and other totalitarian regimes to extend their "Gulag societies." O'Brien argued that no amount of change in the world economic structure would eliminate this threat or the necessity to provide a military deterrent to it. Thus, he ridiculed as simplistic the assumption that money not put into the arms race would automatically go to world development and help to lessen the threat of war. Furthermore, O'Brien charged that the references of the bishops to American involvement in the arms race gave no realistic recognition to Soviet actions which necessitated American responses, and he charged that the bishops ignored what has actually been American leadership toward arms reduction in the face of a Soviet desire for strategic superiority.[33]

Thus O'Brien strongly argued that the debate over American defense policies must be re-grounded on the point which John Courtney Murray had earlier contended provided the context for viewing these questions, that is, the conflict the definition of which constitutes international relations today. It was the old question which some crudely put as "red or dead?" For O'Brien this question still had paramount significance. Its answer required an assessment of what practically constituted the cause of justice and freedom in the world today and what were the threats against it. Only by first answering this question, O'Brien argued, could there be the possibility of having the concrete sense of proportion to use just war principles to measure the moral means of making the right of self-defense a practically functional reality. Because, in his view, the bishops did not adequately address this political context of the issues of war and peace, their moral arguments became an abstract treatment of weapons systems without any grounding in a concrete sense of a just cause that is worth defending. He concluded that you cannot talk meaningfully of applying just war criteria, as the bishops attempt to do, without first being clear on the existence of a just cause.

O'Brien also assaulted the manner in which the bishops aplied *jus in bello* criteria to the use of nuclear weapons. The casuistic distinction employed by the bishops to sever the possession of nuclear weapons for deterrence purposes from the intent to use them O'Brien denounced as insane. He argued that if it is known that a nation considers its nuclear force as morally unusable, it thereby loses its power to deter, for the essense of deterrence is the certainty on the part of a potential adversary that the deterrent weapons will be used if necessary. The doubt that would exist in an adversary's mind by the mere possession of nuclear weapons would not, in O'Brien's view, constitute a deterrent.[34]

Furthermore, O'Brien was critical of the fact that the bishops would tolerate the possession of nuclear weapons designed for purely counter-city warfare (MAD) but reject any weapons development aimed at implementing a counterforce strategy. O'Brien argued that the bishops dismissed the concept of a counterforce nuclear deterrent and war strategy without an adequately justifying argument because of their *a priori* assumption that no use of nuclear weapons could be kept within moral limits. O'Brien contended that to dismiss any nuclear exchange as inherently disproportionate avoided the obligation inherent within the just war tradition to use *jus in bello* criteria to discern the degree of justifiable collateral civilian damage necessary to allow a functional self-defense. His reasoning here reflects his belief that to condemn all use of nuclear weapons as disproportionate would strip the United States of any real self-defense in a nuclear age. Therefore, granting the justice of the American cause, O'Brien's logic demanded that the *jus in bello* criteria must be interpreted to allow a degree of collateral damage commensurate with the requirements of conducting a counterforce nuclear war of defense. In this position, O'Brien was reiterating one of the concerns central to the realist perspective over the past two decades: you cannot grant the right of self-defense without making it morally functional in the actual conditions within which a war would have to be fought.[35]

In explaining the principle by which he would measure the "acceptable degree of collateral damage," O'Brien again reiterated his rejection of the use of the double effect, which the second draft also rejected in its application to the use of nuclear weapons. The draft used the principle of proportionality to reject as morally unacceptable the collateral damage from nuclear weapons, which some just war theorists had used the principle of double effect to justify. O'Brien, who over the past two decades had argued against the traditional interpretation of the principle of discrimination to enshrine non-combatant immunity in Catholic just war thought, also used the principle of proportionality to determine the morally acceptable degree of collateral damage. Thus it was somewhat ironic that after twenty years the American bishops finally followed O'Brien's insistence on using the principle of proportionality in assessing the issue of collateral damage but only to arrive at the opposite conclusion from his. O'Brien admitted that his use of the principle of proportionality to judge the acceptable degree of civilian damage in proportion to the importance of the military target to be attacked would probably allow a greater degree of civilian damage than would be allowed by most traditional applications of the double effect. Yet his justification was the insistence that his method of calculating morally acceptable civilian damage was the only one in accord with the military necessities inherent in the higher moral value of an adequate just defense.[36]

In addressing the bishops' contention that any nuclear exchange must be regarded as inherently disproportionate because of the inability to control its escalation, O'Brien called for trust in the ability of the United States and its NATO allies to work out the means of such control. O'Brien's act of faith in the intent and ability of the Western powers to work out a "controllable, limited" nuclear counterforce strategy may have seemed weak in the face of the technical testimony to the contrary. Yet such an act of faith was essential to O'Brien's commitment to preserving a morally functional and militarily viable defense in an age of nuclear confrontation.[37]

Thus in O'Brien's critique of the second draft, as representative of the Catholic realists' response, can be seen the consistent Americanist concerns of that school of thought. The chief demand of their arguments was to return the debate over issues of war and peace to its political context, rather than to focus on weapons systems. In effect, their demand was for an evaluation of the United States as a society and its role in the world over against the alternative of its chief competitor, the Soviet Union, and what significance the victory of each would have for the world and for the Church. Only with this question clearly settled, they contended, was there a context for evaluating the moral limits of what could be done in the defense of the West. By not rooting their moral teaching in this political context of the issues of war and peace, Catholic realists argued, the bishops became ensnared in an abstracted morality, which served anti-American interests and undermined the bishops' own civilization.

The pacifist response to the development of episcopal teaching was as predictable as that of the realists. As the most prominent veteran of Catholic pacifist thought, Gordon Zahn may well have summarized the feelings of many in his reflection on the bishops' proposed pastoral.

Zahn referred to the second draft as not a disaster, but rather a disappointment. Zahn had always been open to dialogue with

the institutional Church in the hope of moving it toward a
pacifist stance. He saw the proposed pastoral as paving the way
to an eventual total rejection of nuclear weapons by the bishops,
but as it stood, the document, in Zahn's view, still contained
fundamental contradictions. The bishops' skepticism of deterrence, Zahn said, contradicted their toleration of the continued
possession of deterrent nuclear weapons. In effect, from his own
contrary position Zahn charged the bishops with fuzzy thinking
in the same manner as did his realist opponents. For Zahn, the
real question concerning nuclear deterrence was not the abstract question of possession without the intent to use, but
rather the concrete question of the most probable and stated
use of these weapons. Given the stated intent of American
policies and the testimony of strategic experts, Zahn felt that
the bishops' talk of allowing possession without intent to use
was giving themselves permission to be absent from reality.[38]

Zahn charged that a central weakness of the proposed pastoral was its perspective. The bishops' concern to lessen the
danger of nuclear war, he argued, left them open to increasing
conventional military strength as a trade-off for nuclear disarmament. Zahn reasserted that modern conventional warfare
had also moved beyond the limits of traditional morality, and
that it was thus essential for the bishops to face the problem
of war itself, not just the nuclear threat.[39]

In more general reflections on the state of Catholic thought
on war and peace, Zahn noted the remarkable growth of pacifism within the Church in the twenty years since the publication of William Nagle's volume on the "state of the question."
Yet he felt that the criticisms he made in that book were still
valid in 1981. For too many Catholics war was still not an
issue. The most significant change in the past twenty years,
Zahn felt, was that Church teaching through recent popes,
Vatican II, and now the American bishops had brought the
issue of war into open debate in the Church. Yet he hastened
to add that one should not overestimate the degree to which
Church leaders have matched their words with actions.[40]

At the heart of the Church's failure to face fully the issue of
war Zahn placed its continued acceptance of the just war tradition. For Zahn, the greatest sign of the irrelevancy of this

tradition continued to be the gulf between those who discuss the just war ethic and its application and those who actually plan and fight wars. He charged that while ethicians lavish time and energy on balancing military necessity and moral obligation, the tragic truth is that most Catholics will do as they are ordered to do in any case. Zahn argued that the exceptions or allowances made by just war thinkers to the state have historically been used to accommodate whatever was currently judged a military necessity. To tolerate possession of nuclear weapons while rejecting the intent to use, Zahn argued, was only the latest episode in this long line of moral concessions.[41]

Zahn insisted that the Church must focus on the thrust of the Christian message rather than on the academic debate over details of its substance, such as were being conducted over the bishops' pastoral. In the end, he argued, any church committed to the New Testament must adopt a public stance which would never encourage, support, or approve war, and would attempt to persuade its members to avoid co-operation with the preparation for or conduct of war.[42]

In Zahn's reaction to the proposed pastoral were expressed the concerns which had marked the mainline development of Catholic pacifism over the previous two decades. The primary question was not the defense of the West but adherence to the Gospel's mandate of peace, within a worldview hostile to the modern state and the ideological options offered by the current shape of international conflict.

Besides the reiteration of the basic tenets of the realist and pacifist schools of thought given by their chief spokesmen, there were also those who sought to articulate a middle ground, which endorsed the bishops' stance of nuclear pacifism and their desire to maintain an ethical pluralism in which Catholics could morally hold to both the just war and pacifist traditions. Several features of the thinking of representatives of this point of view should be examined here, so as to see the type of interpretations given to the bishops' teaching by some of its major supporters.

The contribution of Father J. Bryan Hehir to the development of the position on the possession and use of nuclear weapons adopted in the testimony of Cardinal Krol, and then in the second draft of the pastoral, has already been mentioned. As a chief staff person for the Bernardin committee Hehir helped to write the second draft and would have considerable impact in its revision into its third and the final form. A significant nuance on Hehir's position was proposed in 1982 by Father David Hollenbach, S.J.. Hollenbach agreed with Hehir that the evidence all points to the moral certitude that it is not possible to talk meaningfully about a limited nuclear war. He urged that nuclear pacifism, rejecting any use of nuclear weapons, should become a firm part of Catholic teaching.[43]

On the question of deterrence, Hollenbach recognized the dissatisfaction which the position articulated in the Krol testimony and the pastoral draft had elicited from both realists and pacifists. The bishops' position violated the basic premise of each school of thought: the total rejection of nuclear weapons (pacifists) and the maintenance of a credible deterrent (realists). Hollenbach sought to place the question on a different level.

He argued that the question of deterrence cannot be settled in the abstract; that is, it is not possible to reach an adequate judgment on the morality of deterrence as a general concept. For Hollenbach the real question was the concrete judgment of whether or not specific strategic options will make the world safer from the outbreak of nuclear war. In effect, he argued that deterrence in the abstract does not exist. There are only specific defense postures involving particular weapons systems and targeting doctrines. In Hollenbach's view the factor which makes the intention behind a particular deterrence policy distinguishable from an intention to use nuclear weapons is a reasoned judgment that the policy in question will actually deter the outbreak of nuclear hostilities. To go ahead with a policy which increased the likelihood or danger of war is to *intend* this outcome. The opposite, he argued, is also true. The moral judgment on the intent behind deterrence policies is therefore inseparable, in Hollenbach's view, from an evaluation of the reasonably predictable outcome of those policies. By focusing on the concrete evaluation of the progress which various strategic policies could make toward preserving peace and fostering disarmament, Hollenbach argued, the intellectual and moral deadlock being produced by the present arguments over deterrence as an abstract concept could be broken.[44]

Hollenbach thought his position was, at least in part, implicit in the stance taken in the Krol testimony and the proposed pastoral. Making the moral legitimacy of the American possession of nuclear weapons for deterrence contingent upon progress in arms reduction negotiations did serve to focus the question on the concrete level which Hollenbach advocated. The threat, however, to reject all possession of these weapons in the event of failure to progress in arms reduction was, in Hollenbach's view, to retreat back again to the abstract level. He argued that the collapse of arms reduction talks should be the occasion not to condemn possession of nuclear weapons, but rather to condemn the policies and attitudes which resulted in the breakdown. Thus the focus of moral judgment would be kept on concrete policies and actions, not on abstract ideas about possession. In this Hollenbach saw himself as doing with the issue of nuclear deterrence what John Courtney Murray had done with the issue of religious liberty—insisting that moral judgments cannot be made unhistorically.[45]

The real danger of the present, Hollenbach feared, was that peoples' judgments about the use of nuclear weapons will be shaped by their feelings about deterrence. Thus, in order to justify the American nuclear deterrence, which they saw threatened by the bishops' possible rejection of possession, many people would move to justify the use of these weapons. Hollenbach felt that his approach could avoid this problem by its focus on specific policies and not the abstract concept of deterrence, which had become the symbolic depository of a wide range of emotions concerning the defense of the United States.[46]

It is important to see some implications of the convergence and divergence of Hollenbach with the position on deterrence found in the Krol testimony and the proposed pastoral. The fear expressed by Catholic realists such as O'Brien was that the return of the bishops to what Hollenbach called the abstract level of judgment, and rejecting all possession of nuclear weapons as a result of insufficient progress in arms negotiations, would produce a radical break between the Church and the state, and remove Catholics from participation in the American defense system. In effect, it would sever the historical alliance of Catholicism and Americanism. This break the realists sought above all to avoid and the radical pacifists to welcome.

In part Hollenbach seems to have offered his own approach as a means of avoiding the emotionally charged controversy which the threat of such a break engendered. In moving to the concrete evaluation of specific defense policies he seems to have hoped to provide a ground on which both just war thinkers and pacifists could enter the public policy debate and work to lessen the chances of nuclear war, without going into ecclesiastical or social schism as a result of a fight over the rejection of nuclear deterrence in itself.

Yet the concrete focus on specific policies, which Hollenbach calls for, entails the necessity of judging the values, intentions, and goals which shape the American role in the world and give birth to specific defense strategies. The necessity of making the same judgment is also implied in the bishops' conditional toleration of the possession of nuclear weapons. Thus Hollenbach and the bishops converge in an approach which, if followed through, could still result in the break between Church and state which Hollenbach seemed to think was avoidable. Such a possible break would then occur, not from a debate over abstract principles and concepts such as deterrence or possession of nuclear weapons, but from a quite specific judgment on the commitments and values which determine the American posture toward disarmament, defense, and world development. In effect the approach clearly called for by Hollenbach and implied in the bishops' stance would lead the bishops to confront more directly the "political context" and the elements making up the "American cause," which both realists and radical pacifists had continuously argued were at the starting point of considering issues of war and peace.

Given the criteria of judgment adopted by the bishops and their rejection of essential elements of American defense policies, it seemed quite possible that, if the bishops took the next step in evaluating American goals and policies, they could arrive at a quite unfavorable judgment. This is not to say that a radically harsh judgment on America's role in the world would be inevitable. For there were those whose agreement with the bishops' nuclear pacifism was clearly joined to a strongly "Americanist" view of the contemporary global crisis. These Catholics reflected an outlook similar to that expressed by earlier critics of American nuclear policy such as Justus George Lawler. While rejecting the attitude of realists like O'Brien toward American defense policies, they would still concur with his basic evaluation of the ideological conflict determining international relations and the necessity of assuring the success of those interests and way of life represented by the United States.

A clear example of this outlook was given by Father Francis X. Winters, S.J., who emerged in the debates over the proposed pastoral as a critic of realist attacks on the document by people such as Novak and O'Brien. Winters applauded the bishops' casuistic distinction between possession of nuclear weapons and the intent to use, and argued that the doubt which even mere possession places in the mind of a potential adversary is sufficient to deter nuclear aggression. He also rejected the traditional reliance on the American nuclear threat as essential to the defense of Europe. Citing the change of opinion by top American strategists such as Henry Kissinger and Robert McNamara, Winters argued that NATO could reject the first use of nuclear weapons and that the Europeans could build a sufficient conventional deterrent.[47] Winters endorsed the stance of nuclear pacifism, contending that the technical evidence overwhelmingly showed that a nuclear war could not be kept limited, and would in fact violate the just war criteria of competent authority, since the government involved would be destroyed, leaving no competent authority to control or end the war.[48]

Yet Winters conceded that those realists gathered around the banner "better dead than red" were correct in grasping that the present struggle over military strategy is at root a controversy over the means adequate to engage in a necessary confrontation with the Soviet Union. He contended that the struggle between the Soviet vision of the emerging world and our own was an inescapable struggle between incompatible civilizations. The question vexing the American Church, in Winters' view, was the choice of the appropriate military and political strategy for pursuing this struggle. Winters saw himself as in accord with the view of John Courtney Murray that a struggle between civilizations, such as that represented in the super-power rivalry, cannot be won by brute force. He argued that we must seek the "high moral ground" of the shapers of our civilization, which Winters saw as fundamentally Christian, and hold that, while the right to armed defense is inviolate, it is also limited. The nuclear strategy which the bishops rejected, Winters contended, only violated those limits in mimicry of our adversaries. Thus, while Winters would allow and even welcome the dissension which the bishops' stance would evoke, he envisioned this dissension as part of the process of calling the American people to be true to their own moral tradition, and not part of a break between the Church and the stated foreign policy goals of the United States.[49]

Thus, for some elements, the endorsement of the bishops' attempt to chart a middle ground between pacifists and realists, and even acceptance of the bishops' nuclear pacifism, was combined with a reaffirmation of America's struggle against communism and the need to uphold American leadership in the world. The Catholic Americanism, which over the past twenty years expressed itself in both the realism of William O'Brien and the nuclear pacifism of Justus George Lawler, continued to breed its dual expressions in a continuing debate over the moral means with which to defend the cause of American and Western civilization.

Thus, the second draft of the pastoral provided a focus on which the schools of thought which made up the American Catholic debate on war and peace converged to recapitulate the major themes which had demarcated their conflicting perspectives for the previous twenty years. The proposed pastoral served to center that debate around the bishops' attempt to grapple with the moral quality of American nuclear policy and the consequent implications for America's role in the furtherance of world peace. The bishops' discussion of the second draft at their November, 1982, meeting revealed that there was disagreement among the bishops over whether the wording of the document clearly ruled out all retaliatory use of nuclear weapons. Yet the strong public impression of the document was that of being at odds with the government's nuclear defense policies. Even though the bishops eschewed identification with any particular nuclear freeze movement, the draft's strong rejection of further nuclear arms development (especially "first strike" weapons) was credited by many as contributing to the administration's difficulty in getting funding for the MX missile.[50] This critical thrust of the second draft galvanized conservative opposition to effect changes in the third draft to be prepared for the special NCCB meeting in May. The subsequent changes made in this third draft served to give the public impression of the bishops backing off from the strong positions in the second draft. This in turn would lead to a concerted effort of many of the bishops who had initially pushed for the pastoral to strengthen the final document's opposition to the development or use of nuclear weapons. The changes that occurred in the third and final drafts of the pastoral evidenced the ebb and flow of the debate within the hierarchy and wider Catholic community, as the bishops arrived at their present official consensus on the issues of war and peace.

THE THIRD DRAFT

Prior to the formulation of the third draft two significant consultations took place. The first was between the drafting committee and members of the Reagan administration. The administration wanted to explain and defend American nuclear policy, and claimed that the bishops were mistaken in believing that it was U.S. policy to target Soviet civilian populations. Yet the consultation made clear the fact that many military targets were located in or near cities. The effect of this consultation was to convince the members of the drafting committee that they were correct in their original assessment that the human effects of a counterforce nuclear exchange would be indistinguishable from those of an all-out nuclear war.[51] Thus, the consultation would serve to strengthen the committee's resolve to speak against any use of nuclear weapons.

The second consultation held at the Vatican involved representatives of the American bishops (Archbishop John Roach and Cardinal Bernardin), Vatican officials, and bishops from

France, Germany, Great Britain, Belgium, Italy, and the Netherlands.[52] There was apparent concern among the German and French bishops that the American bishops' position on first use of nuclear weapons could have a negative impact on NATO. The Vatican also seemed concerned to foster communication and consensus among national hierarchies in dealing with such sensitive issues. While some speculated that the Vatican meeting was designed to blunt the thrust of the American pastoral, the U.S. bishops attending it described the experience as very cordial and collegial.

The major impact which this consultation had on the pastoral was to impress upon the American bishops the need to be clearer on the levels of moral authority in the document's pronouncements. The bishops had to be clear on what was a binding principle of Catholic moral teaching and what was a prudential application of that teaching by the American bishops. Thus, the bishops could not commit Catholic teaching on specific questions such as the actual or deterrent use of nuclear weapons to positions beyond those contained in the statements of Vatican II and John Paul II. Since universal Church teaching did not explicitly reject *all* retaliatory use of nuclear weapons, and John Paul II's 1982 U.N. address conditionally accepted deterrence as a stage in movement toward disarmament, these positions would serve as limits within which the bishops would continue to clarify their own teaching. When the time came to formulate the third draft, the influence of the Vatican consultation was evident in the introduction, which stated that the positions set forth in the document would be of varying degrees of moral authority.[53]

Other changes made in the third draft that are pertinent to this study reflected the desire of the drafting committee to produce a more "centrist" document that did three things: addressed the conservative criticism that arose in response to the second draft;[54] clearly respected the guidelines discussed at the Vatican consultation; and reflected what they saw as the general consensus of the bishops. One of the most significant of these changes was ironically seen by the committee as fairly minor. Committee member Bishop O'Connor, of the military ordinariate, objected to the second draft's call for a *halt* to the pro-

duction and development of new nuclear weapons systems. His
position reflected the arguments of realists that smaller nuclear
weapons could be produced and used in a manner that was both
discriminate and proportionate. He echoed conservative fears
that the bishops' use of language calling for a halt to new
weapons production would add force to the current nuclear
freeze movement in the country, and thus impair U.S. defense
capabilities. To preserve its internal consensus the committee
agreed to change the word *halt* to the less absolute *curb*. Yet
precisely because of the national media's attention to the nuclear freeze movement, particular attention was given to any
language in the proposed pastoral which related to this issue.
Consequently, this change of words would be picked up by the
news media as signalling a significant shift in position away
from the second draft's strong stance against the continued
production and development of nuclear weapons. Because of
this media attention, and the fact that a significant number of
bishops had individually given support to the nuclear freeze
movement, the "curb versus halt" question would become the
issue most symbolic of the debate over the final form of the
pastoral. For it was seen to symbolize the bishops' fundamental
attitude toward the nuclear arms race.[55]

A significant change was also made in the section relating
to the evaluative criteria of the just war teaching, which reflected
the realist criticism that the bishops were concentrating on the
destructiveness of weapons systems without adequate concern
for the causes at stake. The section entitled "Comparative Justice" was added. Comparative justice, however, is not a traditional category of just war teaching. It was actually a redundant
expression of the need for a just cause, but done in such a way
as to allow a favorable comparison of the American political
system over against non-democratic regimes. The section began
with: "Questions concerning the *means* of waging war today,
particularly in view of the destructive potential of weapons,
have tended to override questions concerning the comparative
justice of the positions of respective adversaries." The section
ended with the statement: "The facts simply do not support the
comparisons made at times, even in our own society, between
our way of life, in which most basic human rights are at least

recognized, even if they are not always adequately supported, and those totalitarian and tyrannical regimes in which such rights are either denied or systematically suppressed."[56]

Regarding the use of nuclear weapons, the third draft retained the strong condemnation of counter-population warfare, but softened the section on the initiation of nuclear war. The third draft made clearer that the bishops' rejection of first use of nuclear weapons was a prudential application of principle and not an absolute binding moral principle like non-combatant immunity. More importantly, the language of the section was softened. Whereas the second draft said that the bishops saw no situation in which the initiation of nuclear war could be justified, the third draft stated: "We abhor the concept of initiating nuclear war on however restricted a scale."[57] This revised section also acknowledged that NATO would need time to revise its defense structure to move away from any reliance upon nuclear weapons to deter conventional aggression. The section on limited nuclear war, however, was strengthened by the addition of a mentioning of the just war criteria of a reasonable hope of success in bringing about justice and peace. The draft questioned whether the use of nuclear weapons offered such a hope. The draft's challenging of the rationality of the concept of "limited" nuclear war was also clearly presented as a prudential judgment of the bishops, but it placed a heavy burden of proof on those who would contend that just and limited nuclear war was possible.[58] Thus, while the third draft strengthened the questioning of the concept of limited nuclear war, its change of wording on first use would be viewed by many as a serious weakening of this section of the pastoral. Together with the dispute over "curb versus halt," this change of wording would be a central part of the debate over the whole tone and thrust of the document.

In treating the question of deterrence the third draft mentioned the testimony of administration officials, and quoted both National Security Advisor William Clark and Secretary of Defense Caspar Weinberger to the effect that United States policy is not to intentionally target civilians. Yet the draft also noted that the counterforce targeting policy of the U.S. included 60 "military" targets in Moscow alone, and 40,000 "military" targets throughout the Soviet Union that had been designated for possible nuclear strikes. The draft contended that deterrence policy must be subject to the principle of proportionality as well as discrimination, and that the administration's own testimony showed that any significant counterforce strike would have virtually the same effect on civilians as indiscriminate nuclear war. The draft also stated that administration sources had admitted that part of the deterrent threat was the willingness to launch massive nuclear strikes in retaliation for such an attack on the U.S. Besides questioning the proportionality of counterforce attacks, the draft expressed alarm that counterforce targeting policies were often linked with the notion that nuclear war could be subject to precise and rational limits. This thinking only increased the danger of war.[59]

The draft stated that because of these considerations, and in light of John Paul II's evaluation of deterrence, the bishops' prudential judgment was that nuclear deterrence could only be given a strictly conditional acceptance. The third draft also repeated the three criteria listed in the second draft for evaluating the continued toleration of nuclear deterrence: 1) the development of nuclear war-fighting strategies is not acceptable; 2) the quest for "superiority" in nuclear weapons must be resisted; 3) each proposed addition or change in nuclear arsenals or defense doctrine must be evaluated as to their effect on fostering movement toward disarmament.[60] The language here was somewhat strengthened in that, whereas the second draft said the development of nuclear war-fighting strategies "must be resisted," the third draft said that they "are not acceptable."

The conditional acceptance of deterrence in the third draft was not different in substance from the conditional acceptance of the second draft. Yet the third draft created a significant difference in tone by drastically curtailing the second draft's reference to the 1976 NCCB condemnation of the threat to attack civil populations, and the 1979 Krol testimony on deterrence. The third draft made reference to these earlier statements without specifying their content. This was apparently to avoid charges that the bishops contradicted themselves in tolerating something they had declared to be immoral: the *threat* to use nuclear weapons in an indiscriminate or disproportionate manner. Also, since the Pope had given conditional acceptance to the deterrence system, the reiteration of the condemnation of the threat underlying nuclear deterrence could be seen as at odds with this position.[61] Yet this change, designed to make the bishops look more consistent, would be interpreted by proponents of a strong anti-nuclear stance as the inconsistency of the bishops backing off from their earlier stronger statements against the morality of nuclear deterrence. The deletion of the Krol testimony also served to soften the threat that the bishops could renounce their toleration of the possession of nuclear weapons if the government did not seriously pursue disarmament negotiations. This was also reflected in the section on pastoral guidance, which dropped the second draft's warning that the bishops could, in the future, require Catholics working in the production of nuclear weapons to remove themselves from such employment. This was replaced with: "Those who in conscience decide they should no longer be associated with defense activities should find support in the Catholic community. Those who remain in these industries should find in the Church guidance and support for the on-going evaluation of their work."[62]

The spirit of the changes made in the third draft was also evident in the section on the superpower relationship. The third draft sought to avoid criticism that the second draft was not strong enough in recognizing the Soviet threat or in giving credit to the greater political freedom of the United States. The section was thus expanded with statements acknowledging the depth of ideological conflict between East and West, and, while acknowledging failures in American society, included the paragraph:

A glory of the United States is the range of political freedom its system permits us. We, as bishops, as Catholics, as citizens, exercise those freedoms in writing this letter, with its share of criticisms of our government. We have true freedom of religion, freedom of speech, and access to a free press. We do not imagine that we could exercise the same freedoms in contemporary Eastern Europe or the Soviet Union. Free people must always pay a proportionate price and run some risk—responsibly—to preserve their freedom.[63]

Yet this section also preserved the second draft's insistence that there were objective mutual interests which allowed both superpowers to work to eliminate the danger of nuclear war. This confidence was expressed in the statement: "To believe we are condemned in the future only to what has been the past of U.S.-Soviet relations is to underestimate both our human potential for creative diplomacy and God's action in our midst which can open the way to changes we could barely imagine."[64]

The third draft also continued the linkage of the issues of war and world development. It retained the second draft's insistence upon the need for world economic reform and the creation of a viable world authority. Despite the changes made in the section on U.S.-Soviet relations, the third draft also retained the criticism of the superpower rivalry as ignoring and exacerbating the poverty of much of the world's people. The paragraph in the second draft which referred to American policy toward working with international institutions for world development as "minimalist" and "obstructionist" was dropped. The second draft's insistence on American responsibility for leadership on this issue, however, was retained. The section entitled "Interdependence: From Fact to Policy," in which the internationalist orientation of modern Church teaching was developed, continued to serve as context and balance to the proposed pastoral's treatment of the superpower relationship.[65]

Thus, the changes in the third draft reflected both the impact of conservative American criticism of the second draft as well as the desire of the drafting committee to keep episcopal teaching clearly in line with the present position of papal teaching on nuclear deterrence. The changes in wording in the sections on the use of nuclear weapons and nuclear arms development had the effect of significantly altering the public perception of the whole tone and thrust of the document. Media scrutiny of any semantic change, especially the change of "halt" to "curb," helped bolster the impression of the bishops backing off from what was a more critical view of government arms policy contained in the second draft. This impression was further reinforced when conservative critics such as Michael Novak and administration spokesmen now began to speak favorably of the document. Whereas the second draft had been both praised and criticized as an endorsement of the nuclear freeze movement, the third draft was appearing as making peace with government policy. Perhaps typical of this reception was the *New York Times* headline: "Administration Hails New Draft of Arms Letter—Says Bishops 'Improved' the Nuclear Statement." People with the Reagan administration were claiming that the change of "halt" to "curb" was a rejection of the nuclear freeze movement and a vote of confidence for the administration's policies.[66]

To a great extent, this perception of the third draft was not entirely fair and represented an effort by the administration and Catholic conservatives to co-opt the pastoral's intepretation. While the changes of the third draft did serve to soften some of the proposed pastoral's mode of expression, they did not really alter the substantive positions of the second draft to the degree being claimed. This view was expressed in an NCCB press release given in the names of Archbishop John Roach and Cardinal Bernardin aimed at countering the public impression being formed of the third draft. Their statement claimed that changes in the third draft were the result of dialogue within the NCCB and with European bishops and Vatican officials and not the result of administration pressure. The statement stressed that they "could not accept any suggestion that there are relatively few and insignificant differences between U.S. policies and the policies advocated in the pastoral." Specific areas in which their statement claimed variance with government policy were on the first use of nuclear weapons, and the completion of the Comprehensive Test Ban Treaty. The two bishops also insisted that the change of "halt" to "curb" did not alter the bishops' insistence on an end to the arms race or their call for actual reductions of current arsenals.[67]

Yet, despite the Bernardin Committee's protestations, the damage had been done. The public impression formed of the third draft ensured that the special NCCB meeting in May 1983 would witness a fight to restore the stronger statements of the second draft. As the second draft was seen as rallying conservative and realist forces to blunt an episcopal confrontation with the government, the debate over the third draft would be viewed as an effort of nuclear pacifist bishops to "reclaim" the pastoral. Yet given the wide base of support for the

major changes made in Chicago, and the overwhelming support
for the final document, it seems evident that the final form of
the pastoral was the expression of a fairly consistent consensus
evolving among the hierarchy on the nuclear issue.

"THE CHALLENGE OF PEACE"—THE FINAL VERSION

The major changes made in Chicago in essence constituted
a return to the stronger language of the second draft against
the development and use of nuclear weapons. In the symbolic
"curb" versus "halt" issue, the bishops overwhelmingly voted
to reinstate "halt." Regarding the first use of nuclear weapons,
they returned to the wording of the second draft, declaring that
they could see no circumstance which would justify it. In the
just war section the bishops retained the criteria of comparative
justice, but rewrote it. The final version dropped the paragraph
supporting the superiority of the American system and turned
the whole comparative justice section into an admonition against
propagandistic attempts of nations to claim that "absolute justice is on their side."[68]

On the question of deterrence, the substantive expression of
the bishops' conditional toleration was not changed. Efforts to
reinstate the quotes of the 1976 condemnation of the threat to
attack civil populations, and the Krol testimony calling nuclear
deterrence an evil, were defeated. As a compromise, a quote
from the Krol testimony was incorporated in the final text
expressing unease with the system of nuclear deterrence because of the ever-present danger of war. But the previous quotes
referring to the toleration of deterrence as the lesser of two
evils (compared to the effects of immediate unilateral disarmament), and the threat that the bishops might eventually
have to condemn the possession of nuclear weapons, were rejected.[69] This decision seemed to clearly reflect the bishops' concern to not want to appear as moving beyond the stated limits
of the Pope's conditional acceptance of deterrence. To appear
consistent with this position, it was necessary to downplay
statements which could leave the bishops appearing as tolerating something they had declared to be objectively evil. This

desire to remain clearly within the present limits of universal church teaching was also reflected in the defeat of numerous amendments presented by bishops, such as Archbishop John Quinn of San Francisco, to absolutely condemn any use of nuclear weapons.[70] To have accepted such amendments would have gone beyond the strong prudential judgment of the bishops against the use of nuclear weapons to an absolute moral prohibition against any retaliatory use, which no conciliar or papal teaching had yet endorsed.

Thus, the changes in the final draft concerning the issues treated here committed the bishops to a position very close to outright nuclear pacifism. It is somewhat ironic that the wording changes in the final draft strengthened the bishops' rejection of the use of nuclear weapons, while they softened the expression of the conditional toleration of deterrence. In this, the pastoral heightened rather than resolved the consistent tension in modern Church teaching that arose from increasingly stronger stances against the use of nuclear weapons while tolerating a defense system premised on the threat of such usage.

Despite the addition of language in the third draft to give the pastoral a more critical assessment of the Soviet Union and give greater recognition to the political freedom of the U.S., the pastoral still stressed the call of modern papal teaching to move beyond the East-West conflict to look for common ground to secure peace. The third and final drafts continued the strong internationalism of papal teaching in stressing the need for a viable international authority and the necessity of linking the quest for security with co-operative world development. This theme was somewhat strengthened in the final version by the addition of an amendment calling for the United States to work immediately with the U.N. on a task force aimed at the eventual creation of a truly effective international authority.[71]

As already demonstrated, the pastoral's position on the use of nuclear weapons was clearly at variance with key elements in American and NATO nuclear policy. The conditional toleration of the deterrence system, however, avoided the major break with the American defense establishment that some realists had feared. Yet the continued evaluation of the course of

American arms policy, to which their conditional toleration committed the bishops, still had the potential for future confrontations. It remains to be seen how this will develop.

Many of the changes that occurred from the second draft to the final version of the pastoral, and the debates surrounding them, were in some ways more semantical than substantive. These debates over many of the changes in language represented the effort of the conflicting factions within the Catholic community to give to the pastoral a tone and interpretation that was compatible with its own views. This concern with language however, was not unfounded, for in large measure the tone of the language did reflect the attitude and direction of the bishops' thinking, and the moral climate in which they wished to have their peoples' consciences formed. The sense of this importance of the tone of the pastoral was reflected in the conclusion of the final version, offered as an amendment by Archbishop Hickey of Washington, D.C. This conclusion sought to make a final clear statement of what the bishops had intended as the heart of the pastoral's message:

What are we saying?.... In simple terms we are saying that good ends (defending one's country, protecting freedom, etc.) cannot justify immoral means (the use of weapons which kill indiscriminately and threaten whole societies). We fear that our world and nation are headed in the wrong direction.... The whole world must summon the moral courage and technical means to say no to nuclear conflict; no to weapons of mass destruction; no to an arms race which robs the poor and the vulnerable; and no to the moral danger of a nuclear age which places before mankind indefensible choices of constant terror or surrender.[72]

Thus, the pastoral letter, *The Challenge of Peace: God's Promise and Our Response*, gave expression to the current consensus of the American hierarchy on the major issues of war and peace. The debate surrounding its production also provided the most recent occasion for the conflicting schools of thought which divided American Catholic opinion on these issues to recapitulate the themes which have characterized them over the past twenty years. The production of the pastoral, in one sense, served to highlight the division among American Catholics on the issues of war and peace. Yet it was also an attempt

by the bishops to formulate a common ground of moral consensus to which they sought to summon the factions among
their people. This objective was particularly evident in a final
aspect of the pastoral which should be briefly treated here, that
is, the pastoral's endorsement and treatment of ethical pluralism on the issues of war and peace.

The emergence of this ethical pluralism is one of the chief
legacies of the American Catholic debates on war and peace in
the last twenty years. *The Challenge of Peace* is clearly a just
war document in the methodology it employs in its moral assessments. Yet the position of virtual nuclear pacifism embraced by the pastoral is premised on the acceptance of both
the just war tradition and pacifism as legitimate moral options
for Catholics. In espousing the value of both of these ethical
traditions the bishops followed the teaching of Vatican II and
their own previous endorsements of conscientious and selective
conscientious objection. Yet more than any previous episcopal
document, *The Challenge of Peace* sought to bring together the
value of both ethical traditions.[73]

In part, this acceptance of ethical pluralism was significant
as an attempt to enshrine institutionally the recognition of the
changes which have occurred in the past twenty years, as a
result of which the just war theory can no longer claim the
status of being the sole Catholic approach to the moral problem
of war. As such, the pastoral represented an effort of the bishops
to formulate a common ground on which the conflicting factions
within the Church could come together in a basic consensus
on certain fundamental issues of war and peace. Yet the attempt of the official Church to embrace such an ethical pluralism on issues of war and peace entails its own unique tensions.

One of the strongest and earliest advocates of ethical pluralism on the issues of war and peace was Father J. Bryan
Hehir. Because of his influence on the composition of the pastoral
letter, *The Challenge of Peace*, as well as other episcopal statements on issues of war and peace, it seems appropriate to focus
on his thought as representative of those who advocated the
acceptance of ethical pluralism in approaching these issues.

Hehir acknowledged that the basis of accepting such an ethical pluralism was the simple recognition that the situation of

Catholic thought on war and peace is much more complex than it was at the time of Pius XII. In fact, there are two significant moral traditions entrenched among American Catholics and competing for their adherence. Acceptance of ethical pluralism emerges as an attempt to accept this complexity of Catholic moral thought and sentiment. The question, Hehir argued, was whether such an ethical pluralism could be accepted within the institutional Church without becoming an intellectual and moral contradiction. That is, while on the level of the individual conscience these two positions are incompatible, is it a contradiction for the institutional Church to accept both traditions within the ecclesiastical community?[74]

In answering this question in favor of ethical pluralism, Hehir observed that pluralism is a fact of Catholic life, and not an undesirable fact. Yet Hehir recognized that pluralism presupposes limits, or an underlying consensus; otherwise it simply becomes anarchy. Both the just war and the pacifist traditions, Hehir argued, share a common vision of the sacredness of life and a refusal to allow any claim that war can have no limits. Hehir argued that this common vision provided an underlying consensus of value and concern which could support a pluralism of the two traditions, despite their differing moral methodologies and conclusions.[75]

The question of pluralism, however, involves more than the question of whether both just war advocates and pacifists can exist as members of the same ecclesial community of faith. Hehir argued that it also involves the question of the official stand of the Church as an institution in society. For the Church as an institution must function both on the level of forming individual conscience and also on the level of the public debate over social policy. Hehir acknowledged that it is much more complicated for the Church to take a public policy stance on the basis of its own internal pluralism of ethical opinion. One of the great challenges facing the Church in the present day, Hehir declared, is precisely this problem of formulating a public policy stance out of a pluralist setting within the Church.[76]

A further tension produced by the acceptance of ethical pluralism and the subsequent attempt to have the Church speak to the public policy debate on war and peace is the differing models of the Church's presence in society to which the just war and pacifist traditions have historically attached themselves. The pacifist tradition has historically been related to a sectarian conception of the Church. It has tended to assume a counter-cultural posture which presumed an inherent conflict between the obligations of discipleship and those of citizenship, and willingly accepted a small minority position for the Church as a consequence of this belief. In contrast, Roman Catholic theology has always assumed a model of church-state relations, which accepted the positive role of the state and the role of the Church as a co-operative and supportive institution within society.

Hehir acknowledged the inherent conflict between these two models of church-state relations as part of the conflict within the present pluralistic condition of American Catholic thought on war and peace. He also recognized the significant attempt within Catholic pacifism to combine pacifism with a non-sectarian model of the Church. Hehir was critical of such an attempt as unworkable. He considered Gordon Zahn a prime example of this effort to transform the Catholic Church into a pacifist "peace church." Hehir argued, however, that while Zahn praised the continuing cry for peace in modern papal teaching, the premise of the Church's relation to the state which is at the base of this teaching contradicts the anti-state views which are an essential part of Zahn's pacifism.[77]

The pluralism which Hehir advocates and which he saw presently existing was one in which the pacifist option was accepted for individuals within the Church, but in which the official Church itself did not take a pacifist stance. Thus Hehir rejected the opinion of those who saw the present ethical pluralism as a transitional stage away from the just war theory to a pacifist commitment by the Catholic Church.[78] The pluralism which presently exists would be for Hehir the desired condition of Catholic thought on war and peace, in which both the just war and the pacifist traditions are recognized and allowed to continue their creative tension within Catholic moral discourse. In the perspective of theologians like Hehir the virtual nuclear pacifism adopted in the proposed bishops' pastoral, which was itself based on just war reasoning, would constitute the ultimate blending of the just war and pacifist positions. This nuclear pacifism was offered as the new "bottom line" of Catholic moral teaching and the common ground on which the conflicting schools of thought among American Catholics could continue their debate on the issues of war and peace.

Yet, as the reaction of Catholic realists and pacifists showed, this "common ground," as presented in the pastoral draft, was not accepted by all. The ethical pluralism which many advocated did indeed seem an accurate description of the situation in American Catholic thought on war and peace at the beginning of the eighties. That pluralistic situation, however, came about as the result of the unprecedented growth of the pacifist position and radical critique of American global involvements. The rise of pacifism to such unprecedented prominence was reflective of a major reconsideration by significant elements within the Church of fundamental factors constitutive of the debate on war and peace: the ethical demands of the Gospel concerning the use of armed force; the qualitatively new situation created by nuclear weapons and even modern conventional warfare; the attitude to be assumed by the Church toward the modern state; and the compatibility of the goals and values of American policy with those requirements defined by the Church as essential to world peace and human development. As such this growth of American Catholic pacifism is symptomatic of a process of re-evaluation of assumptions which twenty years ago seemed beyond question. By the opening years of the eighties this process seemed far from spent, and had left American Catholic thought on war and peace issues divided between several radically different perspectives.

Those who advocated the acceptance of the present state of ethical pluralism as the permanent and proper condition of the Catholic approach to war and peace seemed to do so in the hope that these conflicting perspectives could be balanced and controlled within a basically just war framework, committed to nuclear pacifism, and allowing the option of total pacifism. There seemed to be the hope that this framework could provide the underlying consensus necessary to any true pluralism, and allow the debate on war and peace to continue without causing a significant rupture of the ecclesial community. Given the radical conflict on basic assumptions between the different schools of thought making up the American Catholic debate, this hope could also appear to many as illusory. The present state of ethical pluralism may not be, as some would hope, a transitional phase in the Catholic Church's evolution to pacifism, but neither is it clearly the beginning of a state of equilibrium between conflicting factions who are still able to work together, as others would hope. Given the depth of these divisions, the development of the Catholic community's stance toward issues of war and peace in the next decade, and its effects on Church unity and the relation of the Church to society, seems less certain than at any point in the history of American Catholicism. Perhaps the only thing that can be said with certainty of this development is that it will bear the mark of the ancient Chinese curse: "May you live in interesting times!"

NOTES

1. These factors are frequently referred to in the discussions of the arms issue in the early eighties. An example of their significance in Catholic analyses of the nuclear question may be found in David Hollenbach, S.J., "Nuclear Weapons and Nuclear War: The Shape of the Catholic Debate," *Theological Studies* 43 (December, 1982): 577–605.

2. Samples of episcopal statements in this period can be found in Robert Heyer, ed., *Nuclear Disarmament: Key Statements of Popes, Bishops, Councils and Churches* (New York: Paulist Press, 1982), pp. 112–163; also in George Weigel, *The Peace Bishops and the Arms Race* (Chicago: World without War Publications, 1982), pp. 5–18.

3. Ronald Kimelman, "Texas Bishop's Stand against Nuclear Arms Stirs Furor," *The Washington Post*, March 20, 1982, p. B5; Coleman McCarthy, "How The Peace Bishops Got That Way," *The Washington Post*, December 27, 1981, p. D5; Bishop Leroy Matthieson, "Nuclear Arms Buildup," in Heyer, *Nuclear Disarmament*, p. 155; "29 Bishops' Statement that Possession of Nuclear Weapons Is Immoral," in Heyer, *Nuclear Disarmament*, p. 182; Frank P. L. Sommerville, "Seattle Cleric is Willing to go to Jail for Nuclear Arms Protest," *The Baltimore Sun*, November 15, 1982, pp. D1, D3. Other statements of episcopal concern with the nuclear issue in 1981 and 1982 can be found in Castelli, *The Bishops and the Bomb: Waging Peace in a Nuclear Age* (Garden City, New York: Doubleday and Co., 1983), pp. 26–39, 61–64.

4. This concern on the part of many bishops with the attitudes and policies of the Reagan administration is cited in Castelli, *The Bishops and The Bomb*, pp. 14–15. This concern of the bishops, as well as other concerns cited in this chapter, were also evidenced in the author's own experience in working as an assistant to Auxiliary Bishop P. Francis Murphy of Baltimore on the third and final versions of the pastoral and at the Chicago NCCB meeting in May, 1983, for debate on the final text of the pastoral.

5. An effort in 1982 by episcopal members of the Catholic peace organization Pax Christi to enlist support among their fellow bishops for the nuclear freeze movement revealed that almost half of the American bishops gave their personal support for the idea.

6. Castelli, *The Bishops and The Bomb*, p. 16; also from personal interview with Bishop P. Francis Murphy of Baltimore.

7. The other bishops constituting the committee were: George Fulcher (Columbus), Thomas Gumbleton (Detroit), John O'Connor (military ordinariate), and Daniel Reilley (Norwich). The Leadership Conference of Women Religious and the Conference of Major Superiors of Men appointed Fr. Richard Warner, CSC, and Sr. Juliana Casey, IHM, as consultants. Bruce Martin Russet, professor of political science at Yale University, was engaged as the principal consultant for the letter. The committee staff were Fr. J. Bryan Hehir and Edward Doherty of the USCC.

8. The first draft of the pastoral was supposed to have been confidentially distributed to the bishops for comments to be incorporated into the second draft for debate at the November, 1982, NCCB meeting. The contents of this first draft, however, were leaked to the press even before the bishops saw it. Since the second draft contained the most complete initial expression of the positions that became the focus of debate around the pastoral letter, this treatment will concentrate on the second, third, and final versions of the text. Reference to specific content in the first draft will be made where it seems appropriate.

9. *The Challenge of Peace: God's Promise and Our Response, Origins* 12 (October 28, 1982): 307. This issue of *Origins* contains the full text of the second pastoral draft. Examples of Pope John Paul II's statements on war can be found in Heyer, *Nuclear Disarmament*, pp. 43–84. In his statements on war and peace John Paul II stands in continuity with the key ideas of previous papal teaching in condemning the arms race and the allocation of resources for war. Aspects of the Pope's teaching as it affected the development of the American episcopal position will be treated as reference is made to the Pope's teaching in the proposed pastoral.

10. *The Challenge of Peace*, p. 387.

11. Ibid., pp. 307–312.

12. Ibid., p. 312.

13. Ibid., p. 314. In rejecting counter-population warfare the draft also rejected retaliatory counter-population strikes in response to such an attack as irrational.

14. Ibid., p. 314.

15. Ibid., p. 315.

16. The first draft had stated: "If nuclear weapons may be used at all, they may be used only after they have been used against our country or our allies, and, even then, only in an extremely limited, discriminating manner against military targets." (First Draft of Pastoral issued confidentially to the Archbishops, p. 30.) This was dropped in favor of the stronger section of the second draft questioning the real possibility of limited nuclear war.

17. *The Challenge of Peace*, Origins 12 (October 12, 1982) (Second Draft), pp. 314–315. The conclusions of the Pontifical Commission were cited by the bishops as being corroborated by the conclusion of most other scientific bodies who studied the subject.

18. Ibid., p. 316.

19. This message was delivered at the U.N. by Vatican Secretary of State Cardinal Agostino Casaroli on June 11, 1982. This statement had a definite impact on the second draft in making it clear that the Pope had committed himself to conditionally accept the deterrence system for the present.

20. *The Challenge of Peace* (Second Draft), pp. 316–317.

21. An example of episcopal differences over this evaluation of American policy can be seen in the contrast of a letter by Cardinal Terence Cooke of New York to military chaplains, and a statement of Bishop Roger Mahoney of Stockton, California. Both were issued in December, 1981. Cooke's letter based the moral toleration of nuclear weapons on the conviction that the U.S. was sincerely trying to find another alternative. Mahoney outlined the Krol 1979 testimony and charged that U.S. arms policy had gone beyond sufficiency to deter and had become a basis of asserting national superiority. He concluded that Catholics, therefore, had no moral basis to support current U.S. arms policy (cited in Castelli, *The Bishops and the Bomb*, pp. 54–55).

22. *The Challenge of Peace* (Second Draft), pp. 319, 324.

23. The new MX missile was specifically mentioned as possibly qualifying for the condemned class of first-strike weapons. First-strike weapons with "hard-target kill capability" are defined as those nuclear

weapons with the speed, power, and accuracy to destroy enemy missiles in underground silos, and which, therefore, offer the possibility of destroying the opponents' land-based missile force before it could be used in retaliation.

24. *The Challenge of Peace* (Second Draft), pp. 317, 319–320.

25. Ibid., p. 318.

26. Ibid., pp. 318, 320–321.

27. Ibid., p. 321.

28. Ibid., pp. 320–322.

29. In a speech on the 150th Anniversary of the Knights of Columbus in Hartford, Connecticut, August 3, 1982, with Cardinal Casaroli and over a hundred bishops in the audience, Reagan attacked the idea of a nuclear freeze as damaging to the U.S. attempts to get the Soviet Union to agree to arms reductions.

30. Michael Novak explains his own change of attitude in "How I Have Changed My Mind," *The Catholic Mind* 77 (March 1979): 33–44. Novak saw himself as a defender of the American liberal democratic tradition against what he saw as the threat of increasingly anti-American sentiment within the American left. He is presently acting as theologian for the staff of the American Enterprise Institute, and has been prominent in organizing American Catholic opposition to what he described as a deviant anti-capitalist trend in Catholic social teaching. Novak was also appointed by President Reagan as ambassador to the U.N. Human Rights Commission.

31. Castelli, *The Bishops and the Bomb*, p. 108.

32. William V. O'Brien, "The Peace Debate and American Catholics," in *American Catholics and the Peace Debate* (Washington, D.C.: the Center for Strategic and International Studies/Georgetown University, 1982), p. 2, 4–5, 24. This pamphlet is a reproduction of O'Brien's original article in the *Washington Quarterly* along with subsequent articles in response to him and a final response from O'Brien.

33. Ibid., pp. 4, 22–28. O'Brien's views expressed here were also presented in an address entitled, "Just War Doctrine in a Nuclear Context," presented at the Annual Colloquium of Catholic Bishops and Scholars held in Washington, D.C., September 23–25, 1982, pp. 12–14. Michael Novak stressed the same points in "Nuclear Morality," *America* 147 (July 3, 1982): 5–6. He attacked the inadequacy of the bishops' treatment of the political context of war-peace issues. He argued that the period of American nuclear monopoly had been the greatest period of decolonization in the world's history, whereas the Soviets from 1945–1949 had taken over nation after nation. See also James V. Schall, S.J., "The Political Consequences," in *American Catholics and the Peace Debate*, pp. 13–16.

34. O'Brien, "The Peace Debate and American Catholics," pp. 4–5.

35. Ibid., pp. 4–5. "Just War Doctrine in a Nuclear Context," p. 28, 48–51.

36. O'Brien, "Just War Doctrine in a Nuclear Context," pp. 43–44. As examples of his use of proportionality to judge the degree of morally acceptable civilian damage, O'Brien stated that a target of significant military value such as a missile installation would justify significant collateral civilian damage in destroying this target, whereas a target of ordinary military importance would not. An example of such a disproportionate degree of collateral damage was the bombing of Dresden in World War II. O'Brien's interpretation of the principles of proportionality and discrimination was given in chapter 2 of this study.

37. O'Brien in "American Catholics and the Peace Debate," p. 26. These views were also expressed in discussion before the Bishops and Scholars Colloquium. Views quite similar to O'Brien's in response to the second draft of the pastoral can be found in James E. Dougherty, "Nuclear Weapons, Deterrence Strategy and Arms Negotiations: A Catholic Perspective," pp. 30–31, 43. This paper was delivered to the Annual Catholic Bishops and Scholars Colloquium held in Washington, D.C., September 23–25, 1982. Dougherty defended the American participation in the arms race as an attempt to restore a military balance in the face of the Soviet's drive for superiority.

38. Gordon Zahn, "Disaster, No: Disappointment, Yes," *Commonweal* 109 (August 13, 1982): 435–436. Zahn cited a book by Daniel Ellsberg, *Protest and Survival*, which he thought documented that most recent American presidents used the "nuclear blackmail" which we usually ascribe to Soviet intentions. In this crucial sense, he argued, we have been consistently "using" nuclear weapons.

39. Zahn, "Disaster, No: Disappointment, Yes," p. 436.

40. Gordon Zahn, "Afterword," in Thomas A. Shannon, ed., *War and Peace? The Search for New Answers* (Maryknoll, New York: Orbis Books, 1980), pp. 232–234. This volume was dedicated to Zahn and its articles provide a good sample of the "state of the question," although the realist/Americanist perspective of people such as O'Brien or Novak is not represented.

41. Ibid., pp. 231–236.

42. Ibid., p. 240. Also in this volume a pacifist interpretation of the American Catholic peace movement is given by Thomas Cornell, who credited Zahn with being greatly responsible for the push to move the Catholic Church toward pacifism and keeping the Catholic peace movement from becoming schismatic ("The Catholic Church and the Witness against War," p. 212).

43. Hollenbach, "Nuclear Weapons and Nuclear War: The Shape of the Catholic Debate," pp. 588–592. Hollenbach cited as reasons for his rejection of any "limited nuclear war": 1) counterforce strategy presupposes the MAD deterrent as its "bottom line" and could trigger the use of the MAD deterrent; 2) the collateral damage from a major counterforce exchange would be hard to distinguish from a direct attack on civilian centers. Therefore, because a nuclear war could not be called "limited" in any rational sense, it violates the *jus ad bellum* criterion of reasonable hope of success.

44. Ibid., pp. 600–601.

45. Ibid., pp. 601–602. By way of example of how his method of approach would work, Hollenbach expressed his opposition to the deployment of the Pershing II missiles in Europe, as well as the deployment of "first-strike" weapons such as the MX and Trident II missiles. He judged that these weapons were destabilizing to the balance of power and would only further escalate the arms race. Therefore, since they thus increased the likelihood of war, they must be opposed and condemned.

46. Ibid., p. 603.

47. Francis X. Winters, "Catholic Debate and Division on Deterrence," *America* 147 (September 18, 1982): 130–131. Winters refers here to Henry Kissinger's 1979 address to a symposium in Belgium in which he said that some Americans were reconsidering the NATO attitude toward first use of nuclear weapons, and the similar views of McGeorge Bundy, George Kennan, Robert McNamara, and Gerard Smith, who published their views in "Nuclear Weapons and the Atlantic Alliance," *Foreign Affairs* (Spring 1982).

48. Ibid., p. 129; also Francis X. Winters, S.J., "A Fair Hearing for the Bishops," in *American Catholics and the Peace Debate*, pp. 20–23.

49. Ibid., pp. 129, 131. A somewhat different slant on Winters' views can be found in George Weigel, "Testimony Submitted to the Ad Hoc Committee on War and Peace of the National Conference of Catholic Bishops," March 22, 1982; also Idem, *The Peace Bishops and the Arms Race*, pp. 19–26, 45–50. Weigel argued the need to resist both the unilateral trends of the more pacifist thinkers and the tendency of many realists to reduce issues to military arithmetic. He charged that the bishops' tendency to focus on weapons systems was usually at the cost of creative thought about the construction of alternative methods of conflict resolution. Yet the focus of Weigel's exhortations was a strong belief in the role of the United States as the agency both to blunt Soviet expansionism and to lead the way to a greater world political order.

50. Castelli, *The Bishops and the Bomb*, pp. 116, 126; also interview with Bishop P. Francis Murphy of Baltimore.

51. Castelli, *The Bishops and the Bomb*, p. 129; Letter of January 15, 1983 of William Clark (President Reagan's National Security Advisor) to Cardinal Bernardin.

52. The meeting was held on January 18–19, 1983. Attending as part of the American delegation were Msgr. Daniel Hoye, Secretary of the NCCB, and Rev. Bryan Hehir, who functioned as expert consultant for the delegation. Bernardin was made a cardinal prior to this meeting. This account of the consultation is based on the official summary given to the American bishops.

53. *The Challenge of Peace: God's Promise and Our Response*, official text of the third draft distributed to the members of the NCCB, pp. 5–6; Castelli, *The Bishops and the Bomb*, p. 136.

54. Castelli, *The Bishops and the Bomb*, p. 135.

55. *The Challenge of Peace* (Third Draft), p. 90.

56. Ibid., pp. 44–45.

57. Ibid., p. 69. The treatment of counter-population warfare and first use is found on pp. 68–72.

58. Ibid., pp. 72–74.

59. Ibid., pp. 83–87.

60. Ibid., pp. 87–88.

61. Ibid., p. 79. Castelli, *The Bishops and the Bomb*, pp. 102–104, 145.

62. *The Challenge of Peace* (Third Draft), p. 144.

63. Ibid., pp. 116, 114–120.

64. Ibid., p. 120.

65. Ibid., pp. 110, 120–127.

66. Castelli, *The Bishops and the Bomb*, pp. 148–150. "Administration Hails New Draft of Arms Letter—Says Bishops 'Improved' The Nuclear Statement," *The New York Times*, April 7, 1983, p. 1.

67. "NCCB Leaders Cite Pastoral's Differences with U.S. Policies," NCCB News Release, April 8, 1983.

68. *The Challenge of Peace: God's Promise and Our Response, Origins* 13 (May 19, 1983) pp. 18, 15, 10. This issue of *Origins* contains the full text of the final version of the pastoral.

69. Ibid., pp. 16–17.

70. Castelli, *The Bishops and the Bomb*, pp. 162–163.

71. *The Challenge of Peace*, p. 30.

72. Ibid., p. 30.

73. The advocacy of ethical pluralism on issues of war and peace was for many people part of a larger movement in contemporary Cath-

olic moral theology for an ethical pluralism of methodologies and positions on various issues on both the social and personal levels. An example of the advocacy of pluralism in contemporary Roman Catholic theology can be found in Charles E. Curran, *Catholic Moral Theology in Dialogue* (Notre Dame: University of Notre Dame Press, 1976).

74. J. Bryan Hehir, "The Just War Ethic and Catholic Theology: Dynamics of Change and Continuity," in Shannon, *War or Peace?* pp. 23–24.

75. Ibid., pp. 24–25. Hollenbach also upheld pluralism in the same vein as Hehir, "Nuclear Weapons and Nuclear War: The Shape of the Catholic Debate," p. 587. It should be noted here that realists such as O'Brien and Dougherty did not deny the right of conscience for Catholics to choose a pacifist stance. Their argument was over the normative validity which the Church should give to pacifism. Without seeking to have the Church condemn pacifists as such, they argued for the Church to uphold the primacy of the just war tradition as the Church's approach to questions of war and peace.

76. Ibid., pp. 25–26.

77. Ibid., pp. 32–34.

78. Ibid., pp. 34–35. Those referred to here were pacifists such as Gordon Zahn and James Douglass.

8

Conclusion

This study has attempted to set forth the major schools of thought governing the American Catholic understanding of the issues of war and peace during the last twenty years in order to provide a framework giving a general order and unity to the debates to which these issues gave rise. Some final observations and conclusions on the intellectual themes and developments of these years are now in order.

The two traditions of the CAIP and the Catholic Worker movement, which constituted the American Catholic intellectual heritage on war and peace at the beginning of 1960, provided the themes which continued to exercise Catholic thought on these issues over the next two decades. In the differing approaches of these traditions it was clear that the issue of war was always part of the larger issue of culture. The particularly threatening nature of modern war was understood as being not simply the result of developing technology, but also, and even more fundamentally, the reflection of a modern culture and civilization which had destroyed the sense of the human bonding between the earth's peoples and any sense of a universal common good. Thus, for both, the analysis of the issue of war was part of the struggle to preserve or establish that civilization which was compatible with their understanding of the Christian vision of the human person and the community of mankind.

Both the CAIP and the Catholic Worker accepted the traditional Catholic critique of modernity to orient their criticism of society. Yet each combined with this historic Catholic distrust of the moral character of modern society its own particular emphasis and interpretation of modern history and the conflicts defining the current state of international relations. For the CAIP the Catholic critique of modernity was mitigated by the organization's Americanism and commitment to allying Catholicism with the Western struggle against communism. The Catholic Worker conceived the cultural struggle of the modern world to be the establishment of Christian community in the face of the anti-human civilization embodied in both the capitalist West and the communist East. The Catholic Worker's use of the traditional critique of modernity was also modified by the movement's philosophy of anarchistic personalism, which never blended well with the medieval ideals also espoused by Peter Maurin.

In their differing worldviews the CAIP and the Catholic Worker each attempted a synthesis of elements which could not be held together. As these intellectual heritages evolved over the past two decades, each broke down into differing schools of thought stressing different aspects within each tradition. Yet there still continued to be two mainstreams of American Catholic thought on war, differentiated by their judgment on American and Western civilization. This question of the moral and spiritual quality of American society and the global role of the United States is the central question in the recent historical evolution of American Catholic thought on war and peace. This is not to undervalue the importance of other factors shaping Catholic opinion, such as *a priori* judgments on the Gospel teaching on violence, or interpretations of the moral categories of the just war theory. Yet despite the differences between realists and most mainline nuclear pacifists, these two schools of thought were joined by their Americanism in understanding the basic cultural struggles shaping their world. Similarly, it was their rejection of the dominant values and goals of American society which joined the analysis of individuals such as Gordon Zahn, Thomas Merton, and the Berrigans, even though they differed in their views of pacifism and non-violence.

In essence, at the heart of the debate on war and peace was the question which had been at the heart of much of American

Catholic history—the relationship of Catholicism and Americanism, or the compatibility of the Catholic vision of the human person and human community with the controlling values and ideals of American society. Throughout most of its history the American Catholic Church had struggled to prove its compatibility with the main features of American society and its liberal democratic institutions. By 1960 and the election of John Kennedy most Catholics believed that Catholicism was firmly established as an accepted part of the American social and political system.

The evolution of the Catholic debate on war and peace in the last twenty years caused the old question to be raised again. This time, however, the question was not raised by Nativists, who challenged the loyalty of an immigrant and "alien" Church. Rather, the question was raised by Catholics who challenged the morality of their government and the humanity of their society. Beneath the debates on specific issues, such as nuclear deterrence, was always the question of whether the Church would take a stand which would radically sever it from what the state had accepted as essential to its defense. The ultimate implications of such a stance threatened to eliminate any significant participation of Catholics in American society. To prevent such a rupture was an overriding imperative of Catholic Americanists, both realist and nuclear pacifist. To create such a rupture was an essential feature of radical Catholic social criticism. In each case the attitude toward American society and its role in the world was the litmus test of how each school of thought evaluated contemporary Western civilization, and the conflict defining both international relations and the role of the Church in the modern world. It was in their judgments on American society that Catholics demonstrated how they continued to understand the issue of war as primarily an issue of culture.

Yet the tendency of the debates on war and peace to focus on questions of the morality of particular weapons or policies has often obscured this central issue of the evaluation of the spiritual and moral quality of modern civilization. The earlier traditions of the CAIP and the Catholic Worker seemed more successful at keeping the issue of war more clearly in the context of that larger analysis. The breakdown, however, of these traditions into differing schools of thought reflected the inability of these groups to maintain an integrated social vision which entailed a thorough critique of contemporary culture and civilization, a vision of an alternative society, and a model or theory of how to effect social and institutional change. The resulting situation was one in which the differing schools of Catholic thought on war reflected various elements of this social vision, but like their CAIP and Catholic Worker predecessors they were unable to integrate them into a workable synthesis. Much of the confusion in the debates of these years was precisely due to the failure of the advocates of these differing schools of thought to be clear or systematic in developing the presuppositions and the implications of their positions on specific issues for a wider vision directing Catholic social thought and action.

The development of episcopal teaching in the last two decades most clearly exhibits this *ad hoc* approach to the issues of war and peace. The bishops rightly incurred the criticisms of both those realists and radicals who charged them with not adequately treating the political context of the issues which they addressed in their statements. In their statements on specific policy questions the bishops became increasingly critical of key American defense policies, questioned the intentions and goals of the government and its willingness to work for a world authority and economic reform, and clearly placed themselves against the stated intentions of Western nuclear policy. While at times appearing to want to step outside the ideological alternatives of East and West, the bishops declined to join with those radicals and pacifists who would have the Church pronounce "a plague on both your houses," and stand in resistance to its government. And, if it was the desire of the bishops to take an Americanist nuclear pacifist stance, they failed to clearly embrace the Americanist definition of the world ideological struggle.

This is not to reject the moral judgments which the bishops have made. Their judgments on nuclear war and deterrence seem a correct application of just war criteria based on a prudential assessment of the known facts. Their criticism of the

obstructionist character of American policy toward world economic reform and the establishment of an effective international authority also seems a correct assessment. The problem
arises with the bishops' uncertainty of where to go with the
implications of their judgments. They seemed caught between
the desire not to break the historical union of Americanism
and Catholicism and the fact that some of their judgments on
vital defense policies threatened to do just that. In effect, they
have logically followed the moral reasoning of their just war
tradition to the point of placing themselves on the horns of a
dilemma. One cannot escape the impression that many bishops
have not considered the consequences and implications of their
statements, and have consequently not fully perceived the dilemma into which they have moved. In this sense, both pacifists
and realists were right in criticizing the lack of clarity in the
bishops' thinking and their neglect of the larger questions which
their statements have raised, although this attack does not
negate the correctness of the bishops' moral judgments as such.

If the bishops wish to be true to the direction which they
have charted in their teaching in recent years, they must begin
to face the larger political and cultural questions which they
previously left untouched and make a clear commitment of
where they would have the official Church stand in the present
global ideological struggle. This would necessarily involve addressing the discrepancy which the bishops have already perceived between the foreign policy and defense goals of the United
States and those conditions which the bishops and papal teaching have already identified as essential to world peace and
development. Their substantial criticism of the United States
must be clearly integrated into either a participation in the
East-West struggle, or an attempt to chart a Christian stance
outside of these given ideological alternatives.

An essential element of this process would be for the bishops
to develop more clearly the linkage which they have made
between the issue of war and world development. In particular,
they must develop the strong emphasis in papal teaching that
development means not merely economic reform, but the creation of those cultural conditions which foster the full human
development of persons. This, in turn, would entail a re-ex-

amination of the Western capitalist system and the dominant values of American society, which are reflected in the foreign policy objectives of the United States. Similarly, while the bishops have consistently reiterated the internationalist ideals of papal teaching, they must begin to explore the requirements for establishing a world political community and the ways in which both superpowers are an obstacle to it.

It may be argued that the position of the bishops required their more *ad hoc* approach to the issues of war and peace in order to respect the great divergency of opinion within the Church, and to provide a minimum moral framework which would not produce a schism. Yet it was precisely the bishops' criticism of American policy which served as the chief stimulus for the latest round of American Catholic debate on war and peace. If they continue to pursue their criticism, the bishops will themselves eliminate the possibility of their functioning merely to articulate points of consensus in Catholic thought on these issues. Furthermore, representatives of the various schools of Catholic thought have recognized that one of the great inadequacies of the just war tradition has been the historical failure of the Church to apply it to specific wars and public policies. This application of the just war criteria would seem to require more than the application of the principle of proportionality to specific weapons or tactics, such as the American bishops did in rejecting the use of nuclear weapons. It would also seem to require a judgment on the values and goals governing a nation's conduct in the world. Thus, the moral calculus by which the bishops rejected the nuclear policies of the United States still calls for a larger judgment on the complex of values and goals which constitute the cause which is used to justify those nuclear policies.

Similarly, while the bishops stated that they did not wish to focus on the nuclear question in such a way as to make the world safe for conventional war, they did not really face the issues involved in contemporary conventional warfare. This problem was only increased by their apparent willingness to accept greater conventional forces as a trade-off for a move away from reliance on nuclear weapons. Especially absent from the bishops' considerations were the problems and issues of

insurgency/counter-insurgency warfare, which has been recognized as the type of war in which the United States is most
likely to become involved. Yet the issue of insurgency/counter-
insurgency warfare, in which the superpowers conduct their
struggle through their surrogates, only serves to raise the larger
question of the motivating values of this struggle and its effect
on the possibilities of genuine human development.

Thus, the *ad hoc* approach taken by the hierarchy skirted
the cultural and political judgments on American and Western
civilization, which constituted the major dividing line between
the differing schools of Catholic thought on the issues of war
and peace. Yet in both the questions which they addressed and
those which they avoided, the bishops have helped to move the
Catholic debate on these issues in the direction of a confrontation on these larger cultural judgments. The future role of
the bishops in guiding American Catholic thought on war and
peace will in large measure rest on their ability to achieve a
consensus of their own on these cultural questions and to formulate from this a concrete historical ideal for Catholic social
action. Failure to do so could mean that the effort at leadership
demonstrated in the bishops' 1983 pastoral on war and peace
would simply dissipate amidst the renewed conflict which they
helped to stimulate.

The realist school of thought was much clearer than the
bishops on seeing the priority of what they termed the political
context of war and peace issues. Yet the major representatives
of the realist perspective did not develop the analysis of this
political context for which they called. Their analysis of the
cultural conflicts shaping the world did not really go beyond the
assertion of the moral superiority of the American and Western
cause. In large measure this is perhaps because after John
Courtney Murray the most prominent Catholic realist spokesmen were not theologians or philosophers, but political analysts and strategists, who naturally tended to focus on narrower,
technical questions. The CAIP, whose heirs the realists were,
originally attempted to combine its Americanism with an effort
at criticizing Western culture from the perspective of traditional Catholic values. The Americanism espoused by the Catholic realists in the last two decades eliminated any possibility

of developing or even maintaining this minimal critique of American culture. Their rejection of the internationalism of the CAIP and their refusal to consider the issues of war and peace in the context of other issues such as world development reflected the reduction of the issue of war in the minds of Catholic realists to an issue of military defense.

The focus of realist thought became the need to provide a moral and militarily feasible defense for the West in the context of war as it is likely to be fought in the present day, including nuclear war. In this, later realists consciously saw themselves as continuing the task set forth by John Courtney Murray, even though they accepted positions in which it is unlikely that Murray would have concurred. Yet in their attempts to articulate a defense of the United States which was both moral and militarily feasible, Catholic realists stand subject to the judgment that their controlling consideration was military necessity, to which moral limits were accommodated. This is perhaps most clearly evident in the work of William O'Brien, if only because he was the clearest and most systematic in his treatment of the issues. Other Catholic realists might regard O'Brien, at least in some of his positions, such as the acceptance of torture, as a minority view not at all in accord with their own. Yet the logic which O'Brien used to justify even his less accepted positions seems to characterize the general realist approach, that is, you cannot grant the right of self-defense and not make it functional in the actual conditions of war today. In his criticism of the more traditional use of the just war theory by other realists and in his more extreme positions, such as on the use of torture and the bombing of civilian centers, O'Brien reflects more honestly and clearly what has been the controlling concern of realist thinking all along.

The chief contention of the realists was that any moral limits which kept the United States from mounting a militarily feasible war of defense was contrary to the just war tradition of the Church. Theoretically they would admit that the just war tradition placed limits on the use of force beyond which one could not go. Practically, however, the limits which Catholic realists were prepared to accept never contradicted the current definitions of military necessity, even if it meant defense policies the execution of which could destroy entire societies. For example, the realists' willingness to allow the use of nuclear weapons in a counterforce war never answered the objection that the societal effect of such a war would be practically equal to that of a counter-city attack, especially since counterforce strategy allowed the targeting of certain types of cities containing military objectives. Similarly, faced with the fact that the developing strategy for counterforce warfare would itself eliminate the ability to control or limit war, realist thinkers could only make an act of faith that appropriate means of control would be developed.

In the end, no amount of destruction in war could outweigh the realists' abhorrence of the prospect of a communist "victory." The practical effect of their approach left Catholic realism distinguishable from non-Christian, purely pragmatic approaches to war, not by the limits it placed on the use of force, but by the moral casuistry it felt obliged to use to justify the dictates of conventional military wisdom. While Catholic realists maintained a strong sense of the just war tradition's emphasis on the justice of the basic cause, they failed to exhibit an equally effective sense of the moral limits on the use of force to which even a just cause is subject. Consequently, their insistence on focusing on the political context and the justice of the Western cause can be seen as part of the process of their reducing the issue of war to an issue of military defense, and adjusting the just war tradition to accommodate the needs of that defense.

Because Catholic realists viewed the Soviet enemy as intractable and the Soviet system as inherently aggressive, they could place no faith in the use of reason to find common ground and interests which would allow for movement toward disarmament. Yet this pessimism toward the powers of human reason and good will contrasted sharply with the realists' great faith in the power of reason to control and limit even nuclear war. This discrepancy in their belief in the ability of reason to shape and control human affairs was necessitated by the ideological commitment of Catholic realists in the same manner as that commitment shaped the moral calculus which they applied to all specific questions of American defense.

This ideological commitment was also operative among Catholic nuclear pacifists who embraced the same Americanism as those realists whom they otherwise opposed. These nuclear pacifists were more sensitive to the moral limits that must be placed even on a just war if the justice of its cause is not to be compromised. Yet for the most part, their concern for the elimination of nuclear weapons did not lead to a similarly developed analysis of modern conventional warfare and the question of whether it too had passed beyond the tolerable limits of Catholic moral tradition. In choosing to stress the internationalist tradition of the CAIP these Catholic nuclear pacifists also failed to develop any significant critique of the United States and its world role, or to explore the criticism at least minimally made by the bishops. In a sense, these Catholic Americanists could be seen as following John Courtney Murray's emphasis on non-military engagement with the Soviet Union, as opposed to the military emphasis of their realist counterparts. Yet their Americanism meant that this engagement with the Soviet Union could not be linked with an internal critique of the West as well. As was the case with Murray, their sense of the moral superiority of Western liberal democracy caused them to stress the political freedoms of the West without an equal consideration of its injustices. The very passion with which they argued against the realists to preserve the moral character and quality of the West's struggle against communism meant that no criticism of the West could be allowed to impugn its moral superiority as the last hope of Christian and humanist civilization.

In contrast to the Catholic Americanists of both the realist and the nuclear pacifist schools, the radical Catholic social critics of the past twenty years were far more successful in maintaining a focus on the issue of war as primarily an issue of culture, which required a thorough criticism of their own society. In their analysis of the modern state Catholic pacifists and radicals focused on the effects of managerial and technological society on the basic bonds of human community and the sense of personal responsibility. In so doing they preserved the emphasis of the traditional Catholic critique of modernity in its charge that modern society destroys the basis of human community by its materialism, individualism, and the under-mining of basic community units such as the family.

The most significant contribution of radical Catholicism in these years was the attempt of some elements to develop an analysis of American society which integrated the issue of war with other social questions, most especially those of race and economics. The thrust of radical Catholic social analysis, as much of papal teaching, was to see the problem of war as expressive of a cultural crisis in human solidarity. It was precisely the problem of race which provided the most blatant and perfidious expression of this crisis, as well as an avenue for tracing its historical-cultural roots. It was in exploring the nature of racism in American society that Catholic radicals saw the common roots of the race problem and modern annihilating wars in the development of that Calvinist culture which gave birth to capitalism and laid the foundation of the modern world, and which was viewed by traditional Catholic social thought as a nemesis culture. This culture was seen as justifying the egotistical pursuit of greed (capitalism) and necessitating the creation of a racial mythology to justify the enslavement, exploitation, and even annihilation of other peoples. It was this cultural denial of universal human solidarity that many Catholic radicals saw underlying American defense policies based on nuclear annihilation, and foreign policies aimed at world manipulation and control, often resulting in wars such as that in Vietnam.

The view of America espoused by Catholic radicals and pacifists was not shared by the majority of their co-religionists. Yet these radicals were true to the tradition of Catholic social thought in insisting that war, as a social issue, cannot be understood apart from the wider cultural critique which encompasses both sides of the present world ideological struggle. They were in advance of their Americanist opponents in their recognition of the dangers of the Church aligning itself with any particular social system, and that the political freedoms of the West were not a sufficient reason for the Church being an agent of that civilization or the present political objectives of its governments. They also seemed quite correct in their criticism that the Americanism which has historically dominated Catholic thought on war in this country prevented any serious attempt to recognize or account for the many people who remain disenfranchised from the benefits which are used to justify the American and Western cause. Similarly, their revisionist interpretation of American history seriously challenged the reformism of Catholic Americanists, who felt that issues of war and peace could be dealt with without questioning the global objectives of the United States, and who believed that the political freedom of the West exempted it from being judged as engaging in a struggle for global control which was not in the interests of world peace and human development.

Yet American Catholic radicals of these years also exhibited significant failures in formulating an integrated social vision. These failures were in large measure a product of the very type of radical social criticism which they attempted to make, and are failures which radical Catholicism shared with left-wing American social criticism in general. Brian Wicker has observed that one of the characteristics of contemporary radical Catholicism has been a fundamental uncertainty about immediate political policies that has grown along with the radical depth of the social criticism which it embraced.[1] Catholic radicals and pacifists of these years sought to effect a revolution within the Church and eventually the larger society. The first prerequisite of such a revolution is to change the way people see themselves and their world. In the attempt to formulate and offer such a new vision, it is not fair to demand that the vision be immediately accompanied by a detailed specific program for effecting change. Yet eventually any radical social criticism must address the question of implementing its social vision in institutional change, and the success of such an effort is in large measure determined by the adequacy of the social vision itself. Much of the difficulty in addressing the problems of social change evident in radical American Catholic thought on war was rooted precisely in the inadequacy of its social vision.

One of the most salient characteristics of much radical Catholic pacifist thought in these years was its anarchism. The traditional Catholic hostility towards modernity had become

reduced in contemporary American Catholic pacifism to a rejection of the modern state as an inherently totalitarian entity.
In viewing society as a dichotomy between the totalitarian
state and the morally responsible individual, Catholic pacifism
had either forgotten or rejected the tradition of Catholic social
thought which was expressed in papal social encyclicals from
Leo XIII on, and which presupposed the necessity of intermediary institutions between the state and the individual. These
intermediary structures (family, church, occupational associations, and so forth) were envisioned as both limiting the power
of the state and protecting the individual and providing him
with a communal context in which to exist and function. Contemporary Catholic pacifism eschewed any analysis of whether
the modern state was totalitarian because of the destruction
of these intermediary structures, and instead simply assumed
the state *per se* to be totalitarian in nature. Their doctrinaire
pacifism could concede no legitimate function to the state, for
the state was premised on the assumption of a legitimate use
of force, and their anti-institutionalism precluded any serious
effort to create strong intermediary structures to support the
individual and effect social change. Thus, Catholic pacifists
correctly perceived the corrosive effect of modern culture on
the structures of human community, but their own ideological
perspective also kept them from envisioning more than the
conflict between the totalitarian state and the individual. Their
anarchism placed them at odds with the traditional Catholic
social ideals which originally inspired the Catholic Worker
movement through Peter Maurin, even though Maurin set the
stage for this himself with his particular brand of Christian
personalism. Because Catholic pacifists could not go beyond
personalistic protest, they could not adequately address the
question of institutional change.

Closely related to the problem of anarchism in Catholic pacifism was the strongly anti-American tenor of the social criticism and historical interpretation adopted by Catholic radicals
in these years. Two factors involved here require consideration.
The first is that the anti-American social critique of Catholic
radicals often blended with the anarchistic attitudes of Catholic
pacifism to obscure whether Catholic radicals were seeking to

reject the state as such, or a particular social system. The anarchism endemic to American radical Catholicism informed attempts to construct a revolutionary critique of society in such a way as to often make America a symbol of the modern state which was to be rejected. This, in turn, tended to prohibit the development of a social analysis which conceived of America as capable of revolutionary change, and instead fostered a conception of revolution as a sectarian withdrawal from American society. This conception of revolution as withdrawal seemed to go beyond any attempt at organized non-cooperation for the purpose of effecting social change, and entailed a deeper desire to preserve personal integrity by social-political withdrawal.

This, in turn, reflects the second problem with the anti-American analysis of Catholic radicals, namely, the deep sense of cultural alienation which permeated it. Numerous authors have observed that one of the great historical problems of the American Left, and especially the New Left, has been its cultural alienation from the larger working class population.[2] Their radical critique of society expressed their own alienation from it in a way which did not enable them to appreciate or use American cultural symbols to translate their protest into a movement understandable to the larger population. The result was often a form of protest which expressed personal alienation and a desire for personal authenticity rather than the possibility of a genuine cultural and social revolution. Radical Catholics fell victim to the same weakness. The anarchism and anti-institutionalism which was so much a part of the atmosphere of radical Catholicism seemed to permeate its social analysis so as to express disaffiliation far more than identification with the society it sought to transform.

This in no way negates the criticism which radical Catholics made of American society in their attempts to deal with the issue of war. It does mean, however, that if the critique which radical Catholics make of society is meant to be more than an expression of personalist protest, they must face the challenge of relating to American cultural symbols to translate their revolutionary criticism into a social vision which can creatively speak to the personal and social yearnings of wider segments of the American people. The difficulty which Catholic radicals experienced in effecting such a translation is perhaps not unrelated to the difficulty which they exhibited in constructing and maintaining a supportive and enduring communal structure within their own ranks. The experience of the Catholic resistance movement is a case in point. One cannot deny the truth articulated by men such as Thomas Merton and Gordon Zahn in their recognition of the ways in which modern society co-opts and undermines attempts to construct institutional structures capable of supporting counter-cultural movements. Despite their sensitivity to the need for such a communal rooting of revolutionary activity, their pessimism led them to rely on the heroic witness of individuals. Yet neither can one ignore the degree to which the anti-institutional anarchism of Catholic radicals frustrated their own desires for such a communal base and destructively exacerbated their sense of cultural alienation from their own Church and nation. If Catholic radicals are to move beyond personalistic protest and develop a revolutionary vision for American society, they must face the challenge of creating a synthesis of personal authenticity and community, against which their instinctive individualism and anarchism has tended.

A significant part of the tension which the absence of such a synthesis has caused in American Catholic radicalism is reflected in what Catholic radicals and pacifists have seen as the eschatological dimension of their political protest. The social critique which Catholic radicals developed in treating the problem of war and related issues took on extremely apocalyptic overtones. They correctly realized that the depth of human aspirations and the crisis of human solidarity which these issues opened up were not subject to ultimate resolution in this world. The social transformation which was the goal of the non-violent revolution sought by radical Catholic pacifists was not capable of being an historically realizable human project, but required the divine act of human perfection which Christians have traditionally looked for in the second coming of Christ. This was clearly recognized in some like Merton and implied in the language of others, but radical Catholic thought on war, as a whole, carried the sense that history had entered a phase when humanity's self-destructive pursuit of power was reaching its apocalyptic conclusion.

Yet this sense of the apocalyptic nature of the times often served to exacerbate the sectarian tendencies of radical Catholics, and to obscure the deleterious effects of their anarchistic individualism by cloaking it with the mantle of prophecy and religious witness. This is not to deny that the eschatological witness which radical Catholics sought to give is a most important contribution to the efforts to face the global crisis which is made manifest in the threat of modern war. In discussing the role of the Catholic left in Britain Brian Wicker ably expressed the importance of the eschatological witness to contemporary revolutionary attempts to address the modern social crisis:

The whole aspiration of man, in his intellectual, his sexual, his emotional life, is for a mode of experience that will give him back his own unity, and that of the world in which he finds himself. But ... in the nature of the case the attempt cannot succeed. It is simply impossible to state this unity except in terms that are irreducibly dualistic....
If man cannot overcome, by his own initiative, the dualism of the very terms in which his most fundamental drive to unity has to be expressed, perhaps this means that man cannot and should not be content to rest on his own resources. May it be that what is lacking in socialist humanism to make it consistent and acceptable is just that belief in a redemption from beyond man's world which at present cannot be acknowledged? The whole meaning of the rise of the Catholic Left is that it is an attempt to show how that suggestion can be given a valid meaning in contemporary terms.[3]

In order to make that most crucial insight meaningful in contemporary terms, it is necessary for radical Catholics not to allow anarchistic individualism to lead them into apocalyptic withdrawal, or their concern for personal authenticity to negate the task of synthesizing that authenticity with the struggle to transform American culture and institutions.

The major representatives of radical Catholic thought on war in these years were unanimous in their desire not to assume the sectarian posture of the traditional American peace churches. This was clearly reflected in their rejection of the dichotomy caused by the acceptance of the church versus sect models of the ecclesial community's relationship to society. Their Catholicism would not allow them to embrace consciously a sectarian view of the Church or an apolitical pacifism of nonresistance. Yet the attempt of radical Catholic pacifists to combine the church and sect models in a Church which is willing to return to the catacombs in non-violent resistance to the state does not seem at all feasible. For it essentially rests on combining a church model premised on an acceptance of the state with a pacifism which rejects the state. The anarchism of Catholic pacifists left them in the contradiction of making moral demands on the state which their own analysis held the state to be incapable of meeting. This contradiction can only serve to pull radical Catholicism toward the sectarianism which its spokesmen eschewed, and deepen its alienation from Church and society.

The overcoming of this contradiction would require a reappropriation of the Church's tradition of social teaching, which allowed for a legitimate function of the state and insisted on the development of intermediary community structures both to limit the state and to enfranchise the individual socially. An obvious problem which this would pose for Catholic pacifists is that the acceptance of a legitimate role for the state would require a modification of their absolute pacifism. Some, like Gordon Zahn and James Douglass, asserted that they could envision a state run on the principles of total non-violence which they espoused. Their failure to develop what this would entail, however, seems indicative of the fact that it is not possible. In the end, the tension inherent in their combining a Catholic model of church with an anti-state pacifism proves unbearable. The choice left to radical Catholics is either to accept a sectarian apocalyptic witness or to seek a new synthesis of religious personal authenticity and political community. The search for such a new synthesis may prove unsuccessful and the Church could still find itself sent back to the catacombs because of its revolutionary witness. Yet there is a qualitative difference between a church reduced to the catacombs by a state which must repress its revolutionary challenge and a church

whose inability to accept the institutions necessary to human
political community has caused it to chose the catacombs as
its only home. The true apocalyptic attitude would require participation in the political revolution to transform society and
culture, while witnessing to the inability of politics to fulfill
the desire for salvation and human wholeness to which political
revolution ultimately aspires. In this sense Catholic radicals
need to be faulted not on their religious and revolutionary zeal,
but on their lack of subtlety.

Thus the schools of American Catholic thought on war which
developed over the last twenty years contained different elements of the Church's heritage of social thought, but were
unable to produce an adequate vision to guide the Church in
its social mission. American Catholics who less than fifty years
ago felt that they had an integrated vision of their world with
which to address the issues vexing their society, now found
themselves sharply divided on what most saw as the most lethal
and pressing issue of modern times.

The developments of the last twenty years have drawn into
question the historical synthesis of Americanism and Catholicism and made clear that the issues of war and peace cannot
be treated apart from the political-cultural context in which
they arise. American Catholics are faced with the challenge to
go beyond abstract debates between pacifism and the just war
tradition and to address the cultural questions which have most
divided them on issues of war and peace. The latest period of
development in Catholic thought on the peace issue makes
clear that this question can only be meaningfully discussed in
the context of struggling to define and establish a civilization
compatible with the Christian vision of human community. The
debates of these years also reveal the confusion and dissension
among Catholics on the nature of political community and the
Church's role in helping to create it.

Given the depth of these divisions, the prospects for anything
but greater dissension may not be very bright. If progress is
to be made toward a renewed social vision to guide Catholic
efforts to address the problem of war, the history of the past
twenty years would indicate the necessity of certain efforts.
American Catholics must accept the challenge of re-examining

their relationship to their own society and the compatibility of that society's dominant values and goals with world harmony and development. To call for a more radical critique of American and Western society is not to endorse naive unilateralism or to ignore Soviet threats to the United States. It is, rather, to reject the given definitions of the world ideological struggle as normative for the Christian attempt to address the threat which war poses to the human race. A revision of the traditional alliance of Americanism and Catholicism is essential to freeing Catholics to begin an attempt to address the problems of establishing world political community, which will not be subverted by a conflicting commitment to defend the West in a struggle for control of the world's resources. The Americanism which has marked so many of the Catholic efforts to deal with the problem of war has more often than not reduced these efforts to a part of the East-West competition rather than being a challenge to the threat which that competition poses to world peace.

The more radical critique of their society which American Catholics need to develop must also seek to integrate the issue of war with other major social questions such as those of race and economics. To continue to speak to these issues as completely separated phenomena is to ignore the necessity revealed in the debates of the last twenty years to view the issue of war in its larger cultural context. The integration of these issues in the social analysis of American Catholics is essential to their ability to speak to the global crisis of human solidarity which is revealed in the threat of nuclear war.

This social criticism, however, must also avoid the anarchistic individualism which has been endemic to so much of American radical Catholicism. The renewed social vision needed for American Catholics must allow them to radically challenge their society without alienating themselves from the institutions necessary to the political community to which they aspire.

In the end, the issue of war has, in the last two decades, served to challenge American Catholics to reassess their place in the modern world, and to face anew the question of their relationship with American society, which they first encountered in the early days of the Maryland colony. Only by accepting this challenge can they hope to meaningfully address the question which the splitting of the atom has placed before the whole human race.

NOTES

1. Brian Wicker, *First the Political Kingdom: A Personal Appraisal of the Catholic Left in Britain* (Notre Dame: University of Notre Dame Press, 1967), p. 25.

2. Treatments of this problem can be found in: Joseph Holland, *Flag, Faith and Family* (Chicago: New Patriotic Alliance, 1979); Christopher Lasch, *The Agony of the American Left* (New York: Vantage Books, 1969); John P. Diggins, *The American Left in the Twentieth Century* (New York: Harcourt Brace Jovanovich, Inc., 1973).

3. Wicker, *First the Political Kingdom*, p. 62.

Bibliographical Essay

Research for this study encompassed numerous books and periodicals published over the past twenty years. This bibiographical essay, however, will focus on those major sources which are most illustrative of the issues and points of view treated here.

As regards the intellectual heritage of American Catholic thought on war and peace at the beginning of the sixties, there is, at present, no history of the Catholic Association for International Peace. The chief source on the positions of this organization is the series of committee reports and symposia papers published by the CAIP from its inception in 1927 to the early fifties, most of which are available at the Catholic University of America. The Catholic Worker movement, in contrast, has been the subject of more attention and study. The movement's newspaper, *The Catholic Worker*, is a prime source for Catholic Worker attitudes toward American society and the issues of war and peace. Representative selections from this paper can be found in *A Penny a Copy*, edited by Thomas C. Cornell and James H. Forest (1968). Dorothy Day's personal expression of the movement's philosophy is found in her autobiography, *The Long Loneliness* (1952). The most complete history of the Catholic Worker movement is William D. Miller's, *A Harsh and Dreadful Love* (1973). An excellent treatment of the religious and ethical perspective of the movement is given in a doctoral dissertation by John Stuart Sandberg, "The Eschatological Ethic of the Catholic Worker" (The Catholic University of America, 1979). The most systematic attempt to treat the thought of Peter Maurin was given by Anthony Novitsky in an article based on his unpublished doctoral dissertation, "Peter Maurin's Green Revolution: The Radical Implications of Reactionary Social Catholicism" (*Review of Politics*, January 1957).

Among the chief representatives of American Catholic realism, John Courtney Murray's volume *We Hold These Truths* (1960) contains a summary of his views of American society and Soviet-American relations. His influential article on the morality of modern warfare, "Remarks on the Moral Problem of War," was originally published in *Theological Studies* (March 1959). The chief works in which William V. O'Brien set forth his thinking in the sixties were *Nuclear War, Deterrence and Morality* (1967) and *War and/or Survival* (1969). A more recent volume in which O'Brien applied his moral methodology to an evaluation of specific wars is his 1981 volume, *The Conduct of Just and Limited War*. An important example of the research used by realists such as O'Brien to call into question the normative moral status of the principle of non-combatant immunity can be found in the articles of Richard S. Hartigan: "Non-Combatant Immunity: Its Scope and Development" (*Continuum*, August 1965), and "Non-Combatant Immunity: Reflections on Its Origins and Present Status" (*The Review of Politics*, April 1967). Other key examples of American Catholic realist thought can be found in William V. Kennedy, "The Morality of American Nuclear Policy" (*The Catholic World*, September 1964), and James E. Dougherty, "The Christian and Nuclear Paficism" (*The Catholic World*, March 1964). A more recent example of the Catholic realist perspective by one of its prominent representatives is found in Michael Novak, "How I Have Changed My Mind" (*Catholic Mind*, March 1979), and "Nuclear Morality" (*America*, July 1982). A sample of Novak's recent efforts to extend the Americanism of the realist school to an evaluation of the economy can be found in *The American Vision: An Essay on the Future of Democratic Capitalism* (1978). Prominent examples of non-Catholic realist thought which influenced Catholic realists can be found in Reinhold Niebuhr, *Christianity and Power Politics* (1948), and the work of Paul Ramsey. Ramsey's seminal work on modern just war theory is *The Just War: Force and Political Responsibility* (1968). This, together with his volume *The Limits of Nuclear War* (1963), provides an excellent presentation of his very influential thought on contemporary issues of war and peace. Mention should also be made here of the series of monographs published by the Council on Religion and International Affairs (CRIA) during the late fifties and sixties. These served as an important vehicle of dialogue between Catholic and non-Catholic thinkers on defense and foreign policy issues, and were of particular significance for the dialogue between Catholic realists and non-Catholics such as Paul Ramsey. Most of these booklets are available at the Catholic University of America library.

One of the major vehicles for American Catholic nuclear-pacifist and idealist thought was the journal *Continuum*, edited by Justus George Lawler. Many of the editorials and articles in this journal provide a good profile on this point of view as it emerged in the sixties. Lawler's chief work on the subject, which drew together much of his writing for *Continuum*, was *Nuclear War: The Ethic, the Rhetoric, the Reality—A Catholic Assessment* (1965). The nuclear pacifist position developed in the late seventies by Rev. J. Bryan Hehir, which greatly influenced American episcopal statements, is set forth in a book Hehir co-authored with Robert A. Gessert, *The New Nuclear Debate* (1976). For American Catholic pacifist and radical social criticism on the issues of war and peace, the works of Gordon Zahn are of key importance. Illustrative of the concerns treated by Zahn in the numerous articles he has written are: "The Private Conscience and Legitimate Authority" (*Commonweal*, March 30, 1962), "The Threat of Militarization" (*Continuum*, Autumn 1969), and "The Future of the Catholic Peace Movement" (*Commonweal*, December 28, 1973). In a pamphlet published by the CRIA, *An Alternative to War* (1963), Zahn set forth his understanding of nonviolence as both a way of life and a rational method of defense in the nuclear age. His views of the relation of the Christian and the state are also found in his volume, *War, Conscience and Dissent* (1967). Zahn's early studies of German Catholics under the Nazi regime, which served as a background to his analysis of American Catholicism, can be found in *German Catholics and Hitler's War: A Study in Social Control* (1962), and *In Solitary Witness: The Life and Death of Franz Jägerstätter* (1964). Together with the works of Zahn, two books by James Douglass are important for the study of radical Catholic pacifism in the sixties and seventies: *The Nonviolent Cross: A Theology of Revolution and Peace* (1968) and *Resistance and Contemplation: The Way of Liberation* (1972). Thomas Merton's very influential critique of American society in the sixties can be found in his two volumes, *Seeds of Destruction* (1964) and *Faith and Violence: Christian Teaching and Christian Practice* (1968). A compilation of various writings by Merton on issues of war and peace can be found in a volume edited by Gordon Zahn, *Merton on Peace* (1971). An excellent biography of Merton is Monica Furlong's, *Merton: A Biography* (1980). An insightful commentary on Merton as social critic is *Thomas Merton: Social Critic* (1971) by James Thomas Baker.

The formative philosophy of the Catholic resistance movement can be found in the chief works of Philip and Daniel Berrigan: Philip Berrigan's *No More Strangers* (1965), *A Punishment for Peace* (1969), and *Prison Journals of a Priest Revolutionary* (1971); and Daniel Berrigan's *Consequences: Truth and...* (1967), *Absurd Convictions, Modest Hopes: Conversations after Prison with Lee Lockwood* (1972), *No Bars to Manhood* (1971), and *America is Hard to Find* (1972). An historical chronicle of the Catholic resistance movement is given in *With Clumsy Grace: The American Catholic Left 1961–1975*, by Charles Meconis (1979). Some biographical material on the Berrigans is found in *Divine Disobedience: Profiles in Radical Catholicism* (1971) by Francine du Plessix Gray. *The American Catholic Peace Movement* (1968), by Patricia F. McNeal, also provides a brief history of the Catholic resistance movement, as well as an account of earlier American Catholic peace activity by both the Catholic Worker movement and the CAIP. A sampling of American Catholic opinion in opposition to the Vietnam War in the sixties can be found in Thomas E. Quigley, *American Catholics and Vietnam* (1968). Also, interviews with American Catholics prominent in anti-war activity can be found in James Finn's *Protest: Pacifism and Politics* (1967).

Among the various collections of modern papal and episcopal statements on social justice and war and peace, several are particularly useful. *The Gospel of Peace and Justice: Catholic Social Teaching since Pope John* (1982), edited by Joseph Gremillion, provides a complete collection of the papal and conciliar documents on social justice, along with commentary and evaluation. *Nuclear Disarmament: Key Statements of Popes, Bishops, Councils and Churches* (1982), edited by Robert Heyer, provides a sampling of Catholic statements on nuclear arms by popes and bishops, as well as some statements by other churches. A complete collection of recent American episcopal statements on war and social justice is provided in *Quest for Justice: A Compendium of Statements of the United States Catholic Bishops on the Political and Social Order, 1966–1980*, edited by J. Brian Benestead and Francis J. Butler (1981). A more limited sampling of papal and episcopal documents, with some commentary, can be found in *Renewing the Earth: Catholic Documents on Peace, Justice and Liberation* (1977), edited by David J. O'Brien and Thomas A. Shannon.

Treatment of the question of selective conscientious objection, which arose particularly in response to the bishops' statements on the subject, can be found in James Finn, ed., *Conflict of Loyalties: The Case for Selective Conscientious Objection* (1968), and John A. Rohr, *Prophets Without Honor: Public Policy and the Selective Conscientious Objector* (1971). Works which provide a sample of some interaction between the conflicting perspectives of the American Catholic debate on war and peace are: James Finn, ed., *Peace, the Churches and the Bomb* (1965), and James R. Jennings, ed., *Just War and Pacifism: A Catholic*

Dialogue (1973). Two "state of the question" books which bear comparison are: William J. Nagle, ed., *Morality and Modern Warfare: The State of the Question* (1960), and Thomas A. Shannon, ed., *War and Peace? The Search for New Answers* (1980). The Nagle volume reflects the dominance within articulate American Catholic opinion in 1960 of the realist point of view. The Shannon volume reflects how much contrary perspectives had grown within the American Catholic community in the subsequent twenty years after Nagle's book. The current realist perspective, however, is not represented in the Shannon volume.

Index

About the Author

WILLIAM A. AU is an Associate Pastor in the Archdiocese of Baltimore and is Assistant to the Office of the Archbishop for Special Affairs. He is also a consultant to the Archdiocesan Peace and Justice Commission and has taught at St. Mary's Seminary in Baltimore and at Catholic University. He has written for *The U.S. Catholic Historian*.